THE  WAR  CAME  HOME  WITH  HIM

# THE WAR CAME HOME WITH HIM

*A Daughter's Memoir*

CATHERINE MADISON

UNIVERSITY OF MINNESOTA PRESS
MINNEAPOLIS

This is a true story depicting real events and real people. Some of the names and identifying details have been changed to respect individual privacy.

Published by the University of Minnesota Press
111 Third Avenue South, Suite 290
Minneapolis, MN 55401–2520
http://www.upress.umn.edu

Library of Congress Cataloging-in-Publication Data
Madison, Catherine.
The war came home with him : a daughter's memoir / Catherine Madison.
ISBN 978-0-8166-9877-6 (hc)
1. Boysen, Doc, 1923–2002. 2. Madison, Catherine—Childhood and youth.
3. Korean War, 1950–1953—Prisoners and prisons, North Korean.
4. Ex-prisoners of war—United States—Biography. 5. Children of veterans—
United States—Biography. 6. Fathers and daughters—United States—Biography.
7. Veterans—Family relationships—United States. 8. Ex-prisoners of war—
United States—Psychology. 9. Korean War, 1950–1953—Veterans—United
States—Biography. 10. United States—Army—Medical Corps—Officers—
Biography. I. Title.
DS921.M224 2015
951.904'27—dc23 [B]
                                                      2015012240

Printed in the United States of America on acid-free paper

The University of Minnesota is an equal-opportunity educator and employer.

21  20  19  18  17  16  15      10  9  8  7  6  5  4  3  2  1

*For Kristin and Erika*

*My father's story is based on his own words,*
*supplemented by those of the men who shared his experience.*
*My story is my own, as best I can remember.*

# Contents

# Prologue

On this February night, my father is a bag of bones lying on his side under a thin hospital blanket. He is seventy-eight, and his kidneys are failing. His cheeks are sunken and his limbs spindly, like those of an awkward teen in a growth spurt. My fingers, long and thin like his, could encircle his leg. Without his glasses, he squints at the 2002 Olympic figure skaters on a television suspended awkwardly from the ceiling. He peers out at me—his small, nearsighted eyes the blue of robin eggs—from a long face whiskered in white, and he attempts the crooked grin I barely remember.

"I liked that ballet, you know," he says.

Only he doesn't say ballet the usual way, *baallay*. He says the *baal* part like *ball*, as in basketball, the only sport he ever mentioned playing. I don't understand what he means at first, so I have to ask. Twice. He gestures at the graceful movements on the screen and explains that as a teenager he used to travel from Pelican Rapids, the small northern Minnesota town where he grew up, to the Twin Cities of Minneapolis and St. Paul. Where he saw "the ballet, you know."

I didn't know this. I have never heard this before. I can't even imagine this.

In my mind he is ten feet tall with a fist like a piston and a voice like Zeus. Perched on a pedestal of medical skill and military might, he commanded our family with high standards and harsh discipline. He went to war and returned a hero. But he declined to cheer our victories from high school bleachers, celebrate our report card As, or say *I love you* out loud. He reminded us often that we were just like everyone else—he loathed pomp and pretense—yet he stood alone and apart. He used force and fear to push us to be stronger, try harder, aim higher, to survive when someone else might not. Behind his back we call him Colonel Surgeon Father God.

He is my father, but I cannot hug him the way a daughter should. Not now, not the last time I saw him when I spent fewer than twenty-four hours at his house two years ago, and not since I was old enough to know what it means to hug your dad. When I try, he stands ramrod straight, his feet slightly turned out, his hands dangling from skinny arms held close to his sides, his jaw set. I can reach my arms around him, which in recent years I have mustered up the courage to try, but he is like a flagpole. Cold, hard, upright. A patriot, stilled.

I know he wasn't always this way. Before my mother died from lung cancer in 1995, she sent a videotape as a Christmas present, one copy each for my two younger brothers and me. Labeled "Precious Moments," the black plastic cassette contained pieces of old home movies transferred from the 8 mm film in the heavy cans we hauled from one basement to another every time we moved. Watching that video the first time, I saw familiar images of Easter morning in Germany when I wore white patent leather shoes and a wide feathered headband, feeling as awkward as I looked with my new blue glasses and frizzy home perm. The Christmas morning in Texas when I sat sweating in the green felt skirt my mother had appliquéd, pretending to smile as I held up a new scratchy sweater in lieu of the latest Nancy Drew mystery I had wanted. Several birthday parties with hats, noisemakers, and friends whose names I had forgotten. But the video opened with a shocker: a clip of my parents' wedding in my mother's hometown of Boonsboro, Maryland.

My mother had always described September 14, 1947, simply as "god-awful hot." There she was, nervous, looking like Lauren Bacall with wide turquoise eyes and perfectly arched eyebrows, milk-white skin, full lipstick-red lips, and dark brunette hair ringing her shoulders in curls. She wasn't wearing her glasses, so she wouldn't have been able to see except through that early-morning blur that the woefully nearsighted normally correct before they get out of bed. Even though she was wearing ballet slippers (she once confessed this to me in hushed tones, as if she had engaged in some anti-high-heel conspiracy), she was trying hard not to trip down the steep steps of the red brick church in her long-sleeved, boat-necked shiny gown and sweeping train. And there beside her, offering his arm, was my father: a jokester, loose-limbed and laughing, acting the goof.

I hit rewind. There he was again. He kissed her on the cheek and whispered in her ear, right there in public. I had no doubt that after the camera ran out of film he would have not only hugged her but also swung her around in glee, train and all. She would have protested in her alto voice, as she always did, but he would have done it anyway.

I was seeing this, but I could not make sense of it. My mother had told me stories of their college escapades at the University of Minnesota in Minneapolis. The time he drank too much at a Phi Chi frat party and dumped water over his head to sober up, only to have his wet hair freeze solid, sticking straight up, as he walked her back to the dorm. The time he took her sailing on Lake of the Isles, the most romantic date ever, she said, until the wind died and they realized they'd forgotten to bring a paddle and couldn't make curfew, a serious offense. I loved hearing these stories, but they weren't about the man I called my father. That man was stern and serious, principled and aloof, unpredictable. He scared me.

He scares me still. When I drove eighty miles from the Atlanta airport to the Athens hospital, I caught myself gripping the steering wheel of the rented car in strangled fear, the fear I used to feel when I barely came up to his waist and then his shoulder, when he towered over me in army greens and shouted me down with a voice I couldn't match. In the car, I was five again, or fifteen. It didn't matter. It has never gone away, that power he possesses over my brothers and me. As I sit looking at him now, shrunken in his cranked-up bed, I wonder what almighty fire could have forged that steel.

I know, of course, that the answer lies in his past as well as in my own. Some of our past is shared: the years he spent training to be an army surgeon, then commanding army hospitals in Vietnam and Japan. But earlier years he spent as a prisoner of war in Korea are a yawning, silent chasm that wraps us in solitary, shamed cocoons. My brothers and I know only the basics: the existence of a cruel guard called the Tiger, a wintry mountain trek called the Death March, the evil called communism. Shards of his story pierce the silence at odd times in odd ways, perhaps during a postmidnight, wine-soaked ramble, in a note scribbled in the margin of a newspaper article from an unfamiliar city, in an e-mail forwarded by a cousin we seldom see. But for the most part, he does not tell us what we long to know, and we do not ask.

Tonight, as my father squints at Sarah Hughes executing the loop jumps and double axels that will win gold, I sit with my questions. I think of all there is, unspoken, between us. I don't know where to start. I wonder whether it matters anymore. For once, my silence feels voluntary, uncompelled.

A technician arrives to check his vitals and adjust his oxygen. The young man in blue scrubs fiddles with tubes and dials and the blood pressure cuff. His back is to me, so I can't see exactly what he is doing. Finally he leaves. My father giggles a little, as if he can't help himself, and shakes his head.

"What is it?" I ask.

"These people," he says. "They just don't know how to treat other human beings."

He asks me to call the nurse. He has scooted too far down in the bed and can't see the TV. It takes her a while to arrive. When she does, she asks me to help. I go to one side of the bed while she takes the other, and on the count of three we grab the sheets folded under him and lift. It takes two tries to get him to the right spot. I am surprised at how light he is, and how it is possible for me to move him at all. This man, so heavy in my life, weighs less than I thought, less than what makes me afraid. How long has it been this way?

I say good night and drive to his house, sneaking peeks at the map I've laid in the passenger seat but no longer gripping the steering wheel. I sleep fitfully in the twin bed in the guest room.

What I don't realize is that under this same roof, in my father's office, cluttered with ash-dusted stacks of books and papers, medical and workshop tools, and messy piles of bills and empty envelopes, is something that has been hidden away, undisturbed, for nearly fifty years. Mere weeks from now, someone will yank too hard on the bottom drawer of the military gray file cabinet, pulling it all the way out, onto the floor, by mistake. Underneath, where the drawer had been, my brothers and I will discover a fat and faded Department of the Army manila envelope we have never seen.

Across the top, in our mother's handwriting: *The Whole Story!!*

# 1

# Yokohama, Japan

## JUNE 1950

"**D**oc, you got a phone call."

My father's name was Alexander. His family called him Lexy. My mother called him Pete, a nickname that stuck after his childhood friends in Minnesota started calling each other by their fathers' names; his father was Peter. His buddies called him Doc.

It was June 25, and my mother was calling from her childhood home in Boonsboro, Maryland. I was eight months old, and we had been staying with her parents since my father left for Yokohama on May 15. A captain in the U.S. Army Medical Corps, he had volunteered for a temporary duty assignment there, which paid per diem rates in addition to his regular pay. He figured he could live frugally and bank the extra to help us get out of debt.

Doc took the phone.

"North Korea just invaded South Korea. They're calling it a police action," said my mother. "What's going to happen to you? Will you have to go?"

He heard the distress in her voice, but he didn't know what to say. He wasn't even sure how close Japan was to Korea or what the fighting there might mean. He reminded her that he had volunteered to go to Japan instead of waiting to be assigned because the Army Medical Department said orders wouldn't be changed for volunteers. As soon as his ninety days were over, they had assured him, he could return home to Fort Lewis, where he had been stationed to complete a family practice residency. He had finished his medical degree and internship before accepting his officer's commission.

"Don't worry. I got it in writing," he said. "The U.S. Army will keep its word."

She wasn't convinced. She liked to say that worrying is a waste of energy because it doesn't change a thing, but she was worried then. She had just turned twenty-four. Despite her nursing degree, she was anxious about motherhood. Routine anesthesia had knocked her out during the delivery, so she didn't remember my birth. She was self-conscious about her small breasts (bra size 34A, padded) and gave up breastfeeding early because she feared starving me. She didn't relish handling child rearing alone, even for ninety days. And while she could blurt out the truth when necessary, she didn't dare mention her deepest fear—that he would go to war and not come back.

"So what do I do now?" she asked.

"Just go home, and we'll take it from there," he tried to reassure her. "The army will help you if you have questions. I'll be fine. And I'll be home soon."

As I slept in my nervous mother's arms on our flight back to Tacoma a few days later, North Koreans were streaming across the 38th parallel, which had separated the Soviet Union–backed Democratic People's Republic of Korea from the American-backed Republic of Korea since 1945, when thirty-five years of Japanese rule ended along with World War II. Fearing broader Communist aggression and supported by the United Nations, U.S. Army authorities ordered their entire Twenty-Fourth Infantry Division to help defend our South Korean allies. The Twenty-Fourth, then scattered throughout Japan, put all its men on alert but picked the Twenty-First Infantry Regiment's First Battalion as the first to go. On July 1, about four hundred troops, most under the age of twenty, were airlifted to a country many of them had never heard of. The troops were known as Task Force Smith.

At 7:00 a.m. on July 3, Doc arrived at the adjutant's office at the 155th Station Hospital in Yokohama, as ordered. The colonel was just hanging up the phone.

"Get packed, Doc," he said. "You're going to Korea."

The colonel assured the young army captain that nothing in his past actions had prompted his assignment as battalion surgeon, but given his written promise to be sent home after ninety days, Doc's imagination took flight. Had he offended a ranking officer? Made a medical mistake? Was he being punished for standing up to an angry lieutenant who had accosted him in the emergency room a few days earlier? The

lieutenant had demanded sleeping pills for his overworked commanding officer and staff, but Doc had refused.

"No way will I give you sleeping pills. You have to cope with the
stress, and pills will only louse you all up. This is the worst time to rely
on barbiturates," he'd told the lieutenant.

The young officer pleaded with him, then threatened. "I will take
care of you, you SOB!" he said, jabbing his finger at Doc before he
turned around and walked out.

Maybe the lieutenant had reported him. Doc didn't ask, so he never
knew for sure. The colonel wished him Godspeed and a rewarding tour.

Within two hours, Doc had his orders. He started on his to-do
list. He wired $200 to my mother through military channels (or so
he thought—it never arrived). A staff sergeant helped him choose his
combat gear—boots, fatigues, bedroll, poncho, mess kit—and taught
him to pack: nothing fancy, nothing he couldn't carry on his back.

"And you keep it on your back, Doc. Don't trust no one to take care
of it for you," the sergeant said. "That way you'll always have something
to eat with and sleep in. Ain't never learned of any exceptions. This is
war, you know, and piss on that police action crap. When the bullets
start flying, you won't give a damn about what the politicians call it."

Doc sensed he was getting basic survival instructions.

"Don't forget—clean that mess gear good, or you will shit for a
week. Use sand and elbow grease first, then the fancy soap stuff." He
threw in a musette bag for personal items, "to hold the goodies you
might want, but just remember you will probably ditch it when you get
in the field. Don't put anything in that bag unless you can throw it away
and not miss it."

By day's end Doc had packed his meager belongings and joined
throngs of young, confused soldiers milling through the narrow Yokohama streets to catch a train to Fukuoka, a port on the western coast of
Japan, more than three hundred miles away. The train was packed with
sweaty bodies and anxious souls, but Doc slept soundly until he was
awakened in the middle of the night by a medic who had spotted his
medical insignia.

"Come with me and look at a guy who has a problem," the medic said.

Doc followed the medic through the narrow corridor lined with snoring men using their packs as pillows. The patient, lying in a lower berth, was one of several American civilians, evacuees from Seoul, who had boarded the train at a recent stop. No one nearby seemed to know him, but they'd told the medic that he'd seemed depressed and agitated.

"He's psychotic and unresponsive," the medic told Doc.

Doc leaned down and touched the patient's forehead, then felt for a pulse.

"No, he's cold and dead." Doc rummaged in his pockets for a tag to tie on his toe. "First American casualty of the Korean War," he muttered to no one in particular.

By the time the men got off the train in Fukuoka, it was Independence Day back home in the United States. They partied hard that night, knocking back sake and American whiskey and stumbling through the streets. The next day, confusion reigned. After receiving orders to report to one station, Doc arrived only to find that his orders had changed and he was expected to report to another. *Goddamn army. It's always hurry up and wait.* Eventually he flagged down a jeep to take him to the ship to which he'd been assigned. He boarded and stowed his gear. At 1900 hours he stood on deck, watching as the lines let go, and the apprehensive, hung-over troops began their overnight journey across the Tsushima and Korean Straits to Pusan, Korea.

Once they were under way, the Twenty-Fourth Division surgeon ordered Doc to hold a sick call and procure any necessary medications from the disaster chests on deck. The sergeant in charge of these emergency supplies assured him that they were inspected on a routine basis and ready for action. Sure enough, their tags sported the appropriate officer signatures and dates. But ready for action? Not exactly.

The first chest he opened was full of broken bottles, goopy tubes, and saturated bandages. The second contained plaster of Paris, well hardened. Among the World War II–vintage surgical instruments was a pair of forceps, which he picked up and opened. They broke as he closed them. The pair of scissors was nothing but rusted metal. The sutures were useless. He shook his head.

"Let's deep-six the medical chests," he said to the sergeant. "We have no supplies. Period."

The ship docked in Pusan the next morning, spilling its human cargo down the gangplanks. It was hot. Men cussed as rain poured from laden clouds and they got their first glimpses of the stark, monsoon-soaked, treeless Korean mountains. On the outskirts of the city, Doc joined his unit, the Twenty-First Regiment's Third Battalion, and got busy scrounging medical supplies. After filling one pocket with morphine syringes and another with three or four bottles of penicillin, he attempted to conduct a routine sick call. By the time he finished, he'd decided that in war—any war, all wars—knowing how to fight trumps knowing how to practice medicine. He asked around until he found an infantryman willing to show him how to shoot an M1 and a carbine and how to clean and replace the parts of each. The sergeant also showed him a Colt .45 but emphasized the carbine and plenty of ammo.

"Most docs couldn't hit the broad side of a barn, so you better have something to spray your target," the sergeant said.

Doc paid close attention. He asked his new battalion aid station buddies where he might find a firearm but got only shoulder shrugs. Guns were hard to come by.

When the division surgeon pulled up in a jeep the next day, Doc noticed that he had a .45 on his hip, a .38 under his shoulder, and two carbines and an M1 in the vehicle.

"I've got new orders for you," the surgeon said. "You're going to the front lines."

Doc pressed his lips together, tight, as the news sunk in.

"I need a gun," he said.

"We're short on artillery and ammunition, so no guns to spare. Sorry."

*Apparently a pocketful of morphine and a head full of medical knowledge will be my only weapons,* he mused as the surgeon drove off.

As the steamy day waned, Doc joined the troops and equipment that filled the passenger cars and flatbeds of a train headed to the front lines. Local civilians had filled the men's canteens with hot water or tea and roused a band to send them off. As the train clanked and strained its way north, the cramped soldiers noticed similar trains packed with Koreans, some of them clinging to the sides with a single handhold, headed south. Contradictory rumors about Task Force Smith ran rampant—that the

Americans were holding the North Koreans back or that the North Koreans had wiped them out. The train traveled all night, occasionally stopping along the way for reasons no one could determine.

Once while the train was stopped, its passengers and some locals
watched three or four Koreans dig a large hole in the ground. When
they were finished, other Korean soldiers tied the diggers' hands behind
their backs, blindfolded them, stood them at the edge of the ditch, and
shot each one in the back of the head. They fell into the hole they had
dug, and the soldiers and civilians threw the dirt back in the hole to
cover them up. The dirt throwers were nonchalant, Doc noted, and the
Koreans on board the train were unfazed.

As in the subsequent war that sent U.S. soldiers to Asia, it was nearly impossible to tell who was who. North Koreans and South Koreans
looked alike, and the 300,000 Chinese who, three months later, crossed
the border into North Korea, would not have looked much different
from its current occupants, at least not to Westerners. The Americans,
with their tall stature, round eyes, and uncommon skin colors, stood
out, making them easy targets.

The train reached Taejon, about fifty miles from Korea's west coast,
about noon on July 8, and unloading began. But after everything was unloaded, word came down that it had to be reloaded, because the destination was now Chochiwon, farther north. At Chochiwon, the train was
unloaded again. The troops moved out a few miles to a nearby location
and began digging in for the night, but another destination mistake had
been made—no one seemed to have a map—so they retraced their steps.
About eight miles north of Chochiwon, in a long, narrow valley that
stretched between two mountain ranges and contained the single road
and railroad track they were supposed to protect, the disgruntled men
pitched tents and dug foxholes. On his third day in Korea, Doc noted
how hard the ground was, and how bitter the critiques of the president
and Congress back home. Panic reigned as casualties began rolling in.

Doc was running out of penicillin and morphine. He treated a sergeant whose right thumb had been shot off.

"We're going to evacuate you," Doc said, pointing to the litter jeep
that was shuttling casualties to the ambulances waiting about a mile
down the road.

The patient shook his head.

"Look, Doc, I fought all the way through the Pacific, and I've been hit before. These kids out here can't even fire a rifle. They should be fighting their *mamasans* in Japan, not a war," he pleaded. "You can't leave those poor bastards out there alone, and I can help them even with this thumb gone." He picked up his gun and walked back toward the firing line.

Doc treated one wounded man after another, asking each how it was going. The men with rifles complained about having no ammunition. The ones with ammo had no guns. Someone reported that four out of five of the big 105 millimeter howitzers wouldn't fire. Doc rolled his eyes. *Not a happy and glorious battle.*

Throughout the night and the next day, mortars exploded. One landed directly in the center of the battalion aid station, destroying all of its scrounged supplies. Another mortar took out the only jeep. Doc, his medics, and others began walking south, where machine gun fire soon pinned them down in a water-filled ditch. A tank commander rescued them by blowing up the enemy's machine gun, then positioning his tank between the Americans and the gunfire erupting from the mountainsides. Once they were out of immediate danger, the ragtag group hitched a ride in passing trucks and returned to Chochiwon. They reported their experience to a skeptical junior officer.

Later, Doc overheard the officer as he briefed the headquarters crew. "Shit, they're just medics. They don't know our guns from the gooks'. They just got scared and got out. Gooks doing an envelopment? They don't have brains enough to do that. They're trained by Russians and only use frontal attacks. We're going to hold that line, because there's no way they could have gotten behind us."

*I guess we imagined those bullets that hit our friendly tanks. And those North Koreans we saw dug into the mountainside—also figments of our imagination?* Dejected and tired, Doc kept his thoughts to himself.

Doc was sleeping on the porch of a mud hut when a medic awakened him with new orders. The men had found another jeep, more medical supplies, and three carbines they could use to shoot their way through the valley they had just escaped.

"I heard A Company screaming for medics on the radio. They're

my buddies, Doc, and we've got to help them any way we can. I know
it's a suicide mission, but they need us," the medic said.

Doc gathered his wits. He'd been in pressure situations before as a
willful youth trying to convince the world that he could survive on his
own. *But am I up to a mission with no return? Why me? Why here? If I
don't go, can I face my new buddies, my family, myself?* The decision was
quick but not easy. Doc said a prayer and climbed into the jeep.

They took off. Military police stopped them at the base of the
mountain ridge and told them to go back because the enemy was dug
in there thick as flies, waiting for morning. When Doc and the medic
argued, the MPs gave in and explained where to dodge bullets, where to
coast quietly to the next hill, and where to open fire and give 'em hell.

The driver gunned the jeep for all it was worth. Tracers flew by as
the passengers emptied their carbines, shooting up the ridges. The jeep
hit a hole in the rough road and careened on two wheels but stayed
upright. The harrowing ride ended at their former aid station, now a
mass of rubble with wounded men scattered about. They dressed the
wounds as best they could and loaded their patients into the jeep and
every southbound vehicle they could stop.

The sun was dropping as they cleaned out their foxholes for the
night and prepared for a new dawn, whatever that might bring. The
left bank, across the river, did not seem to harbor any enemy soldiers,
but North Koreans flanked them on their right. Doc was confident that
HQ was aware of their predicament and would send reinforcements to
hold the line and eradicate the enemy. *Certainly the U.S. Army and Air
Force will come to our rescue.*

The next morning, July 10, all hell broke loose. A North Korean
tank rumbled in through the heavy fog. Doc kept his head down. Men
ran in circles as guns fired and mortar rounds exploded. As screams for
more guns or ammunition and warnings to get out of the way echoed
off the hills, more U.S. soldiers poured over the ridge.

"Who in the hell are you people?" one yelled.

"Third Battalion aid station," Doc yelled back.

"Get the hell out of here," the voice thundered from above. "We've
been run over. Every man for himself!"

Plunging down the hill, he repeated the order as he passed: "Every man for himself, Doc, and good luck."

"Who in the hell are *you?*"

"Colonel Jensen, your commanding officer. It's no use. Get going!"

Doc followed him toward the road, where, just beyond, American men huddled in bunches in a narrow ravine along the river. Every few minutes, some of them jumped up and tried to race across the shallow river to the rice paddies on the other side, unleashing a barrage of machine gun and mortar fire. Most didn't make it.

Doc took cover in the ravine as Jensen, trying to corral his men, was shot dead.

"If we stay here, Doc, we're sure to get it. The only chance we have is to run the river," said the sergeant crouching beside him. "When I say go, run like hell. . . . GO!"

The two raced into the water as bullets flew. Halfway across, the sergeant yelled that he was hit, but he kept running and made it to the other side. He dropped down beside a ridge in a rice paddy. Doc fell in the next paddy above him, on the other side of the ridge, then crept back to drop down beside him. The sergeant asked for some water. Doc handed him his canteen. Machine guns raked them once more. Mud covered them both. Doc lay still. He asked the sergeant if he wanted more water. The sergeant said no. He asked where it hurt. The sergeant moaned. After a few minutes, the sergeant quit responding to his questions.

Eventually the firing let up and Koreans started yelling. Doc was amazed to see GIs standing up and surrendering. Lying motionless, he watched as they were pushed and shoved into groups and marched north on the road. Remembering the pictures he'd seen on the front page of the *Stars and Stripes*—GIs lying facedown with their hands tied behind their backs, the backs of their heads blown away—he promised himself he wouldn't give up.

It was hours, he figured, before he dared turn his head. The firing and the yelling had stopped. The sergeant beside him was dead. Bodies were strewn everywhere. Estimating that it was midafternoon, Doc finally decided to get up, sprint for fifteen or twenty yards, then drop down again. He tried it. Nothing happened. He did it again. And again.

He had no idea where he was or what direction to go. *East, maybe, and then south.* The moist air hung heavy, stifling. Walking was difficult. Out of shape, he struggled to climb the rugged hills. He dropped his cartridge belt and empty canteen cover to lighten the load. He spotted an isolated farm hut and slowly, hands up, approached the door. A frightened farmer beckoned Doc inside and motioned for his wife to give him water, a bowl of rice, some vegetables, and pickled daikons. After Doc ate, the farmer shooed him away, but not until he had carefully drawn directions in the dirt and pointed out a path across the valley and into the mountains on the other side.

Doc followed the path. He waved to an observation plane flying low over his head, but the pilot only dipped his wings and went on. The sun was falling fast. Doc thought he could hear the distinct hum of American engines just over the next hill, which kept him going, over one hill and then the next, until he collapsed in a clump of bushes and fell asleep.

He rose with the sun and continued on, making sure to cross any trails at right angles. As he made a break across one of them, a North Korean soldier's head popped up just over a small hill about thirty or forty yards away. The soldier looked right at him. Doc ran faster. The soldier yelled. Doc dropped into a small hollow, slithered under some brush, and lay still.

Within minutes, the patrol closed in. Half a dozen Koreans yelled incessantly as they swarmed his hiding place and hit him with their rifles. They pulled off his glasses and stomped on them, spit in his face, and ripped off his dog tags and beloved St. Christopher's medal from his merchant marine days. They emptied his billfold, tossed its contents to the wind, pulled the boots off his feet, and tied his hands too tight behind his back. They mimed their questions. Was he a rifleman? A mortar man? Each question was accompanied by blows, spitting, kicking, and body punches. He tried to tell them he was a doctor. Finally they yanked him to his feet and pushed him to walk along the trail he had tried to cross.

It was July 12, 1950. Six days after arriving in Korea, my father became a prisoner of war.

# 2
# Martinsburg, West Virginia
## 1952

One day when I was three years old, I was playing with my best friend, David, in the apartment across the hall from ours, the doors left ajar so my mother could hear what we were doing. She was sitting in our living room in the forest-green corduroy armchair, then new and plump, scanning the paper for war news, when she heard my footsteps bounding across the wooden floors. I ran into our apartment and slammed the door.

She frowned at me. "Don't slam the door!"

I scowled right back. "Do I have a daddy?"

"Yes, you do."

I stomped my foot. My face flushed. "Then where is he?"

"He's in Korea," she told me. "Fighting a war for our country."

My memories begin there, in the Arden Apartments, not with this recounted incident but that same year, when I had the measles. I was hot and cold and sore all over. My pajamas and my pillow were damp, I got tangled in the sheets because I turned over so much, and the light hurt my eyes. My mother brought me cool washcloths when she was home, and Nonie, my babysitter, took care of me at night while my mother worked as a nurse in the Martinsburg hospital. After a week in bed I started to feel better and was allowed to play in my bathrobe beside my bed on the floor, stretching my legs out on the cool, smooth hardwood planks. Instead of a dollhouse, I had a red barn with miniature accessories—tractors and tools, animals and holding pens, and tiny green Coca-Cola bottles in a yellow wooden case I could cradle in my palm. I liked how it looked perfect except tiny, like real but not real. Cold Coca-Cola was my favorite drink, but I could only have it when I was sick because my daddy said it would settle my tummy. At least that's what my mother told me. I wasn't sure who my daddy was.

Before the war broke out, we lived in Fort Lewis, Washington, in drab converted barracks on barren lots landscaped with tricycles and clotheslines. When the troops were put on alert and needed combat training facilities, the families were ordered to clear quarters, which meant that we had to move out, PDQ.

Although new to military life, my mother had befriended her neighbors, to whom she now turned for solace and help in wading through government protocol and copious paperwork as she made arrangements to leave. Married less than three years and without a job, she had little money and meager, mostly secondhand, possessions. She and Mom-Mom, her mother, packed all they could fit into two cars and drove, caravan-style, across the country to Maryland.

"Cathy has been good as gold, and the old Ford is behaving beautifully," my mother wrote in one of several upbeat postcards she sent my father during the weeklong road trip.

Arriving in Boonsboro around lunchtime on July 26, my mother noticed that Pop-Pop wasn't himself. Normally a jolly, loud, cigar-puffing, plain-talking, daughter-hugging, small-town general practitioner, he frowned behind his round glasses and said little. After my mother put me down for my nap, he handed her a Western Union telegram. Strips of purple block printing, all caps, lined the pale yellow paper.

THE SECRETARY OF THE ARMY HAS ASKED ME TO EXPRESS HIS DEEP REGRET THAT YOUR HUSBAND CAPT BOYSEN ALEXANDER HAS BEEN MISSING IN ACTION IN KOREA SINCE 12 JULY 50 UPON RECEIPT OF ADDITIONAL INFORMATION YOU WILL BE ADVISED IMMEDIATELY CONFIRMING LETTER FOLLOWS.

There was more: the postcard my mother had sent to my father had been returned. "Missing" was written on the front in aqua fountain pen ink by a captain who signed his name underneath. The postcard bore an official purple stamp: Verified Missing In Action.

She had received two letters from my father since he'd shipped out to Korea. She wrote practical letters—what we ate for breakfast, what we planned to do the next day—but his were romantic and philosophical. "This is the most difficult letter I have ever had to write" his July 1 letter began. "You will need a stiff upper lip." He begged her to be brave and insisted that she do the best she could, which would be wonderful and perfect. "So long for a while," he signed off, and added a postscript for me: "Nighty nite, Cathy."

The second letter, on a thin sliver of paper that, folded, became its own envelope, was postmarked July 8 San Francisco APO. Where the stamp usually went he'd written "no stamp available," and alongside the address, "censored" and his serial number. Inside, where the date belonged, he wrote "somewhere in Korea."

"You will have to pardon the pencil my love but it is the best I can do," he began. "Just a note to let you know that I have loved you as I loved no one else. God has been kind to let me have you, even though time was so short. Thank you so much for the memories and all. I know how hard you have tried to please me and I thank you Mommie for all of it. I hope Cathy will be a good little girl for you. Good luck my darling and do the best you can. I will remember you always. Don't forget to thank Mother and Dad. I love you." He signed it in his usual way: "Your husband, Lexy."

All the letters she had written to him that summer were returned.

On August 30, another telegram arrived in Boonsboro. An enemy propaganda broadcast named my father as a prisoner of war. Did that mean he was still alive? No one could say. By the end of July, the Twenty-Fourth Division had lost nearly a third of its men, and 2,400 were missing in action, including their commanding general, William F. Dean. United Nations troops from sixteen nations poured into Korea, but the United States contributed the most—100,000 men and two million tons of supplies and equipment in the first three months.

In mid-September, the U.S. Army launched an amphibious attack at Inchon, a western port about eighteen miles from Seoul, and combined forces captured Seoul on September 26. By October, they'd pushed the North Koreans back across the 38th parallel. Did that mean he'd be home soon?

*Time* magazine published a war photo in its October 2, 1950, issue. In one blurry image, a block of mostly bearded men in bedraggled uniforms stand clumped together in long lines, a troop formation of sorts. They're standing at ease, arms loose, smiles on some of their faces. In the front, just behind five or six men who appear to be negotiating with the guards, is my father. With his mouth shut firmly and his right hand on his hip, he stands half a head above the man on his left. He is squinting in the sun. His glasses are missing. At six feet three inches, he sticks out.

The same picture ran in newspapers. Friends and relatives sent my mother their copies from the *Pittsburgh Press, Des Moines Register, South Bend Tribune, Hagerstown Herald,* and *New York Daily News.* The journalism was careful, the picture captions qualified, as "allegedly" from the China Photo Service of Peiping and "purportedly" showing Yank prisoners, called PWs then. Some captions identified the infantry regiment and division, which were my father's, but that was all.

Then the good news stopped, and the optimistic notes and clippings quit coming. In late October, 300,000 Chinese Communist troops poured over the Manchurian border and headed for Seoul, which changed hands on January 4 when UN forces turned tail and headed south. Bridges were blown up, hampering troop movement, which was difficult enough on roads that were more oxcart trail than highway. At one point the U.S. Army airlifted bridge-building materials to troops that had been cut off so they could get 1,200 vehicles across a 1,500-foot gorge. Fighting often raged at night, when temperatures fell to thirty degrees below zero. Chinese troops, who wore quilted jackets but neither gloves nor boots, were taken prisoner with their hands frozen to their guns.

"It's an entirely new war," claimed Gen. Douglas MacArthur.

My mother found life in her childhood home sour and stifling. The radio was always on—my Scotch-swilling, stamp-collecting, reclusive Mom-Mom never missed a newscast—and three daily newspapers littered the house with discouraging details. In January, to escape her mother and distract herself, my mother found a nursing job at the V.A. Hospital in Martinsburg, West Virginia, about twenty miles away. Mom-Mom took care of me while she worked. While raising my mother, she had been a strict, joyless disciplinarian who was quick to spot flaws and punish for them, and apparently not much had changed. It wasn't long before my mother noticed that I began to burst into tears at little more than the sound of my name. Fearing I was being subjected to harsh treatment, my mother began looking for other arrangements.

By May, she had switched to night shifts and rented a furnished apartment in Martinsburg for the two of us. Two of her neighbors were also solo mothers, Wanda through divorce and Mitzi because her husband was hospitalized with tuberculosis. The three moms shared cooking, traded babysitting, and took David and his sister Jill, Mitzi's daughter Carey, and me on outings. My favorite was an amusement park with a sleek silver train, miniature and roofless, with little bench seats in each car. I sat in it and waved as it chugged around the track. I didn't miss waving to my daddy because none of us had one. Instead I had an imaginary sister, who came with me everywhere. I had to remind my mother to get her in and out of the car and grocery cart, and to kiss her good night when we went to bed.

On one of our outings Wanda drove, and my mother sat next to her in the front seat. David, Jill, and I shared the back. A dog wandered into the street, and Wanda slammed on the brakes. The backseat jerked forward, trapping our legs against the back of the front seat. We all screamed. It hurt a lot. My mother tried to be calm. She grabbed my arm and told me to stop crying.

"Good soldiers don't cry," she said, her face close to mine. "Your daddy is a good soldier. You need to be one, too."

On December 21, 1951, the Communists released a list of 3,198 PWs. The *Washington Post* was thick with names that day, and my mother set the able patients on her ward to search for my father's name. They found it. When she came home, she twirled me around and told me the news.

"It's our early Christmas present!" she said.

But I wanted a new suitcase for my doll clothes.

The war headed into another brutal Korean winter. The UN forces had retaken Seoul in March and crossed the 38th parallel in April. General MacArthur advocated full-scale war and a push into China, but President Harry Truman relieved him of his command and replaced him with Gen. Matthew Ridgway. Cease-fire negotiations had begun in July but were abandoned in August. Some of the most intense fighting in the war was still occurring at places like Heartbreak Ridge and Pork Chop Hill; the opponents made few major gains but instead traded territory back and forth, one steep hill at a time.

Christmas came, and I got a little red suitcase, stamped to look like leather, with a handle on top. I filled it with doll clothes.

In March, a letter arrived with the return address, "Chinese People's Committee for Defending World Peace, Camp #2, Peking, China." Dated "25 January 1952," it was carefully printed in ink and signed with my father's full name and serial number. The letter implored my mother to repay a family friend an outstanding $80 debt. My mother was confused—she was sure the debt had been repaid long ago—but no one else would know the friend's name. My father was alive.

His next letter, written February 12, was stranger. "This has been just another day with rather pleasant weather," he wrote. Even Minnesota-bred stoicism wouldn't dub Korea's frigid climate *pleasant*. "That little girl, Cordy, has certainly grown," he added. "It seems funny to think that the little baby I left two years ago can now talk!" Not Cathy—me—but Cordy, his brother's wife. Had he lost his mind?

He remembered her June 17 birthday, although his greeting didn't arrive until August. It was short: "Happy Birthday. Patience my love, I will come home."

In Korea, talks were stalled. A prisoner exchange was proposed, but the Communists balked when UN leaders informed them that only 70,000 of the 132,000 Communist prisoners wanted to go home. Fighting continued, with massive air raids launched against Pyongyang and power plants on the Yalu River.

The letter that arrived in November was addressed to me. My diligent, dutiful mother carefully followed army orders to restrict her letters to one per month during my father's captivity, and one had included my picture. "Tell your mom that you either want long hair or a permanent, not that hair-do," he wrote. He asked me to make sure she got a single red rose on the fourteenth of every month to celebrate their anniversary, and to send a picture of her in her nurse's uniform. And he added a postscript: "Trish, my darling, words may be lacking but not my love, for 'true love is luminous as the dawn but as silent as the grave.'" He was quoting Victor Hugo's *Les Miserables,* which he must have gotten from the prison library or culled from the literary memories of his mates.

Operation Little Switch, an early release of sick and wounded prisoners, was announced in April 1953. Wanda Ball came across the hall every day to sit with my mother and listen to the radio announcer read names of the released prisoners. My father's name was not among them.

But the last name read on the last day's broadcast was Maj. Marin (Pappy) Green, someone Wanda knew.

"Shall I write to his family and see whether he knew Pete?"

"Would you? Oh, please. I have to know if he's OK. I'm so tired of waiting, and praying, and waiting some more."

While we waited, we took a long vacation, visiting my father's sister's family in Indiana and his brother's family in Ohio. When we got home, my mother set the suitcase down in our living room and ran across the hall. She knocked on the door, then opened it and stuck her head in.

"Wanda?"

"I'm here. Come on in and sit down. Have some coffee."

"Did you hear anything?"

Wanda waved an envelope in the air with one hand, using the other to pour coffee and set it in front of my mother's usual place at the kitchen table.

"I did," she said, smiling as she handed over the letter. "Pappy said that if your husband is tall and blond, wears glasses and is a doctor, you should call right away. Use my phone."

The coffee sat untouched as my mother placed the call to Oklahoma. Pappy told her that Doc was the last person whose hand he shook when he left Camp 2. My mother thanked him, hung up, and broke down, sobbing into her hands. I stood at her elbow, watching.

About a week after the truce was signed on July 27, daily broadcasts of released prisoners' names began again. The North Koreans announced that they would hold the highest-ranking officers until the final days of the prisoner exchange. General Dean, who'd commanded the Twenty-Fourth Infantry Division before he was captured in 1950, would be the last to go.

Every day through August and early September, my mother sat by the radio and listened. Every night, after I said the God blesses at the end of "Now I lay me down to sleep," she added, "and please, God, bring Daddy home safely." On September 5, the last name broadcast was General Dean's. Would there be no more? She called her father, her voice quavering. He called the adjutant general in Washington, D.C. Be patient, he was told. The next day, there was one more broadcast. The announcer read my father's name.

Western Union delivered a telegram announcing that he had been returned to military control in Korea and would be sent home by ship. I don't remember hearing the knock or seeing my mother open the door and sign for the flimsy yellow envelope with the address window across the bottom. Did she stand it against the lamp on the side table and break open a bottle of wine? Did she call her family and friends? Or did she just sit with it in her lap and sob once more?

The night my father came home from the war was at the end of September 1953. I was about to turn four years old. While my mother and father revisited their honeymoon in Baltimore, I was left with my aunt and uncle in eastern Pennsylvania.

Fairbourne, my favorite place to be, was a magical farmstead with a spring house to hide in, a pond to swim in, a creek to listen to, an old barn to be spooked by, and a sandbox where my two cousins and I could play with big orange tractor toys and not have to put them away at bedtime. We ate supper early that night.

"Let's go play hide-and-seek!" yelled Sally as we climbed down from the table. "You're it, Tommy!"

We ran out to the big tree beside the house. Tommy put his elbow up on the trunk, hid his eyes in the crook of his arm, and started counting, loud and slow. "One, two . . ."

I wasn't sure what to do.

"Three, four . . ."

"Go up on the porch," Sally whispered in my ear.

A wide porch fronted the old house, its trellis base hiding the storage area for whatever didn't fit in the fusty basement. I tried not to let the steps creak as I climbed up.

"Seven, eight . . ."

I ran behind a mammoth wicker chair and sank to my knees under the window box. A perfect hiding spot. Tommy finished counting. He found Sally in some bushes and kept looking, behind the sandbox and down by the springhouse.

"Give up?" Sally sounded delighted. Tommy nodded his head. "Olly olly in come free!" she sang.

Victorious, I jumped up, and the sharp corner of the window box opened a gash over my eye that sent blood streaming down my face. My chest ached as I tried to catch my breath. The wound hurt and I missed my mother. I sobbed.

My uncle took me into town to the doctor's office. My uncle was very tall and didn't talk much, but he smiled with his eyes and his mouth both, and the hand that held mine was warm and gentle. After I got my eyebrow shaved and stitched up, we walked down the street to the soda fountain.

"A treat will help the hurt go away, don't you think?" he said. I nodded.

We sat side by side on green stools with silver edges, just the two of us, one big, one little. I swerved from side to side, swinging my feet out, and ordered chocolate pudding. It was served ice cold in a tall goblet. I had to sit up very straight to reach it with my long spoon. I ate every bite. That night, chocolate pudding became my favorite dessert. And my uncle became my favorite relative because he hugged me around my shoulders and his voice was low and kind, like a father's.

# 3
# Pyongtaek, Korea

## JULY 1950

Without boots, his shredded feet bleeding through his socks, Doc marched south along a riverbed, carrying a heavy mortar plate on his back like a packhorse. His captors had fallen in with a larger body of Korean troops and were headed for the front lines. Eventually a jeep overcame them, and Doc was allowed to remove the plate and climb aboard. They drove him to a rural housing compound, a gated area surrounded by living quarters, barns, and storage areas. The driver disappeared into one of the buildings and reemerged with the young man who would become Doc's guard for the next few days.

The guard was a teenager, no more than fifteen or sixteen, with a kind, jovial disposition. He worried over Doc's feet, but Korean shoes were too small, and the tire scraps that some American prisoners tied around their feet weren't available. He managed to procure Doc's first food in twenty-four hours: a package of crackers and a can of Carnation evaporated milk. Supplies of the latter were plentiful, Doc learned later, because it was available through U.S. military sources and the Koreans didn't like it.

The guard poked holes in the can with his bayonet, then handed it to Doc with one hand while he held up his index finger with the other. "*Ichi-ban* American," he said, grinning. Number one American food.

Doc begged for water instead. The guard shook his head, but when Doc insisted, reluctantly went to get some. Returning with a dipper full, he pantomimed the vomiting that would result from drinking too much. After Doc had his drink, the guard pointed to the ground and pantomimed sleep. Doc, who could fall asleep instantly anytime, anywhere, lay down and drifted off.

As dusk approached, he was awakened by Korean soldiers emerging from the various buildings in the complex, talking loudly and stretching as if they'd just woken up. The guard kept them away from Doc, often using his rifle to make his point. Eventually a group formed, with Doc and the guard in the middle, and began marching, double file, out of the compound and straight up a hill through the brush. There were no trails or roads, just gnarly terrain. More men joined the group as it moved, dispersed and ant-like, across the countryside. *"Bali, bali!"* the guard reprimanded Doc when he slowed down. *"Hayaku."* Go faster. Hurry up.

Night darkened, and the guard, distracted by animated conversations with his colleagues, began to move farther ahead in the crowd. Sometimes Doc could spot the back of his head bobbing along, sometimes not. Doc began to think about escaping. He dropped back when he could, working his way to the edge of the group. But just as he was ready to make a break, someone would yell and his guard would reappear, as if by magic. One time, Doc managed to drop down into a ravine filled with bushes, but even there the guard found him, pulled him out, and used elaborate sign language to explain just how dumb this idea was.

They marched all night. As the sun rose, they came upon a tent town. Doc was instructed to sleep and he obeyed, despite his rebellious inclinations. When he woke up, he heard men speaking English. The guard delivered him to another American prisoner and disappeared.

The fellow prisoner now in charge of Doc was known as West Virginia, a nickname derived from his home state. He wasted no time in showing Doc the hole in his thigh, where a burp gun bullet had gone all the way through. Doc inspected it but could offer little aid. West Virginia didn't seem to mind; he had wisdom to impart.

"Been here a few days. Food is OK," he said. He explained that the Americans were being held in the tent town to regain their strength and be interrogated, for what that was worth. "I guess they just shoot you after that, but don't worry—they tell me they shoot you in the back of the head, and it is so fast you don't feel a thing. Might as well get the best food you can out of them while you're still kicking."

Later that night, a silent guard arrived to tap Doc on the shoulder and escort him to one of the buildings, built like a small cracker box. In the main room, the guard pointed to a seat across from three officers at a chow table. Doc sat down. The officer who spoke English brandished U.S. Army manuals and asked many questions, none of which Doc could answer. He didn't know where he was. He didn't know anyone else's name. He didn't know where the American troops were or what they were planning. "I don't know," he said again and again. This was no premeditated strategic answer. The simple line became his refrain because it was honest, and it seemed to work.

The interrogation over, Doc was returned to the courtyard and pushed into a line with four other Americans. The guards used telephone wire to tie each man's hands behind his back, tight, and then roped them together. In darkness this human chain began marching north on primitive roads and across rocky terrain. Every time one stumbled, the others fell, too. Civilians they encountered along the way hit and spit on them. The wire cut into their wrists. Even when their six guards allowed them to lie down along the road, their shackles remained in place, which meant that they couldn't swat the mosquitoes that might be carrying malaria and whose torment, they miserably agreed, was worse than the human kind. While the prisoners tried to rest, an old Korean woman arrived with drinking water and large rice bags filled with straw that she placed on top of them to ward off the droning, biting pests. The guards harassed her, but she pushed them away and shouted at them so persistently that they left her to her mission.

The next morning, after eating breakfast—one baseball-sized rice ball—the men set out again. Eventually they reached a warehouse in Pyongtaek, where they were untied and pushed through the door to join two hundred prisoners already sitting on the floor. The warehouse was supposed to shelter them from air strikes.

Within hours, two British planes strafed the building, and barrages of .50-caliber bullets pierced the roof. Guards went berserk. Prisoners screamed for medics. Doc reached over to help a man near him as blood spurted out, gushing over his hand. The man died within seconds. Another was killed outright. After both the Korean and American shouting had subsided, the guards fired their rifles over the men's heads, to keep them from moving around, and started to haul the bodies away.

Twenty-six men were wounded. Whispering to each other, the prisoners did what they could to help them. Supplies were meager: some gauze and one small bottle of Mercurochrome, a common antiseptic that stung and turned skin a peculiar orange hue. Word was passed that one GI had a piece of steel in his eye. Inch by stealthy inch, Doc moved toward the GI, the other men sliding around on their backs to make way for him. No one dared sit up. Finally Doc got close enough to see the quarter-inch fragment lodged in the soldier's cornea. Tears washed down the GI's face. Doc wondered whether removing the shard would cause the aqueous humor to leak out through the cornea. If that happened, the man could lose his sight, and Doc didn't want to be the culprit. But he doubted the guards would do anything at all, and the man could still go blind. He thought about it for a while, lying there on the floor, and finally decided that the steel would have been hot, searing the edges of the cornea as it went in. *One must do what one must do. Maybe it's worth a try. But it's going to hurt like hell.*

Doc unhooked the captain's bars still attached to the back side of his collar and borrowed a match from a nearby GI to sterilize the pin. Although it was too dim to see well in the windowless warehouse, the .50-caliber holes in the roof allowed the sun through in fine, slanted rays. Again the men shifted on the floor so Doc could push his patient directly under a shaft of light. Willing his hand steady, Doc used the blackened pin tip to pluck out the steel fragment.

"Thanks, Doc," the GI whispered as his tears flushed the wound. *A man with guts,* Doc thought. *If the eye heals, he will have done it himself.* The eye did eventually heal, its sight restored. Doc concluded that nature, with minimal assistance, is a marvelous doctor.

# 4

# San Antonio, Texas

## 1954

Sunlight filtered through the dusty Venetian blinds and made long line patterns on the bare floor of my room in the front corner of our new house. I lay diagonally across my bed in my underpants, reaching up behind me to touch the decorative rivets outlining the new white headboard. They were coarse and cool. I climbed them, finger by finger, like the Itsy Bitsy Spider, over my head. Sometime during the night I had kicked off the top sheet, which lay tangled on the floor next to me. I spit on a spot on the bottom sheet where the rounded mattress edge made it taut, and rubbed the white half moons of my nail beds against it. The cold wet soothed me.

I wanted someone to read with me before it got too hot to sit close and turn the pages. I had a new book, *Petite Suzanne,* thicker than Golden Books, with a wide black binding. A relative had sent it to me in the mail. "It's too old for you," my mother said. I knew it had too many words to read the whole thing out loud, but I still liked to look at the pictures. Some were small and drawn with a pencil, but others filled the page and looked like someone had colored them with sharp crayons.

I listened for movement in my parents' room across the hall. I could see through my open door that their door was almost closed, which meant it was Sunday. On any other day the door would be open, my mother would be in the kitchen clinking juice glasses and stirring the oatmeal, and my father would have already left for work at Fort Sam Houston, where he was training to be a surgeon.

I was glad to have a daddy now like everybody else, even though I hardly ever saw him. After we moved out of the apartment in Martinsburg, we drove a very long way across the country, first to spend Christmas with my other grandparents in Modesto, California, and then to San Antonio, Texas, to move into this house at 335 Ridgehaven Place, which had dirt instead of a lawn and skinny little trees with hardly any leaves. Now that it was summer, it was too hot for pajamas at night, and we had to close all the blinds in the daytime to keep the heat out because we didn't have an air conditioner. My mother wanted one, but my father said not yet, we could do without for a while. He was always doing without. He skipped lunch, which made my mother crabby because, as she put it, she was a three-squares-a-day gal. He said he just forgot to eat. And he liked to sleep on the floor. If it was Sunday afternoon or after supper, he stretched out on the living room rug and my mother had to step over him to get to the kitchen. I was careful to go around because I was afraid.

I slid off my bed and got *Petite Suzanne* from the play table my daddy had built for me in the garage, where he kept his tools. The table was big and square, green and white, with drawers big enough to hide in. I kept my barn and my new dollhouse and toys on top and my books in the drawers, because a baby was coming one month after I turned five, and the baby would want my things. I tiptoed across the hall, the wooden floor cool on my bare feet, and stopped to listen. I heard only loud breathing. I pushed the door open and went in. My father wasn't sleeping on the floor. He was on the bed next to my mother. The white sheet was twisted by their feet. She was wearing her short, blue, sleeveless nightgown that you could almost see through but not quite, and she was curled on her side, facing away from him and me. He was lying on his back, naked. My mother had bought him pajamas, but he left them in the package; he didn't need clothes to sleep.

I took one step forward so I could look at my father's face to see if he was waking up. His eyelids didn't move. He looked funny without his glasses. His arms were crossed on his stomach. He made a little noise every time he breathed out. I didn't know if it was OK to ask for breakfast yet so I just stood there, waiting.

Suddenly his right arm smacked my chest as he bolted out of bed and flung me high across the space between bed and wall. My back hit the wall with a thud, and I crashed in a heap on the floor. My mother screamed. I didn't move because I couldn't breathe.

"He didn't mean to, he didn't mean to," my mother kept crying as she picked me up and took me back to my room and sat me down on the bed. My chest hurt. Sobs were starting to come in gasps. "You just startled him," she said while he was putting on his clothes. *But I didn't do anything,* I thought. I only watched.

Several weeks later, for Valentine's Day we got a puppy, a brown dachshund who wagged his tail a lot and kept peeing in the kitchen, where we put newspapers on the floor and boards against the doorways.

"What's its name?" I asked when my father brought it home. I thought it was very cute, but my mother had never had a dog when she was a little girl, and I could tell when her eyebrows knitted together that she wasn't sure she liked it.

"Pashir," my father said.

"Is that a boy name or a girl name? How do you spell it?"

"P-A-S-H-I-R. He's a boy dog."

I pushed my bangs back and straightened my new ponytail. "Why did you name him that?"

"He's named after a guard in Korea."

"How come?"

"Because I promised him," my father said and walked away.

I knew that Korea was another country, but I didn't know where it was. Sometimes after I went to bed at night I could hear my parents talking about it. Not joking or friendly but serious talk. I'd get up and go into the hall, where I hoped they couldn't see me. I heard words like "capture" and "march" and "prisoner." I pictured my father in a jail, behind bars like Curious George.

Once they caught me trying to listen, and their conversation ended midsentence.

"Get in here," my father said. I did as I was told. The air in the room got heavy and stiff, and I couldn't breathe. "What do you want?"

"A drink of water."

"Go ahead and get one. Then go back to your bed and stay there. This is grown-up time."

In November, my father took me and my pajamas and favorite books across the street to stay with Mac and Lorraine, who had some toys but no children even though they wished they did. They told me my mother was going to the hospital. I was afraid she was sick, but they said no, she was going there to get the baby. A couple of days later, Lorraine and I waited by my front door and watched as our Ford pulled into the driveway. My father was driving and my mother was next to him on the front seat. He pulled up to the garage door and shut the engine off. I ran to greet my mother as she started to open the door.

"Look, it's your baby brother! Say hi to him. His name is Dirk," my mother said as she got out of the car and bent down to show me his face sticking out of some blankets.

"Hi," I said as I ducked underneath her bundle to see if what I had been told was true. It was.

"Your tummy's all gone!" I said, patting the front of her slender skirt.

"Yes, it is," she said and smiled at my father, who was already on his way into the house.

I really wanted a baby sister, but I thought this baby would be OK, too. My mother taught me to give him a bath and change his diapers quickly before his fire hose squirted all over. I liked sitting on the couch reading to him while he squirmed on the pillow beside me. I didn't pick him up because I was scared I would drop him. I was scared of other things, like tornadoes and scorpions, but I was even more scared of doing things wrong. Then bad things might happen, really terrible things, worse than I could imagine.

When I was playing tag one Saturday afternoon after my father got home from rounds, I tripped on the curb and skinned my knee in the street. I wasn't supposed to play in the street. But the blood was dripping down my leg into my sock, so I went inside and tried to sneak into the bathroom. My father caught me. He looked at the blood and shook his head. I bit my lip and tried not to cry.

"Go in the bathroom and take your shoes off," he said.

He followed me into the bathroom and pointed to the edge of the tub. I tugged off my shoes and socks and sat down. He groaned a little as he got down on his knees beside me. I could smell his head sweating through his crew cut. His glasses slid down his nose. He pushed them up with one finger while he used the other hand to turn on the water.

"You sure did a number on your knee, Punky," he said with his kind voice, using the nickname he'd bestowed on me when I was a baby, before he went away. "We have to get it clean so it won't get infected." I could see gravel sticking out of the pockmarks around the raw, red patch where skin used to be. It wasn't bleeding that much, but fluid was seeping out. It stung a lot.

He picked up the nailbrush and rubbed the bristles across the bar of soap, then splashed some water on my knee. He started scrubbing.

My stomach clenched. I didn't want to cry, but it hurt so much. He worked up a foamy lather as pink suds slid down my shin.

"It doesn't hurt that bad," my father said. "Many things could hurt worse. It's your job to be a good soldier. Good soldiers are brave and don't cry." I already knew that. I nodded. He finished the scrubbing and patted the spot dry with a towel.

"Can I have a Band-Aid?" I asked, sniffling.

"You can do without," he said. "Just keep it clean and it will heal just fine."

# 5

# Seoul, Korea

## JULY 1950

Two days after the warehouse strafing and eye surgery in Pyong-taek, the soldiers who could walk set out for Seoul, fifty miles away, leaving behind fifteen wounded men they wouldn't see again. They marched at night, over rough terrain. Like Doc, most of the prisoners had been relieved of their boots. Their feet were crusty and bleeding, and their backs and arms ached from frequent contact with rifle butts. As the column straggled, guards kept up an incessant chatter of *bali, bali* and *hayaku* and forced the men in the rear to double-time, *hubba, hubba*.

It was clear the guards despised the Japanese, whose language they spoke and under whose rule they'd chafed for thirty-five years before World War II ended. At one point the guards told twenty-two prisoners to line up by hair color: black hair (Hispanics, Italians, Native Americans, Asians) on one side, and blonds, browns, and redheads on the other.

"You are Japanese," they said, pointing to those with black hair. "The others are Americans."

The prisoners were hungry and bitter. They continued to rage against the president, the Congress, and the army command for their lack of guns, ammunition, leadership, and preparation. By morning, they had become a stinky, filthy, cussing mass of humanity eager to find a resting place in any barn or garage large enough to hold them.

Nights seemed interminable, hope elusive. For one eight-mile stretch, they were treated to a train ride, but the train stopped when two Russian YAKs flew over. Everyone disembarked as the guards dropped their guns and ran for cover. After the skies turned quiet, the guards returned, sheepish. The GIs who had picked up the guns while they were gone weren't quite sure what to do with them, so they handed them back to the guards.

Whenever they were allowed a break, Doc collapsed on the ground to work his instant-sleep magic. The others would wake him when it was time to go, but it was all he could do to stand up and walk again. The excruciating pain in his feet had moved up into his calves and thighs. After he got moving enough to warm his limbs, the pain would subside somewhat. But then he would step on a rock he was too nearsighted to see, his leg would collapse, and he would fall. The buckling was a reflex, like the shin that kicks when a hammer hits the knee. He realized that he had no control over his reaction, and he sensed that his will to survive was slowly disappearing. *It looks bad,* he thought. *Very bad. But what can I do except keep trying?*

He fell again. And again. Sprawled once more on the ground, he sat in despair, watching the feet of his compatriots trudge past. Then he felt a hand on his shoulder and looked up. A fellow officer, Lt. John Brockman, was gazing down at him.

"Why don't you lean on me, Doc? Then maybe you won't fall so much."

Doc nodded as Brockman pulled him to his feet. He held on to Brockman's shoulder as they walked on. His leg continued to buckle, but usually he could recover and keep going. Sometimes he still fell, but Brockman waited with him and helped him up again.

Brockman pointed out the fires raging in the distance. "That must be Seoul on fire up there, Doc, so it shouldn't be too long before we can quit. Just hang in there a little while longer."

Doc hung in there, leaning on Brockman, stumbling to Seoul, forming indelible memories. When he closed his eyes, he saw a picture as vivid as a slide projected on a screen. In it, a fire raged out of control. But in the upper right-hand corner sat a lady with long hair softly curling on her shoulder, looking down at the baby she held in her left arm, lying against her chest. Her voice quiet, she kept saying, "Don't give up." That image of his wife, his daughter, and the fire in Seoul never faded; he could turn his mind's projector on and off at will. He credited Brockman with saving his life as they pushed toward the Han River.

*Never again would I be as exhausted, tired, or scared as I was that night.*

Late the next afternoon, they arrived on the outskirts of Seoul and crossed the filthy Han on a pontoon bridge, only to be ordered to retrace their steps back to the other side, for no reason they could discern. Assorted debris, including dead humans and animals, floated past them on the sluggish current, but that didn't stop some of the thirsty men from cupping their hands and leaning over to scoop up a drink. They spent the night sprawled on the road, trying to sleep. In the morning they crossed the bridge again and were met by North Korean officers carrying a large banner.

*Ah, a parade. Showtime.* The wily prisoners sent their most bedraggled and barefoot colleagues to the outside lines in a silent plea for sympathy, but it didn't take long for the Koreans to notice and insist on rearranging the ranks. As they marched through the main streets of Seoul, civilians jeered and spit on them. Before they had to endure a second propaganda parade on the north side, however, they were given a bath, a shave, and in some cases, a pair of old shoes. Things were looking up.

Yet the formerly well-fed Americans were slowly starving. Twice a day on their four-day trek from Pyongtaek, four men had shared one can of sardines and one small bag of crackers, the standard field ration for one North Korean soldier. Occasionally local civilians provided dry rice balls wrapped in a large, green leaf or a piece of old newspaper. Some men refused to eat them; others couldn't digest them. The guards refused to provide water. Some prisoners got so thirsty they raided the rice paddies, which had been fertilized with human waste; raging diarrhea ensued.

One GI went to Doc with various physical complaints. Although he had been obese and still packed extra pounds, vitamin and protein deficiencies could explain his symptoms.

"Have you been eating?" Doc asked him.

"Not really. The food's bad."

"Well, you need to eat whatever they give you. Even if it tastes bad, it'll make you feel better."

The GI frowned. "My mother never made me eat rice, and I'll be damned if I will eat it here," he said.

Doc could do nothing but shake his head.

More than two hundred men were quartered in a two-story schoolhouse on the northern outskirts of Seoul. North Korean officers visited them to deliver lectures on the evils of capitalism and assure them that they would be treated well. The Koreans also announced that because Gen. Douglas MacArthur had insisted that captured Americans receive their customary three meals a day, the prisoners would be fed three times, which simply meant that their current rations of unseasoned rice balls, watery cabbage soup, and an occasional piece of melon were divided into three portions instead of two.

The men spent several days housed in the crowded school. Occasionally guards would take a prisoner or two away, ostensibly to make political broadcasts; those men were not seen again. Among the troops themselves, no one seemed to be in charge. One soldier informed Doc that, as a captain, he outranked others and was supposed to be the acting CO (commanding officer), but Doc protested, insisting that a medical officer does not command infantry troops.

Physically, he was suffering. His feet were bruised and swollen, and it was all he could do to walk to the latrine. Mentally, the games had set in, his suspicions repeating in an unforgiving loop. *Why didn't the army keep its promise to send me home after ninety days? Am I being punished for refusing to give sleeping pills to that surly officer? Did I do something else wrong? Or fail to follow orders? Why didn't I receive any letters from my wife while I was in Japan? Was the army holding them back? Did she even write? Am I paying for my past sins? Back home I hit a chicken with the car. And I passed that extra copy of the med school test to my frat brothers. But didn't I already get punished for those things?*

Slowly, as he began to feel better physically, the mental torture eased. His thoughts turned to survival, and he focused on the present moment and whatever he might do to make sure those moments kept coming, for him and for those around him. He asked to assist with sick call, but the Koreans refused. As near as Doc could tell, they had little to work with, shoddy equipment, and meager pharmacy supplies. Once they invited him to join them, but when he showed up at the "clinic," he was asked to pose for a propaganda picture. He refused.

At one point, all the prisoners were escorted into the school auditorium and told to sit. Stiff and stilted, select American officers and GIs read prepared statements asking the men to sign a petition demanding an end to the war. After the prisoners signed, the readers explained, the paper would be sent to the United Nations. The Koreans circulated the petition, a blank piece of paper, and insisted the men sign, which they did, of course, thinking it might help them survive. (Several of the men wrote the same names, such as Mickey Mouse and Donald Duck, but no one seemed to notice.)

One afternoon, the guards summoned the men to the courtyard for roll call. "Come with, come with," the Koreans shouted. The men followed orders, not realizing that they would not be allowed to return to the schoolhouse, where they had stowed what few possessions they had left—tattered Bibles, rosary beads, pictures, whatever extra clothing they had managed to hold on to. As they were marched off to a train yard, they vowed they wouldn't make the same mistake again. From now on, they'd keep any and all possessions with them at all times.

Doc had already lost plenty: his thick glasses, his St. Christopher medal, his shoes. But he also gained much of substance: a new acquaintance named Peppe, who would become a trusted confidant and lifelong friend, and other friends, like Shorty Estabrook, a nineteen-year-old spitfire who made everyone laugh, and Eli Culbertson, to whom he'd been tied with telephone wire that bloodied their wrists. He also gained a new, or perhaps renewed, belief in the existence of a supreme being, whatever its name.

*It's something that makes you believe that your strength is part of a plan devised by someone more powerful than you. It's there like a huge wave just before it crests, powerful and never ending in its beauty as it just keeps rolling along, silent in all its majesty but ever present.*

*It is the faith and hope that sustains you; something you accept and admit you do not understand. Prayer becomes a constant, not a once-a-night event—and not always in words, perhaps, but surely in thoughts.*

*How else can you explain the fact that you survive?*

# 6

# San Antonio, Texas

## 1957

Another brother, Eric, arrived in April. I moved into the little bedroom so my brothers could have the big one. They got my play table, but my father said he'd build me a dresser with a lid so I could hide my girl things in there instead. By then I was seven, and my mother said I was a good helper. I set the table. I put away toys. I reported when Eric needed a clean diaper or when Dirk was wheezing and might need his asthma tent to sleep. She asked me to do the best I could, to remember everything she told me, especially on Wednesdays when the maid came to do the cleaning and stay with us while my mother went to the grocery store. This made me feel tall.

One evening a babysitter came to our house. "You're in charge," my mother said as she hugged me good-bye. I liked her smell, Chanel No. 5 from the bottle on her dresser.

"Bedtime is seven thirty for the boys and eight thirty for Cathy," she told the babysitter.

After the babysitter put the boys to bed, Eric started crying. She started toward their room to check on him.

"No, no!" I ran into the hall to block her. "He's supposed to cry." My mother was very strict about this. Sometimes babies just needed to cry themselves to sleep, she told me when I worried. It seemed to me they cried a lot.

Eric was screaming now. The babysitter started toward his room again.

"NO!" I shouted. "You can't go in there! It's orders! He can do without!"

She sat me on the couch and handed me a book, then sat down beside me. I didn't want her there. *I want my mommy. She'd call me a good girl.* I held the book and wiggled my foot until the crying got quieter and quieter and finally stopped. Even though I knew I was right, it seemed to take forever.

My father wasn't like the other fathers on our block. He left early in the mornings before we got up and didn't come home for supper. (I didn't mind this so much because sometimes my mother let me stay up past my regular bedtime and watch old movies on TV. She confessed that she loved Ginger Rogers and Fred Astaire so much when she was my age that she'd skip her Saturday piano lesson and sneak off to watch them, which surprised me because I thought she always followed orders.) Saturdays were just like weekdays, except he got home in time to barbecue hot dogs or hamburgers. On Sundays he didn't toss balls or play games or fix up the yard. I asked my mother why he didn't at least work on the car in the driveway, where we could talk to him.

"Working on cars can hurt your hands and make them dirty," she said. "Your father needs clean hands to be a surgeon." At supper that night I sneaked a look at his hands. The fingernails were neat and clean.

Instead of playing with us, he preferred to be alone in his garage workshop or makeshift darkroom. Once in a while, on a Sunday while my brothers napped, he babysat us. He would move all the dining room chairs except one into the kitchen and push the table back against the sliding glass door. He got out his cameras and tripod, rigged lights and scrims, and snaked wires across the floor. When he was ready, I sat on the remaining chair. He arranged and rearranged the straps on my sundress so they were just so, and he took extra care with my hair, which my mother had fixed before she left.

My mother didn't like my hair because it was always tangled and in my face. She hated brushing it, pulling hard at the knots in back, grunting as my head bounced with her efforts. Even when the knots were gone, she sighed with every stroke. And although it was blonde now, it had been black when I was born, and she promised that when I grew up it would turn brown like hers. Which was too bad, she said, because brown is a mousy color, instead of pretty and dark like that of true brunettes.

My father liked my long hair. He spread it gently on my shoulders and reminded me not to squint or squirm. I was hot and bored under the lights, but I tried to be good so he would let me into the darkroom later. Once, he did. I watched him swish the magic paper in the stinky chemicals until the pictures emerged, then rinse the pages and clip them to a small clothesline strung across the bathtub. I was too shy to talk, but when he talked his voice went up at the ends of sentences, as if he were asking questions and inviting me to answer them. Sometimes he made little jokes. I couldn't tell if I should laugh.

I was never sure how I should be with my father. He could turn instantly from happy to sad, calm to violent. One Sunday afternoon I was outside playing Mother, May I? with the neighborhood kids. As the oldest, I had organized the game in our driveway and was intent on teaching the little ones how to take big steps and little steps forward and back. My mother came out and told me it was almost time for supper.

"OK, I'll be there in a minute."

A few minutes later, my father came out to remind me. His cigarette dangled precariously from his mouth when he talked.

"Just a minute. It's my turn to be the Mother and then I'll be in."

"You're cruisin' for a bruisin'," he said and cleared his throat, his taut upper lip holding the cigarette in place.

He went back inside, then returned to grab my arm so hard I squealed. His face was red. He pulled me into the house and marched me down the hall into my room, where he closed the curtains, sat on the bed, yanked down my shorts and underpants, turned me over his knees, and spanked me hard.

"You will do what I say," he said, the cigarette still dangling. "Don't you dare talk back to me. Ever."

I could see his white handprint on my red skin when I looked in the mirror after he left. At supper I tried to convince myself that the spreading warmth felt good, like the sun-roasted poolside on a hot summer day, but I had to bite my lip to keep it from quivering.

Every other Wednesday morning in the summer, I was allowed to walk to the elementary school library and check out as many books as I could fit into my red wagon, usually ten or twelve. They didn't have my favorite Nancy Drew or Hardy Boy mysteries, or even Bobbsey Twins books, so I loaded up on biographies.

"Are you going to read all those?" the librarian sometimes asked. I nodded. Usually I did. They had big print.

One Saturday afternoon when I was about eight, my father came home early from rounds. I was practicing the piano, which I hated because I had to do it for one hour every day after school while the neighborhood kids got to play outside. I'd only been practicing for half an hour when my father finished the sandwich my mother had saved for him under a napkin and came to stand by the piano bench. I put my hands in my lap and looked up at him. Had I been cruisin' for a bruisin' again? Riding for a fall?

"Want to come with me to the post library? I need to get some medical books."

My heart skipped a beat. "Do they have children's books?"

"I don't know, but we can check."

Although I was thrilled to go along, I was also scared. It was just us two, and I didn't know what to talk about. We climbed into the front seat of his small yellow car, which he bought used after my mother complained about having to leave us alone while she picked him up from work on the days she kept the car. My face felt hot, but I was happy inside. The guards in the little guardhouse saluted as we drove through the gates into Fort Sam Houston. A long ribbon of parade grounds stretched out in both directions. At one end, majestic in its Alamo way, was the hospital. We went the other way, skirting the parade grounds for several blocks before parking next to a building that looked exactly like all the other buildings around it. We got out and walked up a long sidewalk. "*Bali, bali, hayaku*," my father said. I knew this meant I was supposed to keep up. He had very long legs, so mostly I ran. I wanted to hold his hand, but I was afraid to reach for it.

Inside the library were more books than I had ever seen in one place. Rooms of them. Giant stacks of shelves, taller than I could reach. I followed my father as he went from one section to the next, gathering his heavy, thick books, and took them up to the desk to check out. I waited while the librarian, a jowly, manly woman in a tan uniform, stamped the card inside each back cover.

"I want a book, too," I said when she finished. I wondered if my father had forgotten I was there.

"We don't have children's books," she said. "But over there is our fiction section if you want to look at those."

"Can we?" I asked. My father nodded, and I wanted to hug him for that, but of course I didn't. Whenever I tried, he walked away.

I selected a book I could reach. The print was too small, so I put it back and got another. That was better. It was for grown-ups but only medium fat. The title was something about a long walk home.

"How about this one?" I showed it to him, and he said it was fine. We checked it out: my first grown-up book, which I carried proudly to the car. I was allowed to keep it for more than one week, so I would have time to read the whole thing. The story was sad, but I liked it anyway.

Even when the weather was bad, I walked the seven blocks to and from school. In the mornings the walk seemed long because my side ached from going too fast so I wouldn't be late. But in the afternoons I took my time, and as long as I didn't dawdle too much, my mother wouldn't yell at me. On library days, students could stay after the final bell for a few minutes to check out books. I always reminded her which days were library days.

I was walking home one library day when I noticed three scrawny boys playing catch with a football in a corner yard about two blocks from my house. They wore tattered shorts, T-shirts, and tennis shoes with holes. No socks. I kept my eyes straight ahead as I walked past them.

"Hey, girl!" one shouted. "Whatcha got there?"

I held my books tight and kept walking.

"Hey, didn't you hear me? I asked you a question." The other boys had stopped tossing their ball and were watching their friend. When he kept yelling at me, they started laughing and swearing.

"HEY. Whatsa matter with you, four-eyes? Can't you talk?"

My face burned. I had gotten my glasses a few weeks earlier, after my teacher told my mother that I had to go to the bathroom too many times.

"Why do you have to go potty so much at school?" my mother had asked.

"Because."

"Does it sting when you go?"

I shook my head.

"Do you have to go just a few drops, or a lot?"

"Just a few drops."

"So why do you have to go so often for just a few drops?"

I hesitated. She waited.

"So I can see what she wrote on the blackboard."

After I got my glasses, I loved seeing the chalk words so clear, and also the leaves that grew at the tops of trees. But I hated everyone making fun of me. Now this boy was doing it, and he sounded mean.

He came down the grassy slope onto the street and stood in front of me. His friends went behind me. They were older than I was, and although I was one of the tallest kids in my class, they were taller.

The leader stuck his face within inches of mine.

"Where are you going?"

"Home," I said in an almost whisper.

"You're goin' nowhere. You just go stand up there and stay till we're ready to let you go." He motioned toward the steps by the front door of the house and gave me a push. My feet tangled and I stumbled, dropping my books. They all laughed, throwing back their heads, and slapping their thighs.

"Pick 'em up and get up there!" the leader shouted. The other boys were closing in with a chorus of "yeahs," so I did as I was told. I wondered whether the mom was home and might rescue me, but if she was there, she stayed inside. The boys went back to playing catch, making sure to throw the ball hard, between me and the street.

Tears came into the corners of my eyes, but I willed them dry. I tried to stand up straight. A soldier stands up straight. I had to be strong. I might have to be strong for a long time. I might have to go without supper. My job was to do what I had to do to make it home, even though I didn't know what was going to happen to me or what, if anything, I could do about it. I didn't think something terrible was going to happen this time, not really. It was more like I needed to practice being here, having no power at all.

My mouth was dry. I tried to think about what I did to get to this place. Maybe I walked on the wrong side of the street. Maybe I looked ugly, like someone to pick on. I thought about calling for help, but who would help me? Help would not come. This is how we did it in our family; we accepted what was. We tried to make the best of it. We were brave.

I looked down at my feet to make sure they were straight and lined up. Very carefully, I shifted my books from one arm to the other. I pulled my shoulders back and pretended I was balancing a book on top of my head, like runway models do. My stomach rumbled, and I hoped the boys wouldn't hear.

The boys had quit paying attention to me. They seemed bored with their game. Maybe I could make a run for it. But no, they could run faster, and they outnumbered me. I had to get past them all to get to the street. Then I might fall and skin my knees, and they would laugh again. I stayed put.

"So, you want to get out?" the first boy called to me. I nodded.

"We'll let you out, but you gotta get this question right. OK, here it is. What's three times two?"

My heart pounded so loud I thought he'd hear. I didn't know the answer. I could add and subtract, but I hadn't learned multiplication yet. I had heard other kids talk about times tables, but I didn't know them. Maybe I could figure it out? Three times . . . two. Two times . . . three. Three, two times. Three one time and then another time, so that would be adding them together. I could add three and three: that would be six. But what about the twos? I decided that three of those would be six, too, yet still my heart thumped. If I was wrong, I might not get out. Like in prison camp.

I felt like I'd been standing there for hours. It took a long time to get from deciding I had the right answer to feeling brave enough to call it out.

"C'mon, it's easy. It's just three times two," the boy said. He didn't sound quite so mean. I held my books close, with both arms.

"Six," I said, louder than I meant to.

"Yeah, that's right!" he said. "OK, you can go." I walked down the yard to the street and turned right. It was that easy. But I felt like someone else now, carrying a new dread inside. Somehow I'd passed a test, although I probably didn't get an A.

When I got home, my mother didn't yell at me. She didn't even look at the clock. She told me to change my clothes and asked how school was. "Fine," I told her and went to practice the piano.

# 7

# Pyongyang, North Korea

## JULY 1950

For four days, crammed into two dilapidated coaches, the prisoners rode the rails from Seoul to Pyongyang, the capital of North Korea. They spent daylight hours stopped in tunnels, where they would be safe from strafing aircraft, and moved at night under cover of darkness. Once they reached the city and disembarked at the railroad station, mounted guards surrounded them, and a North Korean guard nicknamed Bullfrog marched them, double-time, through the center of the city. This quickstep parade, sans banners, took three hours, no breaks allowed.

Standard military discipline (following orders issued by those who rank above you) had eroded among these American prisoners. Stateside, the ranks were segregated in many ways on military posts, from family housing areas to swimming pools and social clubs. Here all men were treated alike, regardless of age, rank, or training. They were mostly young, many still in their teens, and ill prepared for the unimaginable; they fended for themselves with little thought for the well-being of the group. Yet leaders, whether or not they were officers, began to emerge on these miserable treks. Some of them reprimanded the more disgruntled ones for their derogatory remarks. Their carping wasn't helping anyone. In fact, it was destroying what little morale remained.

On July 25, 1950, nearly two weeks after his capture, Doc arrived at the tin-roofed schoolhouse that would be home for the next month. His group joined another group of about 125 Americans who had already moved in. About a week later, more soldiers from the Twenty-Fourth Division, also captured during the Task Force Smith fiasco, arrived. All 724 prisoners took up residence on the second floor of the building, which also housed two latrines, a makeshift mess hall and cooking area, an education room, the commandant's office, a room used for sick call, and a hospital room with a platform, built about a foot above the floor around all four sides, where patients slept.

With GI chefs preparing the meals, dining improved in Pyong-yang. Rice and soup made with cabbage, daikons, and occasionally potatoes were served for breakfast. Dog meat—the small bones were the giveaway—gave the soup valuable protein and a slightly sweet flavor. *Tastes pretty good,* Doc thought. But evidently someone objected because it disappeared. Lunch was a two-inch square of bread with onion greens and dried fish that had been boiled. Dinner was just like breakfast. Sometimes the cooks had a little bit of soybean oil and salt available for spicing things up, and occasionally the men got a special treat: an apple apiece. They ate in shifts, sharing one hundred bowls and an equally limited number of chopsticks.

Every morning, the men rose at dawn for roll call and about twenty minutes of calisthenics, called PT (physical training). They were allowed to use local wells for washing and brushing their teeth, and soap and toothbrushes were provided. Twice during the month of August, they had the dubious privilege of walking four miles to bathe and wash their clothes in a river. Some passed up the opportunity, either because their feet were too damaged (many were still barefoot) or, much to Doc's chagrin, because they just didn't want to. *Sheer laziness,* he presumed.

Prison life was dull, punctuated only by an occasional game of cards. Men were forced to sit cross-legged in rows all day. Leaders checked frequently to make sure the rows were straight. They also issued occasional orders for the men to stand up, which they weren't otherwise allowed to do. Five at a time were allowed to go outside and smoke two cigarettes each. Visits to the toilet had to be approved—"*Benjo* OK?"— and were often denied at some guard's whim. No one was allowed to go to the latrine after 10:00 p.m. *Their primary objective is to reduce the human race to a herd of unthinking, unfeeling, impersonal, obedient animals—a race of robots whose only instinct is to obey, whose every human instinct has been crushed and extinguished,* Doc decided, although he didn't dare complain out loud. Because he was an officer, the guards called him into the commandant's office several times to listen to their complaints about the Americans' lack of discipline and inability to keep individuals from doing whatever they felt like doing. They charged him with keeping the men in line and making sure they followed all orders.

*This is insane,* Doc thought. He told the guards to go to hell and told the men nothing.

Individual interrogations were conducted regularly, and the entire group was frequently herded into an auditorium and subjected to fanatical lectures extolling the virtues of communism and expounding on the vices of capitalism. Skipping these lectures was not an option. Blank pieces of paper designated as "petitions" and "peace appeals" were circulated for signatures. Several soldiers were taken away to write and record speeches for broadcast. Complying with this request was considered necessary, but the prisoners shared their own set of rules: Don't say anything suggesting treason or related to surrender. Choose themes that would seem ridiculous to fellow Americans, so the folks at home understand that the speech is being made under duress for propaganda purposes. Pepper the broadcast with bad grammar and military slang expressions such as the dismissive "tell it to the Marines." Finally, to maintain some order in the ranks, make sure an American officer approves the speech before you record it.

One day Mr. Tor, an interpreter, tapped Doc on the shoulder and gestured for Doc and another soldier to follow him. He took them downtown to the local radio station, where Doc was provided with beer, watermelon, cookies, and cigarettes and seated in front of a microphone. He was asked to read a broadcast of about five hundred words, which he proceeded to do in a dull monotone, muffing the words as often as he dared. After a few minutes, the door opened to screaming Koreans and an irritated Mr. Tor, who informed him that this was not the way to make a broadcast. Doc tried it twice more, each time eliciting a more violent reaction. The fourth try brought in the guards, who threw the bolts on their guns and began hitting him about the head and shoulders.

Much to Doc's surprise, Mr. Tor intervened and pulled Doc into a separate room where they sat in chairs facing each other. Mr. Tor, whose English previously had been broken and primitive, now spoke with a cultured British clip. He explained that he was really a university professor who had only recently been drafted into a military with which he did not always agree. Pleading for better cooperation, he suggested some phrase changes that Doc might find more palatable and promised to justify them to his superiors. And this conversation, he added, needed to be kept secret.

Doc never knew whether the man was pulling his leg, lying in order to generate better propaganda, or was sincere in his negotiations. Scratching his head, he returned to the microphone and read his piece as directed, this time with a burp gun thrust into his stomach, two carbines held against his back, and two or three men behind him loudly loading their M1 rifles.

As his feet continued to heal, Doc's strength and resolve returned. Once again he offered his medical skills to his captors, and this time he wasn't turned away. He was allowed to accompany the young Korean doctor on sick call, seeing about twenty prisoners a day, although there wasn't much they could do with a few sulfa pills and some unidentified powders prescribed for diarrhea. The Korean insisted on stuffing wounds with gauze strips, then bandaging them with old bandages that had been rewashed. He did not want to know how Doc preferred to do this or what Western medicine might have had to say about it; that would cause him to lose face. Doc learned to keep his mouth shut when necessary.

On one occasion, the team saw a GI who had been shot several days before and had developed a large, painful hematoma. He wanted it drained. Noting that the entrance and exit wounds from the bullet were healing well, Doc explained to the GI and the Koreans that a hematoma was an enclosed pool of blood that would slowly reabsorb on its own and shouldn't be touched. Surprisingly, the Koreans went along with Doc's explanation and sent the GI back to quarters.

In the middle of the night, a guard woke Doc and asked him to go to the camp dispensary, which by then was staffed by the doctor, a pharmacist, and two nurses. When he arrived, Doc found the Korean doctor pleading for help as he leaned over the GI on the examining table. Blood was spurting from the GI's right thigh. After the GI returned to the dispensary because he was still in pain, the Korean doctor decided to cut into the hematoma. Now the bleeding wouldn't stop. Using candles and flashlights to see, Doc plunged his dirty fingers into the wound, found the bleeding vessel, and tied it off with a piece of string. The patient was taken to a hospital, along with fellow soldiers who agreed to donate blood for a transfusion. It was a direct transfusion: the blood was drawn with a syringe from the donor and injected directly into the patient. The man lived for some weeks, until the bleeding started again as the prisoners embarked on their next cross-country trek.

On another occasion, a guard's gun accidentally discharged and shot a sleeping soldier in the leg. Once again, Doc was called to the dispensary. This time a pressure bandage stopped the bleeding, but the leg also appeared to be broken. When a truck rattled into the compound about an hour later, his Korean counterparts invited Doc to climb aboard and accompany his patient through the winding, empty streets to the city's main hospital, to better plead his case for saving the man's leg.

The men brought his patient into the hospital on a stretcher. While the buxom Russian nurse who met them in the waiting room jabbered on, Doc sneaked away from the group in search of the operating room, which was down the hall, and barged in to check out the facilities. The surgeons, working in white masks, gowns, and pants, were finishing up an operation. They were barefoot. Their patient lay on a painted metal table with a base of painted pipe and scrap steel. A miserable light housed in an old-fashioned operating reflector hung over the table, scarcely illuminating its occupant. Instruments were few and decrepit. Doc was not welcome here; nurses quickly moved to eject him, despite vehement objections from the interpreter.

Not only was Doc kicked out; he was also unsuccessful in his main mission. His patient's leg was later amputated in a guillotine operation, sliced off with no skin flaps left to close the wound. The soldier managed to live through the next phase of the prisoners' journey but died later from malnutrition and dysentery, like many of his compatriots.

As August crawled into September, dysentery—which infects the colon and causes cramping; bloody, mucus-filled stools; and sometimes fever—was becoming a problem. Men who had visited the *benjo* six to ten times a day now had to make as many as thirty trips daily, but only with permission, of course. About a hundred men showed up at sick call every day, and a few with severe diarrhea died. One sergeant became paralyzed from the waist down, which Doc attributed to a tuberculosis-related malady called Pott's disease. Another sergeant apparently suffered a heart attack and dropped dead. The camp commander told Doc to put the body in back of the schoolhouse and leave it there for two hours because it was possible the prisoner would come back to life and be all right. Doc did as he was told, but the sergeant remained dead.

Despite these setbacks, morale improved during their stint in Pyongyang. Bitterness abated somewhat as the men quit talking about the past and adopted an in-the-moment approach to the present. They played cards and told jokes. They quit bashing the government back home. And they cherished whatever military highlights they could grab. One day a nearby tobacco factory suffered a direct hit and went up in flames. The prisoners applauded, despite the fact that the Korean guards would now have a convenient excuse to withhold cigarettes. When a Navy fighter plane knocked an enemy YAK out of the sky just 1,000 yards from the schoolhouse, everyone cheered.

One Sunday afternoon, Doc had finished sick call and was crossing the courtyard to the schoolhouse when he spotted U.S. Navy planes flying low, strafing the countryside. Then the unmistakable whine of bombs falling quickened his steps to the room where prisoners crammed together, talking, dealing cards, trying to nap. *Good. They're bombing the bridges.*

The next bomb sent him to his knees, and the one after that shook the schoolhouse so hard he feared the roof would collapse. All around him men hit the floor, rolled into balls as tight as they could, and covered their heads with arms skinny from malnutrition and disuse. For fifteen minutes bombs exploded, friendly fire, as dust cascaded from the ceiling and the room creaked with the sound of splintering wood.

Then it stopped. No direct hits, all quiet again. No one seemed in a hurry to move. They lay in place, listening for distant guns, perhaps contemplating their wartime fate. Except for one. Capt. Herb Marlatt sat up straight, gazed upward, and sang, in an exquisite tenor voice, "Danny Boy." When he finished, still no one moved. So he sang another, "The Whiffenpoof Song":

> We are poor little lambs who have lost our way,
> Baa! Baa! Baa!
> We are little black sheep who have gone astray,
> Baa. Baa. Baa.

Gentlemen songsters off on a spree,
Damned from here to Eternity,
God have mercy on such as we,
Baa. Baa. Baa.

As the final note drifted away, the men stayed silent, committing the moment, at least in Doc's case, to vivid, unassailable memory.

# 8

# San Antonio, Texas

## 1958

Oyster stew was a holiday tradition in Pelican Rapids, Minnesota, where my father grew up, the sixth child born to Danish immigrants. His father was the town's doctor and their house the town's hospital, so my grandmother cleaned and cooked for patients as well as family. Her Christmas *krumkakke* and *aebleskiver* were legendary, as was her *lefse,* thin crepes she made from leftover mashed potatoes. Whenever she came to visit, we ate *lefse* rolled up with butter and sugar. We begged my mother to make *lefse* at other times, but she said it was too much work. She did not have the cookware to make *krumkakke* or *aebleskiver,* but once a year, she made oyster stew.

"Look what I found!" she said on Christmas Eve, rushing in the front door with two bags of groceries. She pulled out a little plastic tub and held it up. "Oysters! They're even supposed to be fresh." Since we lived in Texas, where oysters weren't considered a Christmas necessity, her hunt took her to local grocery stores she rarely visited. The post commissary, a bleak warehouse with harsh lighting and squeaky carts that echoed in the enormous space, didn't carry such delicacies, and she used canned oysters only as a last resort.

She started unloading the groceries onto the counter, pushing aside the angel food cake cooling upside down over a bottle. That was for Christmas Day, my father's birthday, and we'd eat it with frozen strawberries and vanilla ice cream after a big dinner of roast beef and potatoes and a vegetable—always three things—and sometimes rolls and pickles as extras. But tonight the stew was the star. My father would even come home early in time to eat with us.

"Go set the table, Punky," she said, tying an apron around her waist and bending down to retrieve the iron skillet from the back of the cupboard. I set out the napkins and silverware, then went back to watch her dump the oysters into the pan. It was the first time I'd paid attention to how she cooked them.

"How do you know when they're done?" I asked, trying not to think about the taste or texture in my mouth. *Icky.*

"You heat them in their juice until the edges curl. Then you add the milk."

After the milk she added a hunk of oleomargarine, which was as good as butter and cheaper, she claimed, and turned the heat down to simmer. She didn't add salt and certainly not pepper. Once she tried to sneak pepper sprinkles onto a pot roast, but my father smelled it the minute he walked through the door. He said his mother broke up housekeeping with the same tin of pepper she started out with, never having used it, and he wasn't about to start eating it now.

The stew was ready. We waited. It wasn't long before the door opened and my father strode in, hanging his coat in the closet and washing his hands at the kitchen sink.

"Mmmmmm," he said, sniffing the steam rising from the pan. *"Chop chop ding how."*

My mother ladled the stew into bowls, two small bowls and three big ones.

"Not so much for me," I said, but she put another ladleful into my big bowl anyway.

We all sat down. I stared at my bowl, eyeing the six slippery nuggets and trying not to gag on the aroma wafting up into my face. No one talked as spoons clanked dully against melamine. I could never decide which to eat first, the stew or the oysters. I liked cold milk just fine, but this milk was hot and stunk of fish, like the underside of a dock slimed with rotting seaweed. And there was so much of it. Once I tried holding my breath while spooning it in, but it spurted out my nose and got me in trouble.

Another time I had been sick in bed on Christmas Eve day, but my father said I was well enough to put on my blue corduroy bathrobe and come to the table. My mother must have felt sorry for me because she gave me only three oysters. They were rubbery lumps of misery. I couldn't swallow them whole, and I couldn't chew them. When she wasn't looking, I plucked one out of my mouth and held it under the chair for the dog. He took one sniff and went to sit by my brother's chair instead, so I slid the oyster into my bathrobe pocket. No one noticed. The other oysters followed. I finished the milk as if I liked it.

Now my mother was watching me not eat my oyster stew.

"Remember last year?" she said with a crooked smile.

"What?"

"Your oysters. Remember what you did with them?"

"No," I lied.

"You put them in your pocket. And when I hung your bathrobe on the clothesline a few weeks later, they fell out and bounced across the grass. Hard as rocks."

My father chuckled. "Eat your oysters," he said.

Somehow I got them down.

Not eating was a sin in our family. We ate what was put in front of us, and we belonged to the clean plate club. On mornings when my mother set a large bowl of oatmeal in front of me, my stomach churned as the steam wet my bangs. I detested the grayish muck, no matter how much sugar I added. After three bites I was full, but so, still, was the bowl, and I wasn't allowed to stop until it was empty. I spent the first hour at school praying I wouldn't throw up in the aisle.

I soon developed my own set of eating rules. Number one: Eat bad stuff first. Gulp it down, even if it makes you gag, just make it vanish from your plate so you don't have to dread it. Then you have only good stuff to look forward to. Number two: Eat bad stuff while it's hot. The only thing worse than hot awfulness is cold awfulness. Number three: Save the best till last. If everything left on your plate is good, save the best longest, so you have something to eat when no one else does. If good always follows bad, and full always follows empty, then all will be right with the world, at least for a while.

One night at dinner I got so busy eating mashed potatoes and fried chicken—my mother fixed the best fried chicken in the world, everybody said so—that I forgot my eating rules and let my asparagus get cold. I sat staring at it.

"Don't turn up your nose at the asparagus," my father cautioned. It was his favorite vegetable. It made my pee stink.

Green beans I liked. Broccoli I liked. Carrots I loved. But canned asparagus smelled like the mildew on our porch chairs, and I especially hated the stringiness. I would chew and chew every bite, wondering why my teeth were too dull to sever the strands. The tender spear tip was easier to eat than the woody stem end, but if all of it was cold, it didn't much matter.

I dutifully ate one bite and then a second. By the third bite my stomach was roiling. I couldn't put it in my mouth.

My father looked down at my plate.

"Finish your asparagus," he said.

I couldn't. I really couldn't. But I didn't dare say so.

"Eat it," he said again. "You will stay here until you do."

I wasn't too worried yet. He wasn't clearing his throat, and his face wasn't getting red. He was smoking, not dangling, his after-dinner cigarette.

I looked at the asparagus. Maybe it would taste better colder, I thought. No, it was already colder. I could smell it. I couldn't eat it.

Dirk finished his food, climbed down from his chair, and went to play cowboys with Eric. My mother, silent, cleared the table. My father sat there with me. I stared at the whiteness of the walls, at the crumbs left on the tablecloth. It was quiet in the dining room.

"Men died because they were picky like you," my father said.

"Who?"

"Prisoners."

"But who?"

He wouldn't answer. He puffed on his cigarette and peered out through the smoke at something I couldn't see. My throat was closing. I wanted more milk, but he had a rule for that too: pour water into the empty milk glass and drink it down before filling it again with milk. Milky water tasted bad, but not as awful as cold asparagus. I could hear my mother starting the dishes and knew she wouldn't rescue me. I felt like I'd swallowed a golf ball. I had to do something while I could still breathe.

I put a bite of asparagus in my mouth and chewed. Chewed until I couldn't chew anymore, then swallowed. And gagged. The woody stem had hit a snag. When it wouldn't go down, its friends came back up. I vomited on the plate. My father looked down at the gray-green mound of half-digested food.

"Eat that," he said.

I looked up at him, but I couldn't find Daddy. He looked at me with eyes of blue ice, but I could tell he didn't see me. It was as if I had disappeared. Or he had. I sat alone at that table, my plate before me, with an empty man.

"Eat."

I ate.

# 9

# Manpo, North Korea

## SEPTEMBER 1950

On September 6, the prisoners left Pyongyang. The able-bodied crammed into one train coach and two open gondola cars, while another coach carried the sick and wounded collected from the schoolhouse as well as those who had been in local Korean hospitals. A third coach carried a ragtag group of seventy-five or eighty civilian captives, including American and British missionaries, British and French embassy workers, Russians, and Turks. The North Koreans had arrested any non-Koreans they encountered in the Communist-held areas. Although some of the civilians were children, most were much older; the average age was about sixty-five.

As usual, the train moved only at night and sought shelter from air raids during the day. Civilians along the way provided food: two meals a day of rice and soup, plus, twice, a bonus of pork. On the first day of the five-day journey, the train was strafed while stopped at a small village called Ma Run. Most of the prisoners had left the train for shelter in the woods, but those too ill or wounded to walk had stayed aboard. When the prisoners returned to the train, they found three bodies, including a sergeant and the GI with the hematoma, Doc's former patient, whose leg had later been amputated mid-thigh. His stump had opened up, and he bled to death. The prisoners put the bodies on makeshift stretchers and started up the hill into the woods to search for a burial plot.

"Hey, Doc, I'm pretty sure the sergeant here was Catholic. Do you think we could find someone to conduct a service?" asked one prisoner.

He pointed to a group of civilians watching nearby. Doc had heard the rumor that French missionaries were aboard the train, although the guards had prevented civilians and soldiers from mingling. He was willing to ask if one could perform the necessary ritual but figured he would need an interpreter.

"Go see if you can find a GI who speaks French," he told the prisoner.

"Oh, that's OK—I think I can speak English quite well if the guards allow it," quipped a tall, middle-aged man as he stepped forward from the group. He was Monsignor Thomas Quinlan, an Irish Catholic bishop who had spent many years as a missionary in China and Korea and spoke both languages fluently. He was known among the civilians not only for his compassion and kindness, but also for embedding gleaned news in the made-up songs he sang with a grin as he walked the halls of their former quarters. He convinced the guards to stand back as he climbed the hill and delivered a brief funeral service, the first of many, in a voice that soothed with its quiet tones.

On September 11, the train arrived in Manpo, a place Doc was to dub *kindergarten,* where he learned to separate what was important from what wasn't and where he tried to figure out why some human beings survived while others did not. He thought he knew those things already but decided then, in the autumn before he turned twenty-seven, that he was wrong. All his schooling had not taught him what he needed to know.

On the city's north side, high on a cliff overlooking the Yalu River, the prisoners set up housekeeping and resumed their simple routines in a former prison used by the Japanese during their occupation. The Korean camp commanders called a meeting of officers and explained the rules and regulations. The men were to be divided into squads of eight to ten who would occupy a small, defined space and do everything together: eat, sleep, smoke, visit the latrine. The ranking officer, Maj. John Dunn, was having none of it. An opinionated, tough, stubborn U.S. infantry officer who had previously served in China, the major had been hit in the chin and lost a lot of blood when he was captured, but he was recovering. He stood up to the commanders, refusing to comply with what he deemed absurd orders, and demanded that he be given the authority to run the camp as he saw fit. He agreed to handle work details and administer punishment among his men, but the guards had to agree to leave the immediate premises. Much arguing ensued. Dunn eventually prevailed, earning the respect not only of his fellow officers but also of his captors. Even Doc, a rebel who got his ears pinned back on occasion by his superior, came to regard Dunn as a lifelong mentor.

Morale was generally good. Dunn was allowed to control his troops, and he had bonded with the Korean commander, a former well-known soccer player and American football fan, over their mutual love of professional sports. Yet camaraderie, the esprit de corps that might have helped the men survive the brutality yet to come, was generally absent. Despite Dunn's best leadership efforts, men who were now at liberty to develop new friends and knit together a well-disciplined, cooperative unit failed to do so. Many of the prisoners were peacetime recruits and draftees too new to see the need for military discipline. They defied orders, lied, and stole. While stealing from the enemy was condoned if it benefited the entire group, offenders who stole from their buddies had their cases heard by a board of officers who could sentence them to time in the "stockade," a small storeroom guarded by fellow prisoners. Yet even some of the officers displayed dismissive attitudes and lacked commitment to a unified cause. *Unworthy of their rank,* Doc thought.

One morning during calisthenics, an officer standing in front of the men looked pathetic: cold, miserable, shaking, depressed. Dunn took the officer aside and dressed him down.

"Sure, it's cold, but you don't show your clay feet to your men," Dunn later explained to Doc, who'd seen the reprimand. "An officer leads men. That's what he's getting paid for."

At mealtimes, officers ate last. When the enlisted men complained that they did so because they wanted all that was left, Doc pleaded with Dunn to let the officers eat first, so the angry rumors would stop.

"OK, we'll try your experiment. But I'll bet you that in less than an hour after we announce it, you'll hear that the officers are eating first because the food will run out. Good officers go hungry so their men can eat," Dunn said.

The announcement was made. Less than thirty minutes later, Doc saw a GI during sick call. The chief complaint: "There's a food shortage, and the damn officers are going to be sure they get their share!" When he admitted to Dunn that he'd made a judgment error, Dunn chuckled.

"We will make a soldier out of you yet, Doc."

Prison life at this point was bearable, though not comfortable. The days were warm, but nights were increasingly cold and miserable. The barefoot soldiers still wore the ragged summer fatigues in which they'd been captured more than two months ago. Blankets were rare. As the days, too, grew colder, half of the prisoners were issued either a heavily padded Korean jacket or a pair of pants, while the rest did without. Some got shoes, most of which were too small for American feet.

The Manpo compound contained a hospital building with a room that housed about ten patients, who slept on platforms built about a foot off the floor around the sides. The Americans got permission to construct a bunk bed sort of arrangement and set to work adding a second set of shelves, which accommodated ten additional patients. Doc was allowed to select five medics to bring food to them, keep a fire burning in the stove, and assist in medical care. Two of these medics took night duty.

The building also contained an indoor latrine and two rooms that could be used as doctors' offices. Every morning at ten, Doc attempted to supervise sick call. He would examine the patients queued up outside his door, write his recommendations on a slip of paper, then deliver the paper to the Korean doctor. If the doctor agreed with Doc's suggestions, the patient would receive the recommended treatment. Unfortunately, not much treatment was available. Sulfa drugs, for example, were limited to four pills per person a day, hardly a therapeutic dose, although hoarding the pills to adequately treat one case of pneumonia was permitted. Aspirin tablets were ground up, mixed with talc, and distributed in small paper packets; the same often happened with penicillin and sulfa. More than a hundred men had scabies, a contagious skin infection caused by mites that burrow under the skin and produce intense, allergic itching; no treatment whatsoever was available. Some men were visiting the latrine every half hour to deal with bloody, mucus-filled diarrhea, which Doc attempted to treat with powders that were supposedly an opium derivative; he had no idea what he was really dispensing. Infections were common. Lice ruled.

Doc's frustrations over inadequate treatment options didn't end with his captors. He bristled when his patients objected to making do. The prisoners wanted real bandages, not discarded clothing torn into rags, and real splints, not random pieces of wood. Plenty of hot water was available to soak infections, but they questioned this cure. They demanded medicine that was not available.

The Koreans were quite willing to let Doc do whatever minor surgeries were necessary. He surmised that they recognized that his U.S. medical training was more advanced than their own, although he had not completed a surgical residency. But he couldn't handle everything.

Early one morning, Rudyard Olsen, a private from Bertha, Maine, came stumbling across the compound, his arms draped over the shoulders of two friends. He was doubled over in severe abdominal pain and could hardly move his feet. Doc examined him and decided that he displayed symptoms of acute appendicitis.

"I think you're going to need to have your appendix out," Doc told Olsen. "I will do what I can to get you to a hospital, but all we can really do is hope for the best."

Olsen nodded.

Doc had no antibiotics and no instruments. He found the Korean doctor and begged for help.

"There must be surgeons in Manpo," Doc insisted. "Can't you go and find someone to do this operation?"

The Korean doctor agreed to request permission from the camp commander to go into the city and find help. An hour or two later, he informed Doc that permission had been granted and set off. Eventually, the Korean doctor returned to the camp and said he'd made arrangements for Olsen's surgery. When the transport vehicle arrived, the Korean told Doc to select a medic and climb on board for the ride to the hospital so that both of them could assist with the operation.

That night, Doc and his medic were ushered into a small building on the north side of Manpo. This meager place, which the Korean explained was all that was left after American bombing, would be Olsen's operating room.

Doc was led to a small room where he was given a bowl of water, soap, and a scrub brush and told to prepare for surgery. Before he scrubbed in, though, he was ordered to take off his boots and roll up his pant legs and sleeves. The sleeves he understood; surgeons scrubbed up to their elbows. But pant legs? He had no idea what that was about. He scrubbed for ten minutes, soaked his hands in alcohol, and followed his interpreter and a young Korean nurse into the operating room.

The room measured about eight by ten feet, with cement floors and a single 25-watt lightbulb in an open socket hanging over a field operating table. Doc was directed to the left side of the table. Across the table he saw open doors at both ends of the room and noticed a small crowd of people milling about, chattering, just outside. The interpreter explained that they were townspeople who had come to view the surgery. Eventually a stocky Korean came in, announced that he was the surgeon, and with great fanfare, called for the patient. While they waited for Olsen, the Korean told Doc that he had trained with all the great surgeons in Moscow and began to recite the Communist version of Russia's great world accomplishments.

Without warning, a nurse walked in with a bucket of cold water, which she threw across the medical team's bare legs. The purpose of this, the interpreter said, was to sterilize the operating room. Trying not to laugh, Doc looked down at his filthy fatigues and dripping calves, then up again at the townsfolk flowing in one door and out the other.

Finally, Olsen stumbled in, held upright by two assistants, and climbed onto the cold stainless steel table. He was naked. It was probably between forty and fifty degrees outside, like a late October night in Minnesota. Doc explained what was going on, talking at length to keep the patient's mind off the impending surgery.

"It's all OK with me, Doc," Olsen said. "Let's just get on with it."

The assistants unfolded clean sheets to drape Olsen's abdomen, which had been washed and shaved earlier. They used Mercurochrome to paint the area where the incision was to be made. This accomplished, the surgeon paused to explain the procedure with great flourishes to the moving line of visitors.

"What about anesthesia?" Doc asked. He knew Olsen was wondering, too. A nurse arrived with Novocaine in a 30 cc syringe and explained that this was all that was available due to war shortages. It was hardly enough to anesthetize the skin.

"You're going to feel the knife, but the pain won't last long," Doc told Olsen. Olsen nodded.

The Korean surgeon held the knife over the abdomen, poised to make a midline incision. Doc objected, indicating that a side incision would be preferable. They argued. The Korean finally agreed to make a more lateral incision. He cut. Olsen bit his lips to keep from screaming. There was more fanfare as the surgeon put his finger into the abdominal cavity in search of the appendix while, of course, continuing to chat with the locals.

Then the conversation stopped abruptly. The surgeon became more intent in his search but came up with no appendix. He fired off a terse question to the interpreter.

"He wants to know if Americans have their appendixes on the left side rather than the right," the interpreter said.

"No, they don't," Doc replied. "Same side. Can I try?"

The Korean surgeon nodded. As Doc plunged his bare hand into the abdomen and pulled up a gangrenous appendix, the Korean picked up his animated conversation with the viewers. The entire procedure took about forty-five minutes, punctuated by frequent bucketfuls of cold water flung across the floor. While the surgeon lectured, Doc completed the surgery but stopped short of sewing up the incision. Through the interpreter, he pleaded with the surgeon to leave the wound open, since it had been contaminated and antibiotics were in short supply. He also pleaded for penicillin. He asked to leave the medic with Olsen to make sure that his recovery instructions were followed. His requests were denied.

Several days later, Olsen rejoined his compatriots and reported that although the wound had indeed become infected and he was still very weak, he had gotten the best treatment the Korean hospital staff could offer. Doc never found out whether his instructions had been followed. Olsen managed to survive the next few weeks only to die of pneumonia during the frigid winter of 1951.

While medical emergencies sent Doc's adrenaline soaring, what upset him most was hearing that men refused to eat. Living conditions were becoming more miserable, especially compared to American standards. Prisoners slept side by side on the floor, wedged tightly into cramped rooms, with no blankets and little, if any, heat. The colder the weather got, the more depressed they became. But they did have food. They ate in the central mess hall, cafeteria-style, about a hundred at a time. Three times a day, GIs cooked and served rice balls, boiled dried fish, potato or cabbage soup. Twice, local civilians provided cookies, and occasionally prisoners received a tiny amount of pork or beef. Mostly, though, they ate the same tasteless fare, meal after meal, day after day.

Quantities were extremely limited. Most of the men, particularly the young ones, lost weight rapidly, although Doc considered the food nutritionally adequate. He went to the mess hall to watch them as they ate. Some played with their food, endlessly rearranging it on their plates until it was time to leave. Others offered to trade their portions for cigarettes. Several returned their plates with much of the food left on them.

At sick call, Doc continued to see the once-obese man who didn't like rice. He did everything he could to get the man to eat, including ordering the cooks to make whatever specialties they could devise with their limited rations. But the man refused. One day he collapsed and died, the first casualty at Manpo.

As winter burrowed in, a vicious cycle began, a lethal, random pattern that no one recognized at first. Slowly, a prisoner began losing his personal pride. He would forget to wash his hands and face when he had a chance, and he no longer cared about keeping his clothes and body clean. He refused to go outside and do PT in the morning, and he objected to being assigned to work details. He ignored the daily ritual of picking lice from his clothes. He started complaining about the food and finding excuses for not eating it. The less he ate, the more bitter he became toward his family, his country, and himself. When dysentery set in and he rapidly lost strength, it became easier to die than to live. And so he died.

Doc recognized that not eating led to not surviving, although it would take him much longer to understand that going hungry killed the will to live before it starved the body. He started singling out the men who played with their food and made sure that they were seated in a special part of the dining room where they had to stay until they cleaned their plates. He reasoned that if he could force them to eat a daily ration, he could force them to live—never mind that they spent most of their time and energy swearing at everyone and begging to be left alone to die and get it over with. Friends tried appealing to their pride and love for their wives, families, or life back home, but these attempts were usually met with derogatory, derisive comments: "Go to hell, man. What do you care? Mind your own business." Or, even worse, they were met with no reply at all. Apathy was the enemy. In some cases the men used racial slurs and insults to rile up their buddies; those who got angry enough to vow revenge had a reason to eat.

Doc wasn't about to give up. Brute physical force became his new strategy. He and his assistants grabbed and choked the offenders until they ate, releasing them only when they motioned that they were willing to eat on their own. It was a slow process, sometimes taking eight to twelve hours a day, but after a few meals in the special area, where they could hear the jeers of their peers, many began to eat again. Others kept eating just to avoid the humiliating treatment. This ruthless strategy didn't work when the men were too far gone or too belligerent, but, despite numerous loud protests, the practice continued. The successful cases gradually returned to some semblance of normal, still bitching about the horrid fare but, now that they were eating to live rather than living to eat, feeling more positive about survival.

Doc was force-feeding hope.

# 10

# En Route to Germany

## 1959

In early fall, my father got orders to report to the 2nd General Hospital in Landstuhl, Germany, for a three-year tour. The army told him that he had to go alone for the first year because there was no housing for us, but this upset my mother. On several nights I lay awake and tense in bed, listening to them argue, my mother pleading and getting tearful, my father shouting that orders were orders and there was nothing he could do about it. Besides, there was a Cold War on and the Communists were in Cuba and who knows what Russia might do next. Usually my mother tried to be a good sport, even when her raised chin betrayed her real feelings, but this time she dug in. After several weeks it was determined that we could all go, even the dog, as long as we "lived on the economy," which meant finding and paying for our own German housing until military quarters became available.

We divided everything we owned into three batches that the army would pack and move separately. *Hold* baggage, clothing and other basics, would arrive about a month after we did, assuming it didn't get lost, which our military friends said happened often. *Household* baggage, dishes and nonessentials, would take three to six months to arrive. And *storage*, furniture and what seemed like most of our things, wouldn't be seen again until we returned to the States in three years. Each of us, even Dirk, now five, and Eric, two and a half, was allotted one suitcase into which we stuffed everything we would need for the trip.

"Only what you can carry," my father ordered.

My mother reminded me to choose very, very carefully, because the trip would take nearly two months, plus we'd have to wait one more month for our hold luggage to arrive, and Germany was colder than Texas, so I'd need my warmest clothes. I packed, unpacked, discarded, repacked. I had to sit on the suitcase to latch it.

We waved good-bye to the house on Ridgehaven Place and drove the green Plymouth station wagon to Boonsboro, Maryland, the tiny town in the rolling countryside between Frederick and Hagerstown where my mother grew up and where we would stay for the holidays on travel leave until our ship sailed from New York City in January. The house on Main Street had no front yard, only a sidewalk, but it seemed like a mansion with its many rooms and oddities, including two front doors. It had a root cellar, a steep back stoop with no railing, and a kitchen alcove with a high-sided, red-leather booth for drinking coffee, smoking cigarettes, and working crossword puzzles. A second-floor porch contained only a bed, an old-fashioned dressing table with a long shirred skirt, and a portrait wall displaying family members I didn't recognize. My mother reminded me that we had lived here while my father was in the war, but I didn't remember.

I steered clear of Mom-Mom, who yearned for social status and didn't much like kids, but I liked Pop-Pop, the town doctor. Dressed in starched white shirts with rolled-up long sleeves and a bow tie, he saw patients in his office, which was attached to the house but had its own front door. After office hours, he let me climb on the examining table and sometimes sent me to buy cigars down at the drugstore, slipping me a nickel for a soda fountain root beer served in a frosty mug plucked from the ice cream freezer. At dinner he'd tell raucous stories about the generations of babies he'd delivered and how they'd turned out. Mom-Mom didn't approve of the boisterous behavior that made the rest of us laugh. She'd change the subject to politics, which set my father off.

"These damn politicians, who do they think they are? They've never been in battle, most of them. They don't know what the hell we're fighting for."

Eisenhower was a hero, but Truman made him sputter, and soon came the Lecture.

"You've got to trust the guy in the ditch next to you. It's all you've got. That's what is important in life. Not all your foreign cars and diamond rings, but your character. That's what you need to survive, not all that other fancy nonsense. How many of these yokels have character? Not many, I assure you."

The rest was a blur. I tried to tune out the shouting and table thumping. The Lecture bored me. I hoped that someone would send me to the kitchen for more Scotch.

Afraid that I'd miss too much of the fifth grade, my mother enrolled me in her old school atop the hill where she used to skin her knees while roller-skating down. I was scared because everyone stares at new kids, but my teacher was nice and let me be class newspaper editor even though I'd only be there for three weeks. She ran off pungent purple copies of our first issue on the mimeograph machine.

"How ya doin', girlie?" Pop-Pop asked that night at dinner, squeezing that certain spot above my knee that always made me jump.

"Fine. Look what I did today," I answered as I got up to get my copy of the newspaper.

"Sit down and finish your dinner," Mom-Mom said.

After dishes I went upstairs to finish my homework. I stayed on the third floor, up a steep, narrow staircase that wound past an enormous cage, tall as the roof and deep as the basement crawl space, enclosing a huge, roaring house fan. Northerners used them instead of air conditioning, my mother had explained, but that fan scared me more than a new school. I pictured tumbling through the cage and down the shaft, where the fan would chop me to bits. I hugged the opposite wall as I crept past.

The attic was like a playhouse with deep-sloped ceilings and checkered linoleum floors. A bed was pushed into the corner next to a dormer window where pigeons clustered in mottled grays outside the glass. Mom-Mom's parsley grew in a flat on the other dormer's windowsill. From my pillow I could see across the street to the town clock, which announced the hour in sonorous bongs.

I put on my pajamas and got into bed with my books. The door at the bottom of the stairs creaked open. Heavy footfalls groaned on each step. Around the corner peered my father, who had to stoop almost double under the low ceiling. I wondered if he'd come to check the windows. No matter where we lived, if my blinds or curtains were still open at dusk, he'd stride into my room without a word and yank them shut. But these windows were unadorned, and he didn't seem interested in the rooftop view as he made his way to sit on the small wooden chair next to my bed. He was coming just to see me? My heart danced as I smiled up at him, though I worried that the old chair would break.

"I need to talk to you," he said. He looked straight at me and cleared his throat. He pushed the glasses up on his nose with his middle finger. The lines in his face deepened.

"What about?"

"You know."

"No, I don't."

"You won't get very far in this world if you keep acting like that."

"Like what?" My mind raced through dinner, dishes, saying good night to the grown-ups. What had I done?

"You're just like everybody else, you know. No different. You shouldn't act special, show off," he said, twisting his mouth as he talked. "Don't be a snob. Nobody likes snobs, and nobody will be around to watch your back when you need them."

I tried to think as the pigeons scuffled outside my window. I didn't understand what he meant, so I reviewed: I'd remembered to use my napkin, folded it properly. Set knives, forks, and spoons in the right order. Didn't talk back or dawdle. I was often reprimanded for having my head in the clouds and my nose in a book, but this wasn't about that. He complained about people like my mother's sister, a gourmet cook who wore stylish clothes and fancied society parties, but I wasn't one of them.

"Promise to try harder next time?" he asked as he rose to a half stoop and, sighing, started back down the stairs. I nodded and bit my lip, trying not to cry. It took me a long time to go to sleep. Even the pigeons were restless.

In the morning, six bongs woke me. I sat straight up. My pajama bottoms were wet. Humiliation, then panic, froze me to the chilled spot on the sheet as I tried to think. I'd wet the bed. I couldn't tell anyone. I pulled the sheet off the bed and tried to sneak down the stairs, my footsteps like thunderclaps in the predawn quiet. The hallway was empty. I crept into the bathroom and quickly rinsed the spot in the pink sink before anyone came to investigate. On my way back up the stairs, the fan sputtered and growled into its daytime thunder. I hung my wet pajamas across the chair and rigged the sheet so it could dry before nighttime. Maybe my father was right. Something was wrong with me.

A nasty virus took everyone down for a week. My mother and brothers lay moaning in their beds, with every plastic wastebasket in the house strategically placed within grabbing range. Even my father took naps and refused to come to the table for meals. For some reason I was spared, so I helped Mom-Mom fetch water and ice chips and deliver soup when the healing commenced. By the time we left for New York City everyone was feeling better, although on the train my parents gave Dirk milk of magnesia from the strange blue bottle to get rid of the last bugs and return color to his pasty face.

On the morning we were set to sail across the Atlantic Ocean aboard the SS *United States,* I woke up before anyone else. I lay staring at the smoke-smudged ceiling, the highest I'd ever seen, its dusty chandelier hanging askew. We had spent the night in the dank, dark Hotel St. George in Brooklyn; we had two rooms, connected, with one bathroom and no closets. An armoire with squeaky doors and heavy drawers underneath held our clothes. I could smell the yellowed curtains hanging at the window we'd had trouble forcing open "just a crack," as my father insisted even though the January weather was gray and raw.

When the travel alarm went off I knew we had to go downstairs for an early breakfast. Now everyone was up except me. "Get up," my mother said, shaking my shoulder. "It's time."

I couldn't move. I felt nailed to the bed by the invisible anvil anchored in my stomach. I lay there, blinking.

"Don't make me tell you again," my mother said. She was a crab before breakfast. I turned over on my side and rested from the effort, pushed myself up to sitting, put my feet on the floor. I was dizzy. I had trouble figuring out which clothes were mine, what to wear, what to pack. I moved as if my feet were encased in concrete.

I sat on the suitcase to latch it. I felt like throwing up. Maybe I was just nervous, but nervous had never felt that bad. By the time I got to the table in the hotel dining room, the oatmeal my mother had ordered for me was cold. I could only sit and stare at it. When my father told me to finish and finish now, my throat closed in that familiar lump. This time he had to give up because it was time to leave.

We hauled our five suitcases downstairs, climbed into a cab, and took off. The cab ride made everyone nervous. We started, stopped, started again. Every time we careened around a corner, my stomach lurched. I couldn't see where we were going or the tops of the buildings we threaded between. All around us, pedestrians rushed and jostled while horns blared and signs blinked. Whistles blew, dogs barked, people shouted, and my head throbbed.

It wasn't until we stopped and got out of the car that I understood we'd reached the dock. It wasn't the deck on posts stretching down into the water that I expected; it was a vast sea of concrete with people and carts and vehicles going in all directions. The ship was bigger than any building I'd seen up close. It had rows of decks up its side where what looked like multicolored ants were swarming as if someone had kicked their hill away. Tiny heads bobbed back and forth, up and down. I forgot about my aching head and stomach. I could hardly breathe for the excitement of being there.

At the bottom of the gangplank we handed off our suitcases to official-looking men and hugged my aunt and uncle, who had driven up from Fairbourne to see us off. We threw kisses and shrilled farewells as we made our way up the long gangplank. At the top, a young woman pushed flat yoyos of brightly colored paper into our hands.

"What are we supposed to do with them?" I asked as my brothers unraveled theirs. I held mine tight.

"You'll see. Here, take some more," she said, slipping some into my coat pocket.

On board, we became the ants, bobbing about until we found a place at the rail where we could see my aunt and uncle. I had to go on tiptoe to spot them, waving wildly, tiny down below. From here I could see how big the dock really was, like a long city street littered with crates and barrels and buildings and piers at intervals, stretching out into the water. Paper and box scraps blew around, and dirt coated everything.

The boat whistle nearly blew me off my feet. My stomach dropped like an elevator. People stomped and shouted, on the boat and on shore. Those around me started throwing something at the dock. My mother pointed to my hand, still tightly clutched. I threw one of my yoyos overboard. She shook her head, so I turned to watch how everyone else did it. Oh. I held onto one end and tossed it out. Perfect. It was beautiful as it unfurled. The air filled with bright, spiraling colors. I helped my brothers and found the woman again, to get some more. Streamers were fun.

The noise level rose as we pulled away from the dock with a great grinding and rumble underfoot. I staggered as my father grabbed my shoulder with a strong grip.

"You, young lady, are going to bed."

"Oh, let her wait until we go past the Statue of Liberty," my mother said.

"OK, I guess we can do that."

I held onto the rail as we got underway. It didn't take long to sail out of the harbor, picking up speed. I could hardly see the statue as we zoomed by.

"Now," said my father, steering me away from the rail.

I was feeling worse by the second. My feet were concrete again, and my eyes were trying to shut, so I had to keep my head back and peer under the lids to see where I was going, down stairs, through small doors, following a maze of wide and narrow corridors. The boat rolled, a strange sensation of up and down and side to side, all at the same time. Two or three times I lost my balance and had to grab the rails that lined the hallways.

In the stateroom, which was neat and clean like a fancy hotel room but with special railed nooks to keep things in, my suitcase was waiting. I put on my pajamas and crawled into one of the twin beds. Dirk got the other one. I slept until dark, woke up nauseated, slept again. When dawn came I lay watching the porthole fill first with murky green water, then with sky, first blue, then deep cloudy gray. When I got up to go to the bathroom, everything moved and made me dizzy. I held on to whatever I could grab.

I lost track of days and nights passing, and the porthole didn't always proclaim the difference. I knew it was morning when an attendant in a starched uniform brought a tray with a paper doily and a vase of fresh flowers and dishes of oatmeal and eggs hidden under heavy metal covers. I gagged on the oatmeal. A bite of egg got stuck and wouldn't go down. Nothing seemed to get through my dry throat, not even juice or milk. My father said I could order Coca-Cola, but it tasted funny, or my mouth did, even when it was served with crushed ice, my favorite.

When the attendant came to take the tray away, its dishes and glasses still full, my father came in behind her to check on me. He looked down on me, huddled under the blankets, with stern eyes.

"You have to eat," he said.

He said this again at lunch and again at dinner. I knew he wasn't just being mean. My mother was feeling sick, too. She lay on Dirk's bed and held her arm across her stomach. She told my father she wanted to skip dinner. The boat was pitching and rolling, the porthole filling and emptying in record time. Sometimes I saw lightning.

"No skipping meals," he said. "That's the first thing you learn in the merchant marine. If you're seasick, you'll feel better with a full stomach than with an empty one. Just keep going, and eat as much as you can."

My mother looked like she was ready to throw up any minute, but she went along to the dining room, which I hadn't seen yet. The boys were doing fine, careening from side to side down the passageways as if it were a fine game, and stealing the brown paper barf bags, draped discreetly over the rails at frequent intervals, to blow them up and pop them. When our parents weren't around, Dirk showed me how.

One stormy morning, when we were well over halfway across the rough Atlantic, my father the food scold had had enough. He came in and saw my breakfast tray untouched. He leaned down, put his hands on either side of the bed, and stuck his face into mine. I could see his swirled nose hairs and the pupils in his eyes.

"If you don't start eating now," he said in a cold fury, "the ship's doctor will be in to stick a needle in your arm and hook you up to an IV. Is that what you want?"

I stared back at him.

"Are you going to eat?" he thundered.

I opened my mouth to say OK but nothing came out. I couldn't talk either. No food, no drink, no words. I was shaking all over.

"One way or another, we're going to get some food into you!"

He turned to leave, and the attendant who had stepped into the stateroom behind him darted out the door. When she came back a few minutes later to take the tray, she smiled and touched my hand. "Don't worry," she said. "He just doesn't like to see you feeling bad. I'll bring you something good. Maybe you'll like it."

She brought me orangeade and rice pudding and ginger ale. She sat beside me while I drank a little ginger ale out of a straw. Eventually I got a small bite of pudding to go down, then another. A couple of times a day, between meals, she brought me a little treat. Slowly, I started to get better.

On the last full day of our voyage before docking in Le Havre, France, our first stop, I was allowed to get out of bed. My mother took me to see my brothers in the nursery, where they sat on riding toys with their feet up, giggling as the rocking boat sent them rolling across the floor. I wandered into the library, where I imagined sitting at one of the elegant desks to write a story. I begged to go to the movie, and my mother said yes, but only for a little while. Nearly alone in the theater, I watched the first half of *South Pacific* and decided that "I'm Gonna Wash That Man Right Outta My Hair" was my favorite song.

That night I got to see the cavernous dining room, with its elaborate chandeliers and round tables large enough for families bigger than ours. My mother introduced our three bowing waiters, one of whom seated me in a chair like a living room easy chair and spread the napkin across my lap. Then he strapped the chair to the table. My father laughed at the look on my face.

"It's so you won't go sliding across the room," he said.

Once we were all attached, the waiters pulled up the edges of the table to make a little wall that went all the way around. With a grand flourish, they poured water from silver pitchers all over the tablecloth.

"So the china and silver won't slide." My father grinned at me.

The waiter handed me a menu. Nine appetizers, including caviar and a crabmeat cocktail. Four soups, including kangaroo tail and fresh green turtle. Sherbets. Roast saddle of lamb, filet mignon, pheasant.

"What will you have, Miss?" Not the Blue Point oysters or the Burgdorfer asparagus with sauce hollandaise.

"Steak," I said. "And strawberries. Do you have strawberries?"

"Indeed we do."

As we waited for our food, I lifted the heavy fork and held it across my fingers to see how many it would take to keep it from falling. We had three knives, three forks, three spoons. When the waiter brought us each a silver bowl with a lemon slice floating in it, I questioned my mother with my eyes.

"It's lemonade," Dirk said, pretending to drink his.

My mother rolled her eyes. "That's what your brother thought the first night." Both boys giggled while we swished our fingers in the warm water. My father shook his head.

The waiters swept in, their trays held high above their heads, then set them down and removed the silver plate covers with great ceremony. One waiter set before me a large china plate on which sat a bowl of fresh strawberries, plump and red and perfectly ripe, even though we were here, in the middle of the Atlantic Ocean in the middle of January. He anointed them with cream from a silver pitcher.

"Just for you, Miss," he said. "I'm glad you're feeling better."

"Thank you," I said, and ate every one.

# 11

# The Cornfield, North Korea

## OCTOBER 1950

As the days grew short and cold and the nights long and colder, rumors flew. Somehow the men had received word of the Inchon landing, which began September 15 and, over the next couple of weeks, signified a victory of sorts for the Americans. The prisoners had already buried twenty-eight of their men in Manpo, yet they nurtured optimism. Their captors, however, grew fearful. On October 9, they uprooted the roughly 750 soldiers and civilians and marched them about ten miles west to a village known as Kosan, where they were quartered in two schoolhouses outfitted with double-decker platforms to sleep on. About twenty sick and wounded prisoners were transported by barge. Ten days later, the group moved again to another small village, Jui-am-nee.

"What's going on?" Doc asked the Korean doctor and pharmacist with whom he now had a working relationship. The two Koreans hadn't trusted each other at first, causing much tension, but Doc finally figured out that each had suspected the other was a Communist. Once they learned that neither was even a Communist sympathizer, the mood lifted, and everyone managed to get along.

"The Chinese Communists are invading our country. They're streaming across the Yalu by the thousands," said the Koreans, explaining that the river formed the border between China and North Korea. All these moves—first to the school compound along the road, and then to an old mining camp farther south and more hidden up in the mountains—were made to protect the prisoners. The Chinese, they added, might not be inclined to treat the prisoners as well as the Koreans had.

Doc did not dispute this theory. Despite the lack of food and crowded conditions, the regimentation of daily life had been largely left up to the prisoners themselves. Several of the Korean guards were sympathetic and humane in their way, keeping their distance and subsisting on rations not dissimilar to what the prisoners consumed. Some even asked how they might be treated if the Americans arrived to liberate the prisoners. The Korean doctor and pharmacist were elated to discover that American troops were headed north; they disliked Communists, especially the Russians, and thought conditions would improve under American control. They proposed a reconnaissance trip to see whether American forces were indeed nearby. If so, the prisoners could escape and join the troops. Perhaps the Americans could finalize an escape plan while they were gone.

Three or four days later, the Koreans returned with their report. Indeed, the American forces were not too many miles farther down the Yalu, but sadly, it would be impossible to reach them. Doc barraged the doctor with questions, but the Korean would only shake his head.

"Come, I'll show you," he said, gesturing.

He led Doc and a few other officers on a long trek back through the mountain pass they had crossed previously, then up to a mountain-top that overlooked a valley. They stood on the peak in silence, peering down at the small village nestled in the valley far below. The Korean took out his Colt .45 and fired several shots in the air. Open-mouthed, Doc stared as hundreds of Chinese soldiers swarmed out of buildings like bees emerging from their hives. Whistles blew and bugles blared. He had never seen so many human beings in such a small area. The Korean turned to the Americans.

"As you can see, they are all over the place, and it would be foolish to try to get seven hundred men past them without being noticed. There are thousands of Chinese between us and the Americans. An escape would be impossible," he said. The officers nodded their agreement and scuttled their plan.

Three men did try to escape. One of them was returned to the group as they marched north along the Yalu River. The other two were shot.

On October 25, with United Nations troops less than sixty miles away, the prisoners were moved once more, this time from Jui-am-nee back to Kosan, and the next day they were moved to a cornfield just west of Manpo. Lieutenant Sol, the compassionate Korean officer then in charge, threw open the doors of the Kosan warehouse they had used to store food and invited the men to take whatever they could carry.

Tobacco, which could be used to barter with the locals for more food, was also issued.

Meals had become erratic, but the men were more euphoric than ravenous. They were sure their ordeal would soon be over. Rumor had it that General MacArthur had assured the president that the boys would be home for Christmas. Men were still dying—two here, three there—but sick call had been suspended. Seven prisoners, anticipating liberation, refused to march out to the cornfield and stayed behind in a Kosan police station. They were never seen again.

For five days, the cornfield was home. Temperatures plunged below freezing at night. Although some men had managed to secure hats and gloves, most had none. They used bowls and bare hands to dig holes in the ground, where they slept, or tried to sleep, huddled together under bags of rice. They erected windbreaks out of cornstalks and used other cornstalks to keep small fires going, assigning shifts of fire watchers during the night to make sure the embers didn't go out. After the men had eaten what rice, millet, and cracked corn they had, they bartered for food and stole from each other.

Doc watched Chinese troops marching south in what seemed to be an unending stream. Their cooks, loaded down with food and utensils, ran around the flanks, perhaps to arrive first and prepare the next meal.

On October 31, while friends and families at home celebrated by dressing up in costumes to ring doorbells and collect candy, a new commander arrived, a major for the North Korean security police, a man the prisoners would never forget. Taller than most of his comrades, he had a small face with a pointed chin, bright, restless eyes, and big teeth that stuck out when he scowled. He wore a tight jacket with jodhpurs and high boots. His shoulders were slightly stooped, and he tilted his head forward when he walked. Some said he looked evil. Monsignor Quinlan had run into him before and remembered that he'd been a prison warden in Pyongyang. But no one knew his name, or if they knew, they kept it to themselves. The prisoners called him the Tiger.

About an hour before the Tiger strode across the cornfield to confront his new charges, Lieutenant Sol took Major Dunn aside and warned him about what was coming. The captives, who were military and civilian, men, women, and children, would have to march north to

Chunggang, a remote camp along the Yalu River about 110 miles away, across snow-covered mountains. The march would be cold and hard and long, and the prisoners might not be treated very well. They should also avoid or treat with suspicion three new prisoners who would be joining them. Lieutenant Sol suspected they were Communist collaborators and shouldn't be trusted because they were the only men who had survived a massacre of about three hundred American prisoners. He bid farewell to the grateful American officers, who shook his hand with tears in their eyes.

Darkness was starting to fall when the Tiger took charge. Through Herbert Lord, a British Salvation Army commissioner who acted as interpreter, he instructed Major Dunn to order the men to fall out and be ready to march in five minutes.

"What about the men who are sick? They cannot march," Dunn pleaded with him.

"It makes no difference," the Tiger responded. "All men walk. If they cannot walk, carry them."

Father Paul Villemot, an eighty-two-year-old toothless French priest who walked with a cane, stepped forward from the group of civilians.

"If I have to march, I will die," he told Commissioner Lord, who translated.

"Then let them march until they die!" the Tiger shouted. "That is a military order!"

More orders followed. The men must not carry any food, which would be provided along the way. Nor could they bring weapons. If they defied these orders, they would be shot. He kicked the cane away from Father Villemot.

"That is a weapon," he said.

At about 5:00, approximately 650 soldiers and 75 civilians marched out of the cornfield. Sixteen men remained behind in a crude lean-to their buddies had constructed, some because they couldn't walk, others because they refused to go on. Dunn pleaded with the Tiger that they should be hospitalized. The Tiger agreed, but Doc wasn't buying it. He suspected they would be shot instead. He looked deep into the eyes of the paralyzed sergeant lying on a makeshift stretcher. A man with Pott's disease should never have been sent to Korea.

"Don't cry, Doc," the soldier said. "I know what is going to happen to us who are left here, but it is not your fault. You must carry on to help those who can still walk. May God be with you."

After dark that Halloween night, thirteen sections of skinny, hungry, apprehensive American soldiers trotted as best they could through the congested city of Manpo to another open field on the east side, a distance of about six miles. Two officers were in charge of each group of fifty. About forty or fifty guards kept them in line, waving their guns and shouting at them to hurry, *bali, bali, bali*. Bringing up the rear were the civilian prisoners: diplomats, missionaries, journalists, and family members who hailed from Germany, Ireland, France, Britain, Australia, Austria, Switzerland, Turkey, and Russia. Father Villemot was the oldest. The youngest was a baby less than a year old, carried by his Turkish mother. A six-year-old girl walked, holding her father's hand. It must have been after midnight when the prisoners lay down, huddling close together on the wet, cold ground, and tried to sleep. Some had gotten a handful of partially cooked cracked corn to eat, but others went without. Some slept; most could not.

At daybreak, they rose stiffly when the Tiger called them to attention and issued his orders. They were to keep marching at all times. No one was to fall out of the lines for any reason. Anyone who disobeyed would be shot.

The sections set off briskly, double-timing at a near run. Light snow was changing to sleet, and the mountains lay ahead. Guards herded former litter patients down the road, beating them about the head with sticks of firewood. If they fell, other prisoners were told to carry them. Many of the men could not keep up, and some of those fighting diarrhea dropped out to defecate along the side of the road. After an hour, the Tiger called a halt. He ordered Commissioner Lord, Major Dunn, and the officers whose men had fallen out to stand before him on a small knoll. Seven officers stepped forward.

"Your men are falling out. You have failed to obey orders!" the Tiger shouted. "You will be shot!"

Commissioner Lord pleaded with him, explaining that the officers had asked the guards what to do about their men, but the guards weren't sure what to tell them. It would therefore be unjust to punish them. The Tiger told Lord to shut up or he would also be shot.

"Whose group let the most men fall out?" he yelled.

Lt. Cordus H. Thornton stepped forward and stood at attention.

"Death is the penalty for disobedience in the Korean army," said the Tiger. "What happens in your army when you fail to obey orders?"

"In the American army, sir, I would have a trial," Thornton replied.

The Tiger threw up his arms. He called to nearby guards and other North Korean soldiers passing by on the road.

"What is to be done to a man who disobeys the lawful order of an officer in the Korean People's Army?"

"Shoot him!" the Koreans shouted, roaring their approval.

"There, you've had your trial," the Tiger barked. Thornton didn't flinch. He looked the Tiger in the eye.

"In Texas, sir, we would call that a lynching," he said.

Commissioner Lord remained silent, refusing to translate until the Tiger forced him to. Whether he translated accurately, no one knew. Whether he again pleaded for mercy, no one knew either. The Tiger was not to be deterred. He instructed the other officers to return to their sections.

"Do you want a blindfold?" he asked Thornton.

"Yes," Thornton replied.

A guard stepped forward. He wrapped a towel around Thornton's eyes and used another to tie his hands behind his back. The Tiger marched Thornton about ten feet away from the others, stopped, and faced him. Then the Tiger grabbed Thornton's shoulders and turned him around, put a .45 caliber pistol to the back of his head, and pulled the trigger.

The Tiger, teeth protruding, turned back to his charges.

"You have just witnessed the execution of a bad man. This move will help us to work together better in peace and harmony," he announced in a loud voice. He instructed the prisoners, who had no tools except their hands, to bury Thornton in the partially frozen ground. When they were done, the columns re-formed and the men marched on.

# 12

# Bremerhaven, West Germany

## 1960

By the time the SS *United States* docked at our final destination, I was hungry again on a regular basis. Our last day on the ship was filled with the pandemonium of packing, docking while greeters cheered in a language I didn't understand, and disembarking. By the time we made our way down the gangplank with our luggage, it was early evening. No one was there to greet us. We wore tags indicating our itinerary and rode a bus to the Bremerhaven *bahnhof,* where we were supposed to catch the night train.

I had never seen a train station like this. I stood gazing up at the ironwork of the massive structure, its ceiling high and rounded, the clacking of the train wheels echoing around us. The tracks and trains came inside the station and stopped at numbered platforms with a sound like an accordion squeezing air. I was glad to see that German numbers looked the same as American numbers.

"Don't gawk," my mother said. "And close your mouth before you catch a fly."

Our train wasn't in yet, so we found the station's restaurant and sat down at a table. The waiter brought us menus we couldn't read. I wanted a glass of milk.

"*Milch*?" the waiter asked. My mother nodded. She rummaged in her well-organized large purse, pulled out a German dictionary, and tried to identify menu items. We knew *wienerschnitzel* and *sauerkraut* but not much else. She shook her head when Dirk said he wanted tomato soup and a grilled cheese sandwich. I didn't care what food we got. I just wanted that ice-cold milk that tasted like home.

Service was slow in our new country. The waiter came back twice to ask a question that no one understood. He finally showed up with a tray filled with our food and set my milk down in front of me. I grabbed the glass and nearly dropped it. It was hot. I looked wide-eyed at my mother.

She looked back at me with her no-nonsense eyes and felt Dirk's glass.

"I guess here they serve the milk warm," she said. "It's still good."

It wasn't. I wanted to go back to Texas.

By nine, we were aboard the train, where we slept on narrow shelves and took a long walk down a rocking corridor to go to the bathroom. By morning we were in Frankfurt, where we changed trains and headed for Heidelberg. There we pitched our luggage out the windows to waiting porters and ran, because we had only a few minutes to catch the train to Landstuhl, the sixteenth-century burg nestled at the base of the hill where the Americans had built a sprawling hospital compound in the early 1950s.

A tall, rail-thin, grinning officer in uniform jumped out of a van to greet us at the tiny Landstuhl station.

"Hi!" he said, sticking out his hand to shake my father's. "I'm Jerry Scott. Bet you're all bushed. Hop on in."

"Who's he?" I whispered to my mother.

"Our sponsor," she whispered back.

I didn't know what that meant. In San Antonio we had lived off-post, like normal people, so this was our first military transfer. My father carried a huge stack of orders, identical copies, in his briefcase, and handed them out everywhere. I expected him to get one out this time, but he didn't.

We crammed ourselves into the van and stuffed the suitcases wherever they fit, including on our laps. After driving several miles down a two-lane road, we slowed abruptly in the middle of what seemed like nowhere, and turned right. A newer stucco house stood in stark relief, unpromising, at the end of a rutted dirt driveway. We were home.

As we unloaded the van, the front door opened, and a woman with short dark hair leaned out and waved.

"Hi! Welcome!" called Jerry's wife, Suzy. Peering out from behind her was a girl about my age, thin with long braids and glasses like mine. Sharon became my first army brat friend.

The Scotts grabbed our bags and showed us around the bottom half of the house. It was cold and smelled like the oil stoves that were supposed to keep it warm. It had two bedrooms, a bathroom, a living room, and a kitchen/dining room with a built-in booth and table on one side and an alcove for the sink, stove, and refrigerator on the other. Suzy flung open the cupboards to reveal bread, peanut butter, jelly, and other staples she'd stocked there for us. In the refrigerator were butter, eggs, and an odd-shaped container.

"Milk," she said as if she read my mind. "Reconstituted. Tastes funny, but you'll get used to it."

I looked at Sharon, who stuck out her tongue.

"There's no phone but you can use your landlady's phone if there's an emergency," Suzy said. "She doesn't speak much English, although she understands more than you might think. Oh, and she thinks Hitler was the best thing that ever happened to Germany, so watch what you say."

We trooped upstairs to meet Frau Hocke. A cheerful teenager in a black wool skirt and black turtleneck answered the door and introduced herself and her twin sister in passable English. Behind Frieda and Renate hovered their mother, a gaunt, shriveled woman also dressed in black. Only her face and her hands, which she wrung nervously, escaped the heavy drape. She nodded but did not speak. She pointed to the phone in the hallway and gestured permission to use it if we needed to.

Back downstairs, we said good-bye to our new friends and started to unpack. My room was the living room, separated from the rest of the flat by a heavy door of tinted glass.

"Where's the bed?" I asked my mother.

"There," she said, pointing to a small green settee shoved against one wall, near the oil stove. I sat on the hard bed/couch, wincing when I felt the springs, and stared out the picture window. Unfortunately what it pictured was the edge of a hill excavated by a bulldozer. The machine, crusty and abandoned there, had chopped headlong into the red clay, exposing the hungry roots of scraggly pine trees that leaned dying on each other. Rain had formed rivulets in the clay field, now a desert littered with residue from the somber woods beyond and a campground for huge stag beetles that waved sharp antlers at each other. I got up to get a better look at them, thankful for the safety of the glass between us. I had never seen scary little beasts like these. I hoped they wouldn't populate my dreams.

Inside, the window was filled with flies, not the little black ones drawn by lemonade at a picnic, but big blue ones that buzzed obnoxiously as they battered the pane. If I got too close, they attacked my hair, hands, and elbows. But as dark fell and chilled the window, they slowed and gathered in the corners. I swatted a few with a rolled-up paper, leaving juicy spots on the glass and carcasses upside down on the sill.

That night I climbed into the tangle of sheets that wouldn't tuck in and tried to sleep. I lay hunched against the back of the settee and listened to eerie sounds from upstairs, wailing that rose and fell like notes on a badly tuned violin. At first I thought it was the wind, but no, it was a voice, whether of human or animal I wasn't sure.

The door opened and my father came in, maybe to close the curtains except there weren't any.

"What's that?" I asked, pointing to the ceiling.

"Frau Hocke, I think," he said. "She lost her husband in the war, and apparently she's still sad about it. That's why she had to take in renters, to make ends meet."

"You mean she's crying?"

He nodded.

"You need to wear those, you know," he said, pointing to the shiny new dog tags I'd laid next to the lamp on the side table. It was an odd sort of necklace, with two rectangular tags stamped with name, serial number, blood type, and religious affiliation. Each tag had a hole in one end and a notch in the other. One tag was strung on a long ball chain that fit over my head, and the other had its own small chain looped through the big one.

"Why do I have to?" I asked.

"In case we need to evacuate. In case there's more war."

"Isn't one tag enough?"

He reached inside his T-shirt and pulled out his own dog tags. He never took them off, even in the shower, but I never thought much about it. They seemed to be part of him.

"Well, if somebody goes down, you take this one and stick it in his teeth so whoever finds him will know who he is." He opened his mouth and showed me how to wedge the tag in there, with his top front tooth in the notch. "When rigor mortis sets in, nobody can take it out."

"What about the one on the little chain?"

"You put that one in your pocket so you can turn it in to your commanding officer. That way they will know who died."

"Oh," I said, and thought about this every night as I hid my dog tags under my pillow.

That first winter was bleak, a chill wall of leafless trees, red clay, damp cold, and expatriate isolation pocked with small tragedies. Every morning, the house was freezing. The only warm room was the bathroom, where I got dressed after waiting my turn in the hallway, clutching my pile of clothes. Every night, the high notes of Frau Hocke's mourning haunted my homework.

My father got orders to go to Bremerhaven on TDY (temporary duty) for a few weeks, leaving my mother in charge. Things seemed to fall apart when he was away. She hurt her leg tripping over a short fire hydrant and limped for weeks. She had a fender bender with our car, a yellow and white Ford Taunus station wagon, miniature compared to our Plymouth. Eric, now three years old, got his finger stuck in the chain of Dirk's bike. My frantic mother stood on the road and flagged down help, which arrived in the form of an elderly German man riding by on his bicycle. He used the tools in his pack to dismantle Dirk's bike and extricate Eric's crushed fingertip.

On our way to the commissary to buy groceries one Saturday morning, we heard a thump and a loud squeal as we backed down the driveway. My mother got out to investigate. Our favorite kitten from Frau Hocke's litter lay just in front of the rear wheel, crushed flat.

"Oh no!" she screamed. She started crying and fished in her purse for the little pack of Kleenex she always kept handy. "I checked, I always do, but I didn't see it. It must have been sleeping on top of the wheel." Frau Hocke came out with a shovel and scooped up the cat. We climbed back into the car. My mother fished in her purse again and gave us each a peppermint Lifesaver. She always kept those handy, too.

"I don't know why your father has to be gone again," she said. "Sometimes we need him more than the army does."

But we managed. Dirk walked to a German kindergarten with his lunch in a little red *essen tasche* on his back. I was still in fifth grade, this time in the K–12 military school at Vogelweh, near Kaiserslautern. Landstuhl had its own American elementary and junior high schools, but I had no way to get there, so my mother arranged for me to ride the high school bus to Vogelweh instead. Every day it wheezed to a stop at the end of our driveway, and I climbed on with my arms full of text-books, praying I wouldn't stumble and drop them. Cool, coifed juniors and seniors stared at me as I, embarrassed by my frizzy home perm and one-suitcase wardrobe, searched frantically for a seat. Often there was none, and I stood at the head of the aisle as the bus jerked down the road. Sometimes the driver forgot to stop for me and I was left standing, shamed, in its exhaust. Unless it was Thursday, when my mother drove my father to work so she could use the car, I would have to miss school.

School was harder than I was used to. The math class was well into fractions, which I hadn't started. I'd never even heard of civics. I didn't understand the swear words I heard on the playground and saw carved into the baseball dugout. Fortunately my teacher, Mr. Fisher, was pa-tient and generous. He decided that I should edit our fifth-grade news-paper—another smelly purple publication—even though I was new and didn't know anybody. Maybe he figured it would help me adjust.

I was slow to make friends. Always worried that I'd say the wrong thing, I kept silent. But if someone talked to me, I talked back. I liked gregarious kids like Sondra, who talked to me in the cafeteria even though she was older, in sixth grade. When she showed up in a Girl Scout uniform, I told her I'd been a Girl Scout in my old school. She asked if I wanted to come with her to her next meeting.

"Where is it?"

"Oh, just up the hill behind the school. We can walk. It's right after school every Wednesday."

"I'm not sure." I looked down at my saddle shoes. "I don't know how to get home afterward. My mom can't come get me."

"You can ride the regular army bus to Landstuhl and just tell them where you want to get off. I'll show you where to catch it. C'mon, it'll be fun."

"I'll have to ask my mom, but OK."

It was arranged. We agreed to meet at the top of the stairs by the footbridge at 3:30 the following Wednesday and walk up the hill to-gether. The area I could see from the school was spotted with identical buildings crouched together. I had no idea where to go and wasn't even sure which hill she meant, but she would show me.

By Wednesday I was nervous. I spotted Sondra in her uniform at lunch, and we waved. "See you later," I called across the long tables. She nodded. The afternoon dragged as I muddled through schoolwork and rehearsed saying hi to a troop of strangers.

At last, the final bell rang. A crush of students knocked into me as they catapulted toward the doors. I tripped on the stairs but caught myself. At our appointed place, I found a safe lookout spot where I could see everything: shouting faces, hundreds of them. Flattops, long braids, pigtails, curls, grease, hairspray, bleach jobs with dark roots. Books, lunch boxes, jackets over shoulders and around waists. A few scout uniforms, but not Sondra's.

The flow of kids thinned to a trickle as, one by one, the teachers emerged from their empty rooms and locked their doors. One stopped to ask whether anything was wrong. "Oh, no," I said. "I'm just waiting for somebody." Ten minutes went by, then another ten. The halls were deserted. Did Sondra forget? Since lunch? What did I do wrong?

I went out onto the footbridge. I thought we were clear about meeting at the top of the stairs, but maybe she got mixed up. No one was there. I started up the nearest hill and looked at the buildings. No one was there, either. I couldn't see any building signs or numbers, not that I knew what to look for. I turned around and went back, hoping that Mr. Fisher might still be in his room. He could help me figure out what to do next. But all the doors were locked. I couldn't get back into the building.

My throat tightened. My books were heavy and my shoulders hurt. I couldn't call home and didn't know where to find a taxi, plus I'd used all my lunch money. Sondra had said there were buses, but I didn't know when they ran, where to catch them, or whether one would drop me off at the lonely house in the red clay pit. Not likely.

I decided to walk. I knew where the main gate was, and once I got outside I could follow the main road. It might take a couple of hours, but I would survive. That's what we did at our house; we survived. I passed the PX and the motor pool. The MP at the gate nodded to me but didn't ask questions; he was busy waving cars through with his white-gloved hand. I walked out the pedestrian entrance and turned left. A grassy strip alongside the main road stretched long and straight.

The trees that arched over it might have offered welcome shade on a sunny day, but the afternoon had turned cold. Gray collected in the distant sky. I held my books closer to my chest and wished I'd found a bathroom before I left.

I walked for more than an hour. It was beginning to rain. The path beside the road had ended, yielding to clashes of weeds, and my shoes were getting soaked. The trees dripped on my head, every drop large and surprisingly hard. I tried to imagine what my hair looked like now: plastered to my head with flat, wet polka dots that turned blonde to brown. Cars whizzed by occasionally. I wondered if the drivers noticed my bad hair or how wet I was getting.

I tried not to think about Sondra and how few friends I had at school. I thought about the homework I'd have to do when I got home.

I had spent the previous night sequestered in the chilled living room, wrestling with math. I liked math, but I didn't understand fractions at all. Why was adding no longer adding and subtracting no longer subtracting, and why did you have to change the numbers before you could do anything with them? Turn them upside down? Make those little crosses, bottom to top? What was a numerator anyway? I was trying hard, but it all seemed like nonsense. I had put down my pencil and paper and laid my head on my arm on the edge of that hard little couch. Tears fogged my glasses.

"Mom! Punky's crying!" Dirk was spying on me through the door. Snoop. Tattletale. Usually I was the one telling on him. My mother, wiping her hands on a dish towel, poked her head in the door.

"What's wrong?" she asked, the furrow between her brows deepening. She looked at my paper. "Are you still having trouble with that?"

I couldn't answer. I was trying not to cry anymore, so I had to keep my mouth closed.

"Pete!" she called. "Can you come in here?"

My father had gotten home early that night. We'd had dinner in the booth, and I had cleared the table and rinsed and stacked the dishes. Then I'd gotten excused to go finish my homework while my mother washed and dried. Of course I'd finished English and civics first and saved math until last. Already it was past my official bedtime.

His frame filled the doorway as he ducked his head to enter. My father made the room seem smaller. He perched awkwardly on the other end of the settee and looked at my book and papers spread out on the small coffee table. The dim lamp near the window cast gaunt shadows.

"What seems to be the problem here?" he asked, not unkindly. His day must have been pretty OK, not awful like sometimes. I kneeled down on the floor beside him, so I could see the papers. I took a deep, uneven breath.

"I just don't get how to do this."

"It's easy," he said, hinting at a smile. "You have to think of pieces of a pie. Two halves make a whole. Four pieces, four quarters, make a whole. If you only have two quarters, that makes half a pie. See?"

I nodded. I got the pie part. But what about three-sixteenths and five-twelfths? When do you use the top of one number and the bottom of the other? And what the heck is a lowest common denominator? I didn't say any of these things. He didn't seem scary tonight, yet I was afraid. He was waiting.

"How do you do this problem?" I asked, pointing to one.

"Well, that's easy," he said. Everything was easy for him. "Here. Watch." He picked up the pencil and it flew across the page. Tiny numbers appeared as if by magic. He paused, satisfied. "There," he said. "See?"

I didn't see. I couldn't even remember how to multiply. My mind raced, and I felt ashamed and stupid. Stopped tears were hot behind my eyes. I heard the flies buzzing slow in the light-warmed corner of the window that didn't open.

I lied to my father and nodded yes. He handed the papers back to me and stood up. His knees creaked. He said good night and left, closing the door behind him and leaving emptiness that hovered like a ghost, haunting me until I finally fell asleep, my homework incomplete.

Now as I trudged under darkening skies, I decided my math book was the heaviest of them all. Was it going to pour? My books would get wet. I'd have to pay for them if they got ruined. More cars zoomed by. I shifted my load onto my right arm and pushed up my sleeve to see my watch. Nearly 5:00. My mother would be expecting me home soon. I had no idea where I was, no landmarks to guide me, and I really, really, really had to pee. *Can bladders burst?* I wondered.

I was on a march. He had been on a march, my father. It's what gave him those odd feet, with the black and purple blotches by the ankles and the curled, yellow toenails. I didn't see him barefoot very often and he never wore sandals, but once when I was small and he'd been sleeping on the floor without his shoes and socks, I asked him why his feet were weird. He didn't say anything. He got up and went into the other room. My mother said it was because they got frozen on the Death March and now go make your bed.

This was no Death March, for sure. I was shivering, my hands stung with cold, my shoulders ached, my feet were going numb, and I was miserable but just a little bit. It was nothing. I kept looking for a place to pee, but the trees beside the road were too thin to hide behind and the ditch too shallow to crouch in. People would see me and think I had no manners and was trying to embarrass my mother and my father who had been on the actual Death March. I was just marching home and I would be OK when I got there. If I put my shoes by the stove, they would dry by morning. If my mother yelled, cheery, from the kitchen, "Hi, honey, how'd it go?" I would yell back, "Fine," then barricade myself in the bathroom, change into dry clothes, and not talk about being forgotten. So that's what I did when I finally got home, half an hour later. My bladder hurt even after I peed, but the bathroom was warm and sheltered no flies.

# 13

# Death March, North Korea

## NOVEMBER 1950

Hundreds of captive men, women, and children trotted as best they could to keep up with the Tiger's blistering pace. Most were still dressed in tattered summer clothing. Those who could lift themselves above their physical pain took note of the natural beauty of this foreign land, its steep mountains and winding narrow valleys, the stands of lush pine, the gentle falling snow that marked their passing. Such blissful mental escape seldom lasted; eventually the traveler had to look down and also note the red streaks in the snow, bloody footprints left by those with holes in their shoes or those who wore no shoes at all. Doc was one of the latter.

The snow was also speckled with grain that had drained out of holes jabbed in the sacks made of rags that some of the soldiers carried on their backs. The Tiger had ordered them to dump any food they had brought along from the cornfield, and now they knew he meant what he said when he threatened to shoot anyone who disobeyed. But they held onto whatever bag or bit of blanket they could scrounge, wrapping it around their shoulders as they walked, and using it as meager cover when they stopped to rest. Whistle blasts called a halt every three or four hours. The prisoners sat on the ground, atop their sacks if they had them, during breaks that Doc thought lasted too long. Their limbs became so stiff that it was all they could do to stand at the next whistle.

The Tiger's orders were repeated often. No one was to fall out for any reason, not even to squat beside the road. Because their subsistence depended on partially cooked, often rancid, corn kernels with bits of husk still attached, most of the prisoners suffered severe diarrhea, but stopping long enough to defecate meant dying from a bullet to the head. Liquid feces ran down their legs as they jogged. When someone couldn't walk or keep up, two men in his section were assigned to help him in whatever way they could: cajoling him, hoisting his arms over their shoulders to share the load, or carrying him piggyback. Whatever they did to keep him moving was preferable to the constant harassment, swearing, and beating by the guards and their rifle butts. And if he died, they were to carry him still. Tiger's orders. No bodies left behind as evidence.

Not all of the Korean guards relished their duties. A few, especially those who had dropped back with their struggling charges and could safely stay out of sight, quietly tried to encourage the men to keep moving. They raised their voices and guns only when the Tiger was close by.

Nights were worse than days. Sometimes shelter was available, but seldom was there room for everyone. Some men stuffed straw in their pants, tied the legs shut, and stood all night, moving around to stay warm and hoping to catch bits of sleep as they marched the next day. Yes, they learned, one could fall asleep on one's feet.

They stopped one night at a schoolhouse with three rooms, one designated for civilian diplomats, another for women and children, and the third for everyone else. The soldiers crammed themselves into the third room until no one else would fit, at which point the guards kept pushing more men in, the way gloved attendants sometimes shoved Japanese riders onto trains in Tokyo so they could get the doors shut.

Lying down was impossible that night. Jammed so close together on the floor, the prisoners were in excruciating pain, sitting on their tailbones, knees pressed against their chests, feet and hands hovering in midair because there was no room to put them down. They had no way to maintain their balance, so pressure from their neighbors flopped them forward, backward, or sideways. After some time had passed, one man who couldn't take it anymore went berserk and began screaming uncontrollably. The guards threatened to fire their guns into the room until silence reigned. Quiet ensued for about half an hour, then more screaming from the first soldier and others. And again, angry threats from the guards standing outside. Finally Major Dunn ordered the prisoners to remove the screamers by passing them overhead and depositing them outside the door. Two or three were ejected that way, sentenced to spending the night outside with those who hadn't fit into the room in the first place. The men who stayed indoors, where they gulped scarce oxygen and gagged at the stench of rampant diarrhea loosed from men who couldn't move, at least stayed warm.

In the morning, the Tiger took much delight in throwing open the door and issuing, with a grin, his first-ever good-morning order: "Everyone stand up!" Of course, no one could stand. Line by line, they fell forward and crawled on hands and knees through the door. It took several minutes for the numbness to wear off so they could rise up, stiff and sore. Some who had spent the night outside on the ground, snow blanketing their torsos, never got up at all. After eating a meager breakfast of grain that had been issued to make a substitute for coffee the night before, those who were still alive were forced to collect the corpses and set off on another day's march.

Major Dunn had spent his marching hours haggling with the Tiger through the interpreter, pleading the cases of his weakened men and the burdens they faced. Most of them could hardly stumble along, much less keep up a trotting pace, and they certainly couldn't be expected to carry their dying (or dead) brethren. Commissioner Lord suggested a more humane plan: one of the prisoner doctors could certify a death, and the body could be buried or remain beside the road until an oxcart arrived to collect it. The Tiger had a better plan: if someone was thought to be dead, the prisoners should tell a guard, who would shoot the man in the heart to certify his demise. Those who couldn't walk any farther, he added, could stay by the roadside and wait for the oxcarts to take them to the People's Hospitals. He also ordered an oxcart to carry Father Villemot and two of the women. Dunn appeared to be making progress with his humanitarian goals.

On November 4, the fourth day of the march, conditions worsened. Heavy snow began to envelop the long line of marchers as they made their way up a steep and narrow mountain pass, leaving bloody tracks on the switchbacks. Icy conditions meant slipping and sliding. Those who could keep going were soon trudging through more than a foot of snow, faces down against the wind, arms held close to bodies to contain whatever warmth remained. They helped each other when they could. A Turkish teenager used a rope to drag his family's suitcase behind him up the steep incline.

The sound of a gunshot ricocheted off the cliff walls. Then another and another.

"What's all the shooting about?" someone asked.

"I suppose they are shooting the dead," someone else answered.

One of Doc's fellow Task Force Smith survivors, Lt. Wadie J. Roun-tree, was still fit enough to carry a disabled prisoner on his back, using a fireman's carry. He transported Private Ambrose in this manner for an hour before realizing that Ambrose had died. He kept going for another thirty minutes until a break was called and a medic could confirm the death. While others were preparing for a quick roadside burial, a guard with a burp gun fired at least fifteen shots into the body.

Doc counted twenty-one rifle shots echoing across the forlorn valley that morning. By this time, he understood that People's Hospitals didn't exist, that the men who had stayed behind in the cornfield had been shot, and that no oxcarts would be collecting the sick, wounded, or dead. The guards merely kicked bodies over the edge of the chasm, removing all traces.

The next morning, the interpreter, Commissioner Lord, added a postscript in English to his daily announcements: "Gentlemen, this morning I am reminded of good news: 'Yea, though I walk through the valley of the shadow of death, I will fear no evil; for Thou art with me.'" He repeated the entire Psalm 23, which became a mantra for many who survived.

Through blinding snow and sleet, soldiers and civilians kept plodding skyward. Some, now comprehending their fate, would simply stop in the middle of the road and sit, waiting for their fellow prisoners to pass them by and leave them heaven-bound. They asked for cigarettes and called out last messages for loved ones. One pleaded for a gun so he could shoot himself rather than wait for the guards to do it. Another exhausted soldier finally dropped the man he had been carrying and left him there to continue on. The downed soldier didn't protest when the man who had carried him returned to confiscate his tattered shoes. Someone sang "God Bless America" through tears. When four men carrying a litter were forced to put it down and leave it, a passing soldier plucked the wounded man from the litter, slung him over his shoulders in a fireman's carry, and kept going.

When the column stopped to rest, the Tiger assembled those who couldn't walk and thus were slowing the pace. He was overheard instructing the guards to bury them in unmarked graves.

On the other side of the pass, it was just as hard, maybe harder, to keep one's footing on a downhill slide as it had been to climb up. But conditions were improving. The sky was starting to clear, and hope fluttered. As the group approached the city of Chasong, the Tiger told them that they would have the remainder of that day and part of the next to rest. They spent this time listening to his lectures about how the difficulties they faced represented atonement for their capitalist sins. During their respite, Major Dunn persisted in his cajoling. Finally the Tiger agreed to arrange truck transportation for the old men, women, children, and five sick and wounded POWs. That night, all were sheltered in a schoolhouse and given straw to sleep on.

Each morning, the marchers who were still alive rose to their feet, put one in front of the other, and went on. They were headed for Chunggang, about 115 mountainous miles from where they began. Those who could keep going covered about 10 miles a day at a slackened pace, while others reached their own final destinations. Doc counted seventy-six prisoners who were shot during the ten-day march. Another five died of exposure. *A man would carry a buddy today, collapse tomorrow, and meet his end a hero, but one never to be known.* And the torture wasn't over.

# 14

# Landstuhl, West Germany

## 1962

I hurried through my homework and went into the kitchen to see how dinner was coming.

"Is it time to set the table?"

"Not quite. Your father isn't home yet." My mother looked tired, her tight-curled hairdo limp, ready for the weekly shampoo and set that was her special treat. She was chopping celery into perfectly even pieces to add to the pot roast. She was an easier mark than my father when it came to granting permission. She usually started with *no* but sometimes edged toward a reluctant *I guess so*.

"I was wondering if maybe I could go to the dance tonight?"

"What time does it start?"

"Seven o'clock."

"I'm not sure if we will be done with dinner."

"Well, if we are, then could I go?"

"Is Gary going?"

Gary Lawson, an athletic, blond ninth-grader on whom I had a secret crush, lived across the hall. Since we'd moved into the four-story stucco apartment building on "the hill" a year ago, his mother had kept us abreast of every family feud and personal annoyance. We'd hear raised voices, then Mrs. Lawson would burst through her door just before she pounded on ours and swept in, breathless with her story. My parents were amused and sometimes offered advice, but what she really needed was an audience. Since I'd never lived so close to so many people, the borrowed drama fascinated me.

"I don't know if Gary is going. Does it matter?"

"You could walk with him. *If* you go. We'll see," she said.

I didn't want to miss a school dance because I never wanted to miss anything, but I wouldn't be walking with Gary. The army post was a small town with only 135 students in junior high. Few of us had TVs, which broadcast only one American show, a weekly episode of *Bonan-za*, so we hung out together, playing pool and Ping-Pong, dancing to stacks of 45 rpm records, and swigging Nehi at the teen club. If Gary walked me to the dance, people would talk.

I didn't explain this to my mother. As soon as my father walked through the door, I flew into table setting. It was after six when we sat down. I winced when my mother announced my plans, but my father—did he even know the word *yes*?—said nothing. Then, after an extend-ed period of chewing, he launched into an animated political rant that somehow invoked the Gettysburg Address.

"Do you know what that is, Punky?"

My mouth was full. I gulped. I dared not shake my head.

He glared at me. "I asked you a question."

"Um, didn't Abraham Lincoln write it?"

"Well, yes." For a moment he seemed pleased. "But what did it say?"

"Um, four score and seven years ago, something. Maybe about slavery."

"You mean you don't know what the Gettysburg Address said?"

"Well, not exactly." I never knew how to handle his challenges, which he clearly enjoyed. *Yes* wasn't exactly true. *No* could launch a ti-rade. The right answer always eluded me. He was still looking at me, expectant.

"I'm only in seventh grade, and we haven't studied that yet."

"That's no excuse. You live in a democracy, and you better under-stand how that works and why. Not everyone in this world is free, you know. They don't have food on their table every night or clothes on their backs. You kids are so spoiled, and you don't even know it. What do you think I do every day? What do you think the army is all about?"

*Must have something to do with the Gettysburg Address, but this is a question I can't answer correctly, no matter what. Better not try.*

"When we're through with dinner, and after you've done the dish-es, I want you to write a two-hundred-fifty-word report on the Gettys-burg Address and give it to me."

I looked at my mother, begging in silence.

"But she's going to the dance," she said.

"Not until she finishes her paper."

"May I please be excused?" I asked.

"Not until everyone is finished."

It was 6:30 already. Hopeless. It seemed forever before I could clear the dishes. In the kitchen, my mother whispered that she'd finish up so I could get started on the report. From the bookcase I hauled out the brown *Compton's Encyclopedia,* volumes *G* and *L,* which, being household baggage, still smelled musty. In my room I read the entries and wrote with a blue fountain pen on three-holed paper. Two hundred fifty words was a lot; I kept stopping to count. Finally I had enough. I washed my face, hoping my eyes didn't look red, and handed in my work to my father, still sipping coffee at the table.

"Sit down!" he ordered. I sat. He took his time reading. He'd calmed down. A smile played with the corners of his mouth.

"I guess this is OK," he said, peering at me over the top of his glasses. "You think you can remember it now?"

I nodded. He told me I could go. I ran out our door, took the half flight of stairs down to the entry in a single jump, and jogged most of the way to the school gym. I was embarrassed about being so late, and once I got there, embarrassed about my outfit. School dances were special. Boys tucked their shirts in. Girls dressed up in clean blouses, pointy bras stuffed with old nylons, short skirts cinched with wide belts, and shiny flats with stockings. I was wearing a fat pleated skirt that covered my knees, no belt, no bra, saddle shoes, and what utterly humiliated me: ankle socks.

My mother wouldn't let me wear nylons, not even the ninety-nine-cent kind bought on the economy instead of in the PX. I was too young, she declared, and the bobby socks my friends wore to school would stretch out my shoes. I had to wear thin white socks like hers. Convinced I looked stupid, I went into a bathroom stall and stayed there, sniffling, until a pair of feet stopped in front.

"What's the matter with you?" asked Jenny Morris, a popular eighth-grader. Her mother wore thin ankle socks like my mother, but Jenny wore nylons.

"The socks," I said, opening the door and pointing to my feet.

"What's the matter with them?"

"I hate them."

"So why do you wear them?"

"Because my mother makes me."

"Why don't you just take them off?" she asked. "Your mother isn't here. Put them in your pocket and then put them back on when you get home."

"I can't."

"Why not?"

"They'd kill me."

Jenny rolled her eyes, finished teasing her hair, and turned to leave. "No, they wouldn't," she said. "Just do it."

But I was afraid. What if my parents found out? My mother would just yell, but my father? I'd been forbidden, and if I disobeyed orders, he would be more furious than I could imagine. Disobeying orders was not a choice.

Now that my father lived close enough to walk to work and could return for evening rounds if necessary, he seldom missed dinner. Our dinner table was general headquarters for discussing issues, settling disputes, and learning manners. He placed a smudged, palm-sized, pink stuffed piglet in front of whoever slurped spaghetti and delivered a stern "children should be seen and not heard" if anyone spoke out of turn. We were getting used to frequent admonitions: Stand up straight. Hair out of your eyes. Hands out of your pockets. Keep off the grass.

Lately, our dinner discussions had revolved around the possibility of hosting a young Danish woman for six months, evidently a common practice here. She would help with cleaning, cooking, and babysitting. We'd help her with English and maybe we'd learn some Danish, my grandparents' native language. She'd sleep in a dormer room on our building's fourth floor and have one day off every week. We (my father said *we* even when he meant *I*) decided this was a good idea.

Arrangements were made. Anticipation was high. Weeks passed, and one day Else arrived. Nearly six feet tall, slender, with blonde hair that fell below her shoulder blades, she was the most beautiful girl I'd ever met. She was shy, especially with her English, but she could understand us, and I liked her. I think my brothers' high-energy antics frustrated her, which made her yell at them sometimes, but she was nice to me.

The next couple of weeks brought smiles all around the dinner table that now seated six, but the pleasure didn't last. One evening after Else had gone to her room, my parents called me into the living room. It was odd for them both to be there. Usually after supper my father disappeared into the bedroom, where he was using every inch of floor space to build two huge stereo speakers, nearly five feet high, to fit the corners of the living room. It was a particularly messy pet project, especially when he decided that the speakers would sound better if he packed the woofers in sand that he swiped from the playground and baked in the oven. I wondered if Else had complained about not being able to get into the bedroom to clean.

"Sit down," my father said.

"Tell us about Else," my mother added.

"She's nice. I like her."

"But what does she do when we're not here?" My father, the gruff interrogator. I didn't like the look on his face.

"Nothing. I mean, she takes care of us."

"Is she mean to your brothers? Does she hurt them?"

"No. Sometimes she yells at them when they're bad."

They wanted details but I couldn't think of any. I'd heard them lecturing her loudly at night after I went to bed, but about what, I wasn't sure. I didn't want to get her in trouble. I just wanted the tension to go away.

"What about guests? Has she had guests?"

"Well, she did have one friend over. She introduced us. He was fine."

At this, my father blew up. He never used the F word, but *goddamn it all to hells* and *sonofabitches* colored the air. I knew the rules for when my parents were gone—no one in, no one out—but I thought they were only for me. I was confused. On one hand, I felt bad that I might have betrayed her. On the other hand, being asked to testify graduated me from silent childhood, and that felt good. My father finally calmed down, and my mother told me to go to bed.

After that, the tension grew. Despite her markedly improved English, Else quit trying to converse at dinner and stared at her plate instead. When my father tried to pry words out of her, she looked ready to burst into tears. His lips drew a straight line across his teeth. My mother knitted her brows. When Christmas came, we gave her a small present from all of us. She gave each of us our own presents, carefully chosen. Mine was a jade bracelet so delicate and grown-up it made me gasp.

One Sunday afternoon my father asked Else to come in even though it was her day off. He sat at one end of the table and told her to sit at the other. My mother sat down, too, and I was ordered to sit in my usual place. I didn't know why I had to be there, but I knew better than to ask. Dirk and Eric grabbed their leather pouches of aggies and went outside to play marbles.

The grilling began. My father asked Else where she went on her days off. Did she go out with a man? Who was that man? An American GI? An enlisted man? Where did they go? And where did they go after that? Did they hold hands? Did they kiss? What?

She tried to answer, but he kept interrupting. His face was red and he slapped his hand on the table, jumping the coffee cups. My stomach hurt, listening.

"Yes, I have a boyfriend," she said.

"Are you sleeping with him?"

She didn't answer. Maybe she didn't understand, but I hoped she was standing up to him. Inside, I cheered.

"Did you bring him to our house?"

She shot me a look of surprise and hurt. I felt awful.

"Yes, he came here. But he came after I was done with my work."

"You don't bring men here."

"It was my day off. We were supposed to go to the movies, but you needed me here, so I came."

"You don't go to their place either."

"On my time off, I can do what I want."

"No," my father bellowed. "You cannot do what you want."

"Yes, I can!"

Her face was red, too, but she didn't flinch. He was on a tirade, half off his chair, spittle collecting at the corners of his mouth. Sometimes it sprayed the tablecloth. He pointed at her while he shouted. *Bad girl. Bad, bad girl.*

He said that she was immoral, that we couldn't trust her. That trust is the most important thing. That she wasn't supposed to date soldiers.

That she'd slapped us in the face after we'd invited her here and given her the benefit of the doubt. That we had no choice but to send her home.

Else, her eyes filled, had stopped trying to talk. I was clenching my teeth. Part of me wanted to sit tall beside my father, to take his side because he was always right, to blame her for being all those bad things girls aren't supposed to be. I practiced this inside my head and pretended to match his face, as my mother was doing. She had a way of tilting her head and holding her mouth in a grimace that said she was resolved to stand beside him, no matter what he said or did or what she really thought. She wasn't going to fight him on this. I wasn't going to say a word, either, even though the other part of me wanted to hug Else. I didn't want her to go home, but I wanted this cruel time to be over. She left a week later. I found a good-bye note, written in her careful European script, in my jewelry box.

The Else incident prompted another Sunday afternoon meeting at the table.

"Do you know what menstruation is?" my father, a professor this time, emphasizing the *stru*. I shook my head. He fetched medical books and *Compton's* volumes, splaying them on the table and pointing out vagina, uterus, ovaries, clitoris.

"Oh, you mean periods," I said. Of course I knew what those were. My friend in the next stairwell had gotten hers and explained Kotex in messy detail. My mother had placed a box of beginner's pads in the hall closet and left pamphlets on my bed.

"Or falling off the roof. On the rag." He started to smile, then stopped. "It means you could get pregnant, but not if you keep your legs crossed. No one will want you if you're not a virgin. A man will get his pleasure from a slut, but he won't marry her. So if you want to marry a good man, you have to save it for him."

This was an order, I could tell. My mother, sitting across the table with a pained expression, had nothing to add. When he launched into an abstract philosophical discussion of true love, sacrifice, and honor, I think we both zoned out. He never mentioned birth control, although I knew my mother used a diaphragm because I'd found it in a blue plastic case in her bedside table.

The truth was, boys freaked me out, ever since John Andrews rang my doorbell and handed me a marshmallow-filled chocolate heart for Valentine's Day in the third grade. I took one bite and hid the rest in the bottom of the wastebasket. Last Christmas, Tommy Wilson gave me a miniature, wooden Bavarian grandfather clock, painted red, with a wind-up key in the base's tiny cupboard. I couldn't open the gift until Christmas morning—family rules—and doing so in front of my parents was excruciating. I couldn't look at Tommy after the holidays, although I did enlist two friends to help stamp WE LOVE YOU TOMMY into the ballfield snow, so everybody could see it from our school's second-floor windows.

No boy would want me, I was convinced. I was, according to my mother, flat as a pancake. What little breast tissue I had spread wide, not forward, so I couldn't begin to fill a pointy bra. My mother bought me a training bra, but for training what? The fabric was so taut that breasts couldn't possibly grow; I stuck my foot in the cup areas to stretch them out, but that didn't help. At least I finally had bra straps that showed through my gym blouse, like the popular girls.

That winter my father decided I should learn how to shoot a gun. We didn't own guns, and no one we knew hunted, except my uncle's friends in northern Minnesota who complained that my father always passed up the good shots. Nevertheless, he was adamant that I learn how to handle a rifle, and my mother made no objections that I heard. She calmly set about arranging a car pool and made sure it included at least one other girl so I wouldn't feel weird. I still felt weird.

Every Saturday morning through the gloomy winter and reluctant spring, my mother woke me in her singsong, sardonic "rise and shi-i-ine," the one phrase that made me think about using the gun I cradled weekly in awkward arms. Neither of us was an early riser like my father, who liked to throw open the bedroom doors on weekend mornings and shout, "Front and center! Up and at 'em!" I much preferred to stay snuggled under the covers with whatever novel I was reading at the time. No matter. I was expected at the breakfast table by "0700 hours," to consume my hearty, hot breakfast in time to catch my ride to Ramstein Air Force Base, a half-hour trip we shooters endured in sleep-sodden silence.

The firing range was in a long, narrow building, gray and dull as the February sky. Inside it was dark and cold, its odor acrid, like the charred remains of a campfire. We kept our jackets on. At the front end we sat on metal folding chairs, watching an instructor point to the parts of a .22 rifle on a cardboard diagram. Then we took turns attaching a paper target to a clip and cranking it out on a squeaky clothesline contraption to the other end of what looked like a bowling alley lane. Groaning, I lay down on the freezing concrete and leaned on my pointy elbows to aim the gun. This hurt. I was supposed to look down the top of the barrel and line up the little V-thing at the end with the big black circle on the target, but I had a lazy eye that wandered off on its own, a malady that also made cameras and binoculars a nuisance. Since I had skipped my prescribed eye exercises to read Nancy Drew mysteries instead, I figured I deserved this cold concrete punishment.

The target flapped in the breeze created by the clothesline contraptions in the adjoining lanes, and the gun liked to dance. Up, down, sideways. Try as I might, I couldn't hold it still. I would wait until it floated past the target, then pull the trigger. No. Squeeze the trigger. While holding my breath. Trying to keep one eye open. *BLAM!* My ear went numb. I didn't just miss the target; I missed the paper it was printed on.

"Try it again!" the instructor shouted. When my turn ended, I reeled the target in. It had only a few scattered holes, one just nicking the target's outer edge. The instructor laughed. I stuck one bullet in my pocket as a souvenir. I liked its heavy, smooth feel in my hand.

This weekly ritual lasted almost until the end of the school year. I was one of the few kids who didn't get sick or drop out. I stuffed cotton balls in my ears, and I improved. The gun still did its own thing, but I managed to earn my National Rifle Association Marksman medal and patch, and Marksman First Class, and Sharpshooter with bars. I kept them in a box in my underwear drawer. I never showed them to my father. He would think I was showing off.

"So what did you learn in school this week?" my father asked as he ladled a large scoop of baked beans onto my plate. I didn't like baked beans, but he did, even cold and straight out of the can, which is how he ate them when my mother ate dinner with the Officers' Wives Club.

On Saturday nights she doctored them with brown sugar and onion browned in butter to accompany the ritual hot dogs or hamburgers.

"Not much. We're supposed to do a science fair project."

"So what are you doing for yours?"

"I don't know. I don't have any ideas. What do you think?"

He chewed a few mouthfuls of hamburger-with-everything-on-it.

"How about evolution of the transistor?"

"What's a transistor?"

Without a darkroom or a shop to build something more elaborate, he had taken up electronics. He was building a radio from a kit, for which he enlisted my mother's help because he was color-blind and couldn't identify the color-coded components. Radios, he said, used to be large because they needed vacuum tubes. With transistors, they could be smaller, which changed everything. I didn't really get it, but I treasured the transistor radio I had gotten for Christmas.

"So if I did that, would you help me?" I asked.

"Sure."

"OK," I said without expression. Inside, I sighed with relief. Now I would be able to tell my science teacher, Mrs. Patterson, that I had chosen a project; maybe my chronic nervous stomachache would go away. I glowed with the promise of help from my father, who had become a local hero after spending six weeks commanding Operation Ida, the U.S. relief effort in Iran, where he helped build an emergency hospital in the sand after September earthquakes killed 12,000 people and injured many more. My mother saved pictures of him with the Shah from the *Stars and Stripes*. He had brought me a little carved box, a silver-filigree pin of tiny shoes with toes pointed up, and an Iranian doll whose face, except for the eyes, was covered with a thin black veil. It took the place of the geisha doll he had bought for me in Japan on his way home from Korea, the one we put in storage back in the States.

On Monday morning, I turned in my idea to Mrs. Patterson, who nodded absent-mindedly. I thought about it constantly, at school and when I couldn't fall asleep at night, but I had no idea where to begin. I looked up transistor in the encyclopedia but found only one paragraph about the inventors. I was afraid to ask for help.

"How's your project coming?" my father asked one night at dinner.

"OK," I said after a pause. "But I'm not really sure how a transistor works exactly."

"Here, I'll draw you a picture," he said. He grabbed a pen and a piece of scrap paper and drew a diagram.

"Thanks," I said.

I still wasn't sure what to do. Mrs. Patterson marked days off on the calendar posted at one end of the blackboard. With two weeks to go, my fellow students were buzzing about their projects. I sat glum and silent, wishing I'd never heard of the transistor. The following Saturday night, I sat staring at the heap of baked beans on my plate.

"What's the matter with you?" my mother asked.

"Nothing."

"Then eat."

"I can't."

"How come?"

"The science fair. There's only a week left, and I haven't gotten anywhere on my project."

"Whose fault is that?" my father lectured from his end of the table. "If you've got something to do, then do it. No one's going to do it for you. The world isn't here to wait on you. The science fair isn't really very important, but it's an example of what will come later on a larger scale. If you learn that now, you'll never regret it."

"So what do I do?"

"Go tell your teacher the truth: that you didn't get it done."

I was a failure. I always knew it. My father was a Tiger survivor, and a hero on top of that, but not me. On Monday morning I sat in science class, nauseated with shame, waiting for a chance to approach Mrs. Patterson's desk. Finally I tiptoed up and whispered that I wouldn't be turning in a project because I hadn't really started.

She smiled and touched my arm. "Oh, of course you can do it. You've got a few days yet, and I'm sure you'll do a fine job. Just get started and don't worry about it so much. OK?"

Relief buckled my knees. That afternoon, my mother took me to buy a piece of poster board. I taped a transistor to it and carefully re-created my father's diagram in magic marker. I added some block headlines and wrote a little report about the inventors in large script. On science fair day I wrapped it in a plastic bag and carried it to the gym.

That evening most of the kids and their parents gathered around my classmate's egg-hatching demonstration, an elaborate exhibit that covered an entire table. The boy's father excitedly explained how they'd worked so hard on it, the whole family. I stood beside my poster and stared off into space, wishing I could be somewhere else. A couple of visitors stopped to look at my project; one asked a polite question. But my parents stayed home.

Every summer more friends left for the States, their suitcases stuffed with as many bags of gummy bears as their parents would allow. In 1963, it was our time to return to the land of doorknobs that turn, two-stick popsicles, and American TV. No elite passage on a fancy ocean liner this time. In Bremerhaven we boarded a troop ship, smaller and cruder, painted in browns instead of crisp blue and white. Troops stayed on one end and families on the other.

At night, quartered in a windowless bunk room with other girls my age, I tossed and turned in the heat and tried not to think about my queasy stomach. Meals were served in shifts, and my father, again reminding us that an empty stomach is a sure invitation to seasickness, ordered me to show up on time. About a week into our ten-day passage, I arrived at our designated table. By then I'd gotten my sea legs and was feeling OK until I saw my plate, which held a slab of gray beef and the biggest baked potato I'd ever seen. I liked baked potatoes, but this one was thoroughly burned, black and crusty, which was no excuse not to eat it, my father said with his eyebrows. I tackled the monster with my knife and fork and was chewing my second bite when nausea attacked without warning. I bolted from the dining room, headed for the deck, grabbed the rail and upchucked over the side. My whole meal spewed right out of me, smelling pretty much the same as it had smelled on the plate. I noticed at least half a dozen other passengers, at discrete distances, doing what I had done. I wiped my mouth on the napkin still clutched in my hand, returned to the table, and finished my meat and potato.

At dinner on our last full day on the boat, my father announced that we would all get up before dawn the next morning.

"Why?" I whined.

"To see the Statue of Liberty," he said.

"I don't want to see the Statue of Liberty," I said. "It's too early. Besides, I already saw it."

He clenched his teeth and I shut up.

The next morning up on deck, it was still dark and damp with dew. Mute and ghostlike figures began to fill the empty spots behind the rail in silent, shifting layers. Some grabbed life jackets to ward off the chill. Our family huddled together as I watched the water, a deeper gray than the sky, rolling in hills and valleys. I no longer had to work to keep my balance.

Then she pierced the mist with her torch, chin held high in the breaking light. We were closer than I had imagined. A woman along the rail started singing "God Bless America." I looked up at my father's face as he stared, rapt, while other voices joined in. I wanted him to reach down and put his hand on my shoulder, but he did not. I stretched tall, as if to be more beside him, and found solace in the fact that so many of us stood there together, about to end our voyage, strangers no longer.

"Land of the free," my father said, so only we could hear.

We were home.

# 15

# By the Yalu River, North Korea

## NOVEMBER 1950

Early on the morning after the Death March ended at Chunggang, the Tiger ordered everyone outside to do calisthenics. It was November 10, predawn black and biting, with temperatures in the single digits. Father Villemot had to be carried because he could not stand.

"Exercise is good for health!" the Tiger proclaimed.

Commissioner Lord accused him of madness, given the general condition of the exhausted, starving marchers huddled together in yet another abandoned schoolhouse. The Tiger said nothing in response; he merely held his pistol to Lord's head. After more entreaties from Lord, he allowed Father Villemot to be carried back inside but forced two other priests in their seventies to stay outside for jumping jacks. Villemot died the next day, and the priests two days later. Monsignor Quinlan continued to offer not only last rites, but also inspiration for living and Bible verses for comfort.

Five sick prisoners who had been transported by truck were placed in a separate room where American medics were assigned to tend them. The night after they arrived, a fire broke out in their malfunctioning stove.

"Water! We need water!" the medics shouted to the guards as they left the patients and ran to find a bucket and water to extinguish the flames. While they were gone, the guards extinguished the fire themselves and locked the door.

"Please, let us back in," the medics pleaded when they returned. When the guards refused, they begged to be allowed to go find help. That request was also denied. The guards stood steadfast in front of the door.

The next morning, Doc convinced the guard to unlock the door so he could check on his patients. Smoke filled his nostrils as he entered the room. It didn't take him long to realize that all five prisoners had frozen to death.

After about a week, the prisoners were moved to a more secluded area, away from the strafing warplanes, about four miles north. They called their prison compound "the shacks." About twenty rickety structures and a schoolhouse occupied an area that stretched half a mile along the Yalu River, which separates North Korea from China. For the first month or two, the guards occupied themselves by shuttling prisoners from one shack to another, for no reason anyone could determine. At one point they tried to group the men according to their maladies: those with scabies in one shack, those with severe dysentery in another, etc. But the haphazard system remained just that.

The civilians were sent to live in dilapidated houses, some of which were designated as hospitals. Being sent to a hospital—unheated and lacking floors in some cases—was considered a death sentence. One victim was Bishop Patrick Byrne, an American missionary who died November 25. His colleagues burned millet stalks to soften the frozen earth and dug a grave six inches deep. Monsignor Quinlan wrapped the body in the cassock Quinlan had worn since his capture, hoping that the red cloth-covered metal buttons and piping might later identify the body. Rocks and dirt piled in the shape of a cross marked the grave.

Winter in Korea was like the worst of the Minnesota winters Doc remembered: dark, frigid, relentless. Temperatures plummeted to forty degrees below zero. When frostbitten toes turned black, men used fingers or pliers to snap them off. One man's feet froze and the skin fell off, exposing the bones. None of the shacks offered reasonable living conditions to those stuffed inside. An average shack measured eight feet by twelve feet and held between twenty and forty men. Doc estimated that each had about four square feet in which to spend the short monotonous days and long miserable nights, cramped, hunched, and shivering.

More than one hundred men were crammed into an eighteen-by-twenty-foot shack with four windows on the north side and a door on the south. By day they sat cross-legged in order to fit. At night they divided themselves into four rows, one row with their heads toward the north wall, one toward the south wall, and the other two butting heads in the middle of the room, their limbs overlapping those of their fellows. They slept back to belly, so when one man turned over, they all had to. They shared a single blanket, which was usually given to those nearest the door, who had to chip away the ice that framed it during the night.

Their rice diet contributed to nocturia, which meant having to pee about a dozen times a night. They dreaded going to the outdoor latrine in cold that froze the insides of their nostrils, and they dreaded returning to quarters where ice lined the ceiling and inside walls. They were living in hell.

Doc realized he was getting an education in human nature and survival that no school could offer. He was critical of those who failed to keep clean until he woke from a nap soiled by his own excrement. When the man holding Doc's ration of mush saved him only one bite, he learned that trust is hard-won. Despite MacArthur's promise, Christmas came and went. Men died. All he could do was observe and fight to stay alive. *I'd been hungry but never that hungry, cold but never that cold, tired but never that tired.*

In the evenings, wood details broke the monotony for the three or four men from each shack who were selected to trudge through the snow about a mile each way to fetch bundles of brush for the small stoves that served as sources of heat. The resulting warmth was a mixed blessing. The poorly ventilated stoves filled the rooms with smoke, causing eye and lung irritation and generating arguments over whether to shut the door so those who were near it wouldn't freeze, or keep it open to provide some relief from air pollution.

The men were filthy. When they had first arrived in November, they were allowed to bathe once with warm water in an open room dubbed the bathhouse. Each man stood on thin boards laid across the ice-coated floor and threw a few bowls of water over himself. No more washing was allowed until April. Scabies infected nearly all of the prisoners, many of whom developed festering lesions, some so pervasive that it was too painful to move; they could not raise their arms to feed themselves.

Every morning before daybreak, the prisoners were still required to line up outside for PT, often conducted under bright moonlight. Many of them performed their exercises barefoot because their shoes had worn out or been stolen by their fellow prisoners or, more likely, the guards, whom Doc considered stupid, ignorant, arrogant, and cruel.

The tyrannical Tiger's diabolical underlings maintained strict standards. No access to water. Limited and scheduled mass visits to the latrines. No visits to latrines after 10:00 p.m. The majority of the prisoners suffered from dysentery as well as nocturia. They had to go when they had to go, no matter what time it was or where they happened to be. Liquid feces ran down their legs as they swayed in long lines, waiting for their turn at the latrines. The infuriated guards rubbed it in their faces. The rooms and hallways, not to mention the clothing they wore or discarded, were splattered with human excreta, which sent the Tiger into predictable rages. "You are responsible!" he shouted at the officers in charge of each soiled shack. It took the officers more than a week to convince the Tiger to allow nighttime toilet privileges.

The blame game supplied the guards with frequent amusement. The officer in charge of water detail was held responsible when the well chain broke and sent the bucket plunging to the bottom; for hours the guards made him kneel in the snow while they poured cold water over his bare back. Men who defecated on the ground when the latrines were full were punished. So were men who urinated on the ground, despite the fact that the guards did the same.

Two of the shacks served as kitchens, one for corn and the other for millet. A guard called the Quartermaster was in charge of the GIs who served as cooks. They didn't have much to work with. Besides rice, millet (used for birdseed in America), and whole kernels of corn, they had daikons (large radishes), cabbage, and occasionally soybeans. They were allowed to celebrate Thanksgiving, but instead of turkey, the meal consisted of one millet ball each and one bowl of soup made from nine heads of cabbage, each about the size of a small celery stalk, one cup of soybean oil, and enough water to serve five hundred. The cooks carried the soup to the schoolhouse mess hall in wooden crocks and a fifty-five-gallon drum that had been cut down. About two hundred metal bowls were available to be shared, but they got rinsed out only once a week. Many prisoners ate their meals from their own dirty hands.

Slowly, they were starving. Monsignor Quinlan was sometimes spotted sitting next to a skeletal prisoner, scooping part of his rice into the prisoner's bowl. Doc figured that between the end of October and the end of March, each person consumed about 400 grams of carbohydrates a day, but only a total of about 100 grams of protein, equivalent to the amount in one pound of steak, for the entire five-month period. One day the Tiger summoned Major Dunn and other officers, including Doc, to his quarters. He announced that he would allow the men to grind corn to make fried bread. The officers said they thought his idea was an excellent one, except that no one was strong enough to push the grinder and no oil was available for frying. *Typical*, thought Doc. He was tired of being ordered to do something that he would not be able to do. But he could do nothing to change the system.

By late December, most of the men had lost all the hair on their bodies. Vitamin deficiencies left them with permanent goose bumps. In addition to dysentery and scabies, they suffered from malaria, pneumonia, influenza, mouth lesions, and wet beriberi, a vitamin B1 deficiency that, left untreated, leads to swollen limbs and heart damage, coma, and death. Worms infested them, sometimes crawling out of their mouths or emerging from their rectums in large white globs that, when they hit the ground, sent worms about seven or eight inches long slithering in every direction. Masses of wiggly maggots also infested their wounds beneath the bandages, making the bandages appear to be alive, but that was a good thing. Maggots ate pus; they were nature's vacuum.

The men were dying in greater numbers, as many as eight a day. Frozen bodies were stacked like cordwood outside the shacks. The Tiger frequently reprimanded Doc: "You are an American doctor, and you are responsible." But Doc was not allowed to treat the men, nor was he able to do anything that might prevent their deaths. He mourned Lieutenant Brockman, whose life he had been unable to save in return for his own.

Two Korean doctors nicknamed Squint Eyes and Butcher, two nurses known as the Bag and the Bitch, and two aides who went by Kong and Pork Chop provided medical care to the prisoners. Doc first met this staff in November, when he was helping Major Dunn complete the death certificates for those who died on the march. The Koreans, knowing that the officers had attempted to record the names, serial numbers, and units of those left behind, asked them to write a summary of each case. But the officers could use only prescribed words and diagnoses. They tried to use phrasing that would remind them of the real circumstances of the death, such as "cerebral hemorrhage" for Lieutenant Thornton, although this was one reminder no one needed. They succeeded sometimes, but if the guards caught them veering off the mark, they had to start over again on a new certificate. The Tiger insisted that the most frequent diagnosis,

*dysentery,* be changed to *enteritis,* a seldom-fatal inflammation of the in-
testines. Doc never figured out why. Despite many false starts, the team
managed to complete eighty certificates.

Eventually, after persistent pleading, Doc was allowed to assist Kong
by following him around, carrying a ten-inch-by-twelve-inch tray with a
dilapidated pair of forceps, tweezers, probes, and two half-pint jars, one
filled with alcohol swabs and the other with Mercurochrome sponges.
Both the alcohol and Mercurochrome were diluted with so much water
that the former had only the slightest scent of alcohol, and Doc was convinced that the latter served better as ink than as antiseptic. The available medicine consisted of about a hundred weak aspirin tablets and
some diarrhea powders. On one occasion, two bottles of an American
preparation of penicillin were delivered to the camp, each containing
200,000 units of the antibiotic. The Koreans diluted it with water and
gave 10,000 units to a soldier who had pneumonia. Since a normal dose
is one to five million units, the soldier did not improve. After four hours
of arguing about dosages, during which someone produced a brochure
that specified the dosages Doc was recommending, Doc gave up.

He was often appalled at the lack of medical knowledge. Pork
Chop, who had never seen a stethoscope before, used it over the patient's clothing, which rendered it virtually useless. The Butcher, who
handled the surgical cases, was sure he knew what to do when he found
an open wound: stuff a rag in it. Any rag would do, including one that
had been discarded by another patient. Thanks to this treatment, small
boils often became large abscesses that involved entire limbs. The use of
water for cleansing was strictly forbidden.

Since he couldn't actually treat anyone, Doc concentrated on treatment strategies. If seventy-five men with dysentery showed up at sick
call, the Koreans would accuse them of lying and treat no one. But if
only ten or twelve showed up, the Korean medic assured him, they
would be given some diarrhea powders. The powders did not work very
well on the diarrhea, Doc knew, but they could have a powerful placebo effect and boost the morale of the sufferers. He tried to see patients
before the Koreans did, to select those who would most benefit from
treatment, placebo or otherwise. He also advised prisoners with boils
and open wounds to hide them from the medics, thus avoiding the rag

treatment and its more serious complications. Doc treated them with hot stones instead. Some followed his advice; others did not. Sometimes all he could do was carry a bowl of water reddened by a capful of Mercurochrome and pretend that it would somehow help the men whose scabies lesions he painted, even though he was well aware that his greetings and reassurances had better curative powers.

One day in January, as wind gusted through the scattering of mud huts, it was so cold that Doc paused only momentarily to gaze across the frozen Yalu at a deserted cluster of cement block buildings. He wondered why he never saw people in the lighted streets. He had been making his Mercurochrome rounds and was now on his way back to his own hut to distribute the evening rice among the men who sat, their backs against the wall, holding up their bowls. Each got a spoonful. There, and there, and there.

"Hey, Doc," one of them called out. "Can't you see that guy is dead?"

Doc must have been dreaming, perhaps of top sirloin and mashed potatoes with butter and sour cream, but he didn't miss a beat. He picked up the corpse's bowl and redistributed the rice among the other men. They thanked him. No one bothered with the body. The next day, it would be strung over a pole hoisted on the skeletal shoulders of whoever was on corpse detail and piled with the other frozen slabs alongside the hut, awaiting burial when the ground thawed. Right now it was too cold to go out unless absolutely necessary.

When the rice was gone, the conversation disappeared as well. The men stripped and lay side by side on the floor, using their infested jackets as coverlets and making the lice crawl farther for their dinner. Without warning, the parchment door flew open, and a young guard called for Doc to *Hayaku, hayaku, bali, bali.* Come with, come with.

Doc got up slowly so that he would not get dizzy and fall. He made his way across the floor, trying not to step on assorted hands, feet, and faces. A few assists from the guard's rifle butt encouraged his progress out to the road. He was taken to another hut, where he entered a room and found the Tiger sitting on the floor. A cotton wick extending from the side of a bowl of oil lit the room, and the interpreter stood nearby.

The Tiger was having a hissy fit. Doc stood before him, hands at his sides. Without his glasses, he saw only the blur of a pointed chin and large teeth exposed by a raging scowl. Doc's weight had dipped below one hundred pounds, but his frail frame still rose more than six feet. The Tiger looked up at him. Doc stood soldier stiff, containing any fear and fury behind tight lips he refused to lick. His fists were closed, protecting future surgeon fingers. He cleared his throat and focused straight ahead.

The Tiger was irate. He had often accused Doc of shirking his responsibility to the dying prisoners, but somehow this was different. He stood up and grabbed the Colt .45 pistol from his holster. He placed the muzzle on the back of Doc's head. He began shouting questions, pushing the muzzle against Doc's skull to emphasize his points. Doc answered as honestly as he could, his mouth parched. But as suddenly as he had placed it there, the Tiger removed the gun from Doc's head, emptied the chamber, replaced the round in the clip, put the gun back in his holster, and sat down. He exchanged words with the interpreter.

"You can go now," the interpreter said. Doc turned toward the door.

"Stop!" the Tiger shouted in English, then continued on in Korean.

"The Commandant wants me to tell you that he was about to shoot you," the interpreter said. "But now he knows that you and your major do not lie and are true soldiers like he is. So now you can go."

Doc went. All the way back to his hut and many years beyond, he wondered what that was all about. He had no idea. He forgot what the questions were. He could think only about his mother and father and how strict they had been when, as the family's youngest child in a small Minnesota town, he had gotten punished for telling lies or half-truths. So he took a chance on the truth. And survived one more night. *It was just my God, my character, and me.*

Shortly after that episode, inexplicably, the Tiger was gone.

# 16

# Rockville, Maryland

## 1963

"Cathy, come here a minute," Miss Dorfman called to me from the equipment room next to the gym. Everyone else had headed for the showers, but I was stalling, looking for errant basketballs. I didn't like Miss Dorfman. Short, dumpy, and grumpy, the PE teacher wielded her whistle like a clarion, commanding cowed obedience from even the most recalcitrant ninth-graders, and barked endless rules and corrections. I tried to stay out of her way, especially during classes in trampoline, vaulting, and tumbling, none of which I had tried before. Uncoordinated and hopeless, I was humiliated when her exasperated critiques echoed off the gym walls. The only thing that mortified me more was the shower-room gauntlet, which required us to march single file and naked, arms held high, through a maze of facing showerheads, as she crossed off our names, scowling, from behind a window. I skipped showers whenever I could get away with it.

So far, Miss Dorfman and her sadistic drills had been the hardest part of fitting into Broome Junior High. Finally back in the States, we had rented a three-bedroom split-level house on busy Veirs Mill Road with a vaulted living room, fireplace, and fenced backyard, where finding three four-leaf clovers in the first twenty minutes convinced me that this would be a lucky place to live.

It seemed so at first. The person sitting behind me in civics class had tapped me on the shoulder, asked my name, then nominated me for student council vice president. I didn't win, perhaps because I didn't realize campaigns required posters, but Jane Sims did, and I liked Jane. I also liked my English teacher, who told me to join the two hundred girls trying out for cheerleader. I couldn't do tricks, but I could jump high and yell loudly, and I figured the tryouts would help me make friends. Standing dry-mouthed in a throng of hopefuls straining to read the list of finalists, I was shocked when I saw my name. I was even more surprised, after competing solo, to be named to the squad.

My cheerleading success had not fazed Miss Dorfman, whose glances in my direction remained dismissive. She cut me no slack. What did she want now? What else had I screwed up?

"Yes, ma'am, I'm coming," I called back. I walked into her smelly cage, empty of other students and assistants, and handed her a basketball I had found under the bleachers. Perched on top of a low shelf full of equipment, she leaned toward me, her eyes wide.

"Do you know what happened?" she asked.

"No, ma'am." My face must have paled as my mind raced through infractions awful enough to elicit this intimate conversation. She gestured toward a radio on the windowsill.

"The president," she said. "He got shot."

Those waning days of November found our family, all five of us, in the downstairs TV room, glued to our new TV. Since it had arrived, we had seldom turned it on. In the assassination aftermath, we seldom turned it off. We carried our plates from the kitchen and ate our meals on tray tables. No one asked how school was or what we planned to do on Saturday afternoon. The mood was dark and sullen, veering to angry. My father steamed and swore as we watched the same scenes over and over. My brothers and I tried to escape notice.

The Sunday after John F. Kennedy was shot dawned gray and rainy, as if the world were weeping. My mother gathered us kids together, dressed us in layers, and drove us into the District, where we met up with the Scotts, our former sponsors. We stood in silent throngs along the route to the Capitol. I couldn't see over the heads and shoulders and umbrellas of the people in front of us, but I could hear the clip-clop of the horses' hooves and the creak of the caisson as it went by, heavy and sad, bearing the remains of JFK. My mother held my brothers' hands while I stood by myself, overwhelmed by the hush of the huge crowd, 300,000 silent mourners, which penetrated as deep as the damp cold. My father, who loathed crowds of any kind, was elsewhere.

At home the TV stayed on for days, while schools and businesses closed down and the shooting of Lee Harvey Oswald played repeatedly. Even when normal schedules resumed, our home did not return to normal. Pashir would not eat and started having seizures on the kitchen floor near his bed, where he soon died of distemper. My father left the house as my mother sat with the Yellow Pages, looking for a dog cemetery, and told me to take care of Dirk and Eric, who had gone upstairs to their room, whimpering. I stuck my fists in my eyes so I wouldn't cry.

As winter closed in, misery refused to leave. My parents had made a pact to quit smoking for one calendar year; gone was their comforting habit of lingering at the dinner table over coffee. I had no doubt that my father, always a towering example of sternly touted principles, would adhere to this self-imposed discipline, but he was not himself. He hardly said a word at dinner unless one of us misbehaved. He shoveled in his food, then folded up his napkin and delivered his dishes to the sink, even if the rest of us weren't finished. More often than not, he left afterward, slamming the door on his way out. I was never sure where he went.

"What's the matter with him?" I asked my mother one evening as we cleared the table. She sighed. She stayed quiet so long I thought she might not answer.

"He can't stand the traffic noise on Veirs Mill. It never stops. And he doesn't like driving in traffic either, to and from work. It makes him very irritable."

"What about his job?" He was stationed at Walter Reed Army Medical Center, although he did not take call or make rounds, so I knew he was not practicing surgery. But he never said exactly what he was doing.

"It's OK," said my mother, who was not going to tell me. "He just doesn't like cities."

My mother was not herself, either. Her clothes didn't fit. All that good German beer made her fat, she said, so she was working her way through a book of Air Force fitness exercises, marking her progress on a chart. She was also limping after stepping on a nail in the backyard that pierced the sole of her cheap PX shoe. And she smelled like cigarette smoke. Sometimes when I came home after school she bolted out of the laundry room, slamming the door behind her. I found the pack of Salems she had stashed behind the laundry detergent. Kent was her usual brand, but my new best friend Rosalie explained that menthol was supposed to smell less, so I figured that was why she switched. I felt guilty on her behalf, guilty for knowing, guilty for having no control. And I felt strangely unprotected. It was as if she were as afraid of being punished as I was.

For all my sympathy, I was also mad at her. This year, more than ever before, I yearned to be part of the crowd. My schoolmates were not army brats like me, although many of their fathers worked for the government. Most of them had grown up here, in tended houses with landscaped lawns and swept driveways on curving, tree-lined streets. Their clothes did not come from the Sears catalog and their slip-on shoes were stylish. I still wore saddle shoes with bobby socks and was not allowed to shave my very hairy legs.

"You'll grow up too fast," she told me.

"What are you talking about? Everyone else shaves, and they don't have as much hair as I do."

"I don't care. You don't want to start too early."

"Why not?"

"Because once you start, you'll never be able to stop."

This made no sense to me, but I was afraid to defy her. I confessed my hirsute embarrassment to Rosalie, who was a gold mine of creative ideas.

"You think saddle shoes are bad? What if your mother forced you to wear Hush Puppies? Of all the ugly shoes, they're the worst," she said one day as we walked home.

I looked down at her feet. She was wearing Keds, soiled and full of holes but cool enough for school.

"Well, you don't think I actually wear those suckers, do you? Of course not. Every day I stash them in a bush near my house and put these on instead. Just do what you want and don't worry about it."

I could not imagine sneaking shoes out of the house every day in a brown paper bag. But one Saturday night in the bathtub, I used my mother's razor to shave a silver-dollar-sized patch on my shin to see what it felt like, and took to rubbing the smooth skin with my fingertip whenever I was anxious or worried.

Many nights I lay awake long past midnight, listening to my parents' raised voices drifting up two levels. I could not hear the words, but I could hear the anger and imagine the flying spittle. I heard objects slamming: pots, pans, cupboard doors, the front door, a car door. On nights when my father got home late from work, tension mounted while we waited. On the nights he called and told us to eat without him, we breathed freer and told knock-knock jokes at the table.

One night after dinner they got into an argument, nasty and abrupt. I tried to be extra noisy putting the dishes in the dishwasher so I would not be able to hear them. My mother's cheeks were taut as she held onto the table and shouted back whenever he stopped ranting to take a breath. He was leaning over the table toward her. He got so violent with his voice and his hands, slashing demons in the air, that my brothers bolted for the stairs. I ran after them and found them huddled in the bedroom hallway.

"It'll be OK," I said, kneeling down and trying to get my arms around both of them. They leaned into me, Dirk quietly blubbering and Eric sobbing. A few tears found their way down my cheeks.

"What's going to happen?" Dirk asked, with a gasp for air. I was afraid he might have one of his asthma attacks, although he had outgrown them long ago.

"I don't know. They're just having an argument."

"But they always yell. Are they going to get a divorce?"

"I'm not sure. I don't think so."

"I don't want a divorce," Eric wailed.

I wiped their eyes and pressed their faces into my stomach so my father would not hear them and charge up the stairs after us. The shouting downstairs quieted eventually, morphing into heated conversation—or maybe that was the TV?—but we did not go back. I made sure all the curtains were closed and read bedtime stories. We turned out the lights early.

It was an April Friday, one of those days when it was impossible to concentrate on anything except the intense pea green of the new grass and the translucent clouds brush-stroking the sky. Usually during PE, boys went to one field and girls to another, but today we were all together, sitting in clumps on the side of the hill that sloped down from the parking lot. Our teachers were chalking off start and finish lines in the flat area below us where we planned to run the races we had practiced all week. We wore gym uniforms: for girls, a white pullover blouse and blue bloomer shorts with an elastic waist and roomy legs that showed your underwear if you weren't careful. I sat with my arms wrapped around my legs, hoping no one would notice the hair.

Miss Dorfman's shrill whistle started the meet. My stomach knotted as I waited for my turn at the fifty-yard dash. Usually I was a good sprinter, but this was my first real race. I tried to remember to breathe. I checked my shoelaces and made sure my blouse was tucked in. I wondered whether I should try the starting position that someone had just showed me, but I was afraid I would trip over my feet and mess up. I wanted to win.

Miss Dorfman called my name. I went to the starting line. I decided to run the way I always did, nothing fancy, just faster. The whistle blew, and I took off. I felt the wind rush past my ears and the ground slide under my feet as if I were hardly touching it. My glasses stayed on my nose, and even though my side vision was blurry, I could tell that I was ahead of everyone else. I had never run this fast before, and the finish line was there, right in front of me. I was going to come in first.

Then I was down. On the ground in a heap, hot pain searing my ankle. When I tried to lift my head, I almost threw up. I tasted acid. My limbs quivered. I looked back to where my foot was twisted in the grass. I had stepped in a hole I never saw.

"Don't get up," said Miss Dorfman, crouching beside me. "Wait until we can get help. We need to call your parents."

I did not want that.

"I can walk," I said. I started to pull myself to a sitting position but quit when I tasted vomit.

"No, you can't," she said in a low voice, not barking. "Just wait a minute."

Teachers flurried about while one of them strode off to make a phone call from the office. I glanced at the other kids, most still in their places on the hillside, a few waiting for the next race. They were watching me, and I tried not to notice. After a few minutes the adults grabbed my arms and legs and scooted me off to the side, where I was out of the way.

"We got hold of your folks. They will be here in a few minutes to take you to the doctor," Miss Dorfman said.

That surprised me. My father was at work and my mother had errands to do that day. She wouldn't be home until school was out, another hour or so. Within about fifteen minutes, however, I spotted my father emerging from between parked cars at the edge of the parking lot. He strode down the hill toward me, his arms swinging. He didn't have his uniform on. What was he doing home?

"What did you do?" he said when he got to me. It was a professional question.

"I was running and I fell," I said.

"Looks like you really did a number on your ankle," he said with a chuckle. He thanked the teachers for calling and said he would take me home. They offered to help get me to the car, but he said it wasn't necessary. He leaned over, grabbed me with both arms, and flipped me over his shoulders in a fireman's carry. There I was, a red-faced spectacle, head down on one side and feet bobbing on the other, butt hanging out of my shorts behind his neck. He climbed back up the hill, winding his way through the kids sprawled on the grass. I was sure they were snickering. If I could have run off in the opposite direction, I would have done so, but my father kept a tight grip.

We headed for the hospital through the afternoon traffic he hated. He joked with the doctors, telling them what to do and making me glad he was still around to take care of me. He drove me home and carried me, in the conventional way, to the couch in the living room, where my brothers signed my cast and took turns playing with my crutches. I missed our class trip to the New York World's Fair, and Rosalie got everyone to write me funny postcards. When my father announced in June that we were moving back to Texas, I thought that even though I would miss my new friends, bidding that bad-luck year good-bye might be a good thing.

# 17

# Camp 7, North Korea

## FEBRUARY 1951

One day in the Tiger survivors' camp beside the Yalu River, when the temperature was about fifteen degrees below zero, Doc went to check on the sick men in shack 7. He found a skeletal prisoner standing naked in the corner of the shack nearest the door.

"What are you doing here?"

"Hell, Doc, I have to wait until the wind stops blowing because I want to go to the latrine," the soldier said. "And if I get between the two buildings, the wind will blow me over."

Doc shook his head. The man was right. The wind would have blown him over.

Doc considered shack 7, which housed the most severe dysentery cases, the camp's most oppressive sight. About ten feet by ten feet, the one-room shack contained between ten and twenty weak, emaciated patients whose clothes had been taken away because they were continually shit upon and impossible to clean. The men lay naked on the bare floor, huddled together under shreds of old blankets and comforters until one of them got bold enough to brave a frigid latrine run.

The camp commander who replaced the Tiger had ended the practice of shuttling men from shack to shack and established some degree of order. Shack 12 housed the officers. The sergeants occupied shack 4. Enlisted men took over 2, 3, 5, and the schoolhouse. Shacks 6, 8, and 9 became the so-called hospitals, although Doc thought that calling them that was a mockery. Surgical cases were housed in 9 (Doc was not allowed to go near that one), while seriously ill patients were taken to 8 and respiratory cases went to 6. In truth, the men suffered from the same diseases in all of them. Whoever died in whichever hospital shack was quickly replaced by another sick soldier on his way down his final road.

One shack 9 patient Doc was not allowed to see had fallen while on wood detail and hurt his back. He became paralyzed and was treated as

121

an invalid. The Korean medics told Doc that nothing could be done for the man, and the patients around him reported that he could not move his legs. A few months later he was moved to a different shack, and Doc went to visit. He set a large wooden crock down near the man's legs and noticed slight movement. *Hysterical paralysis.* He got a percussion hammer to test both the man's reflexes and his own diagnosis, then leaned over in the man's face.

"You can walk any time you want," Doc told him. "Help him up when he's ready," he said to the prisoners nearby. A week later, the man was walking normally.

By now almost everyone suffered from dysentery, visiting the outdoor latrines as many as twenty times a day. When they squatted over the hole, they had to make sure that they had something to hang onto so they could pull themselves up by their arms, because their legs were too weak to help them stand. Doc's efforts to treat them failed more often than not. The commandant often rebuked him for interfering with the Koreans' medical practice by urging the prisoners to hide their minor ailments. These harangues were long and bitter, sometimes lasting for an entire day. Doc thought he understood what was behind these episodes. The Communists were making every effort to degrade the officers in the eyes of their men, to undermine what little discipline still existed in the ranks. Yet they held the officers responsible for the behavior of their men. For Doc, this meant sitting through hours of abusive verbal threats. For others, it meant severe beatings that sometimes resulted in death.

But who got punished and for what? Determining the consequences of one's actions from a Communist point of view wasn't easy, Doc decided. Say an enlisted man was caught stealing. If he confessed, he would exhibit the self-criticism the Communists revered and thus would receive little or no punishment. But if he didn't confess, his superior might—or might not—be punished severely for not controlling his men. Once the prisoners figured this out, some of them ignored orders and escaped punishment altogether by refusing to confess, thus passing the buck to the officer in charge. This lack of discipline and absence of loyalty was a sin Doc never forgot or forgave.

The starving men had become animals. They stole. They betrayed their friends. They begged their captors for cigarettes. Some hoarded their smokes and sold them to their compatriots for food. Occasionally a few would band together and attempt to physically prevent one prisoner from exploiting another weaker one, but that did not always work. Guards would throw down a cigarette butt just to watch men too weak to stand fight each other for it. Not only were there no angels in a prison camp, Doc concluded, but hunger destroyed all virtue in some men and some virtue in all men.

Now that a new commander was in charge, Doc vowed to launch yet another campaign on his own behalf. So far, he was not proud of his track record. The Butcher was still stuffing used rags into dirty wounds. One of Doc's attempts at covert medical intervention involved a sergeant with cellulitis, deep inflammation that was spreading in the man's leg. Doc put heat on it and looked for a long knife to steal so that he could incise and drain the infection. But Pork Chop got to the sergeant first. The Korean medic put tar ointment on the leg, bandaged it, and moved the sergeant into a shack from which Doc was banned. The patient subsequently died. Three months later, when another soldier developed an abscess the size of a grapefruit on his back, Doc again pleaded for permission to make an incision to drain the wound. This time, the new commander agreed to allow the treatment and offered a bonus: if Doc succeeded, he would be allowed to work alongside his Korean counterparts.

Nervous, besieged by scurrilous remarks, and fortifying himself against the assistant commander's blatant disapproval, Doc sliced into the abscess, washed it with the dreaded water, and applied a pressure dressing. Then they waited. For days.

*God be with me,* Doc prayed.

The abscess healed, and not only was Doc allowed to openly treat patients, but he also enjoyed an extra bonus when the Butcher quit practicing medicine for the remainder of his stay in camp. Still, Doc was not able to do much. Rumor had it that water spread scabies, so men refused to wash even when water became more readily available. Doc painted the lesions with whatever he could find: Mercurochrome, house paint, and white lead (a pigment once used in oil paints) from a half-gallon drum. He also tried mixing rendered pork fat with sulfur to make a salve, but the quantities were so severely limited that he made little headway in relieving the sufferers.

And as always, lice ruled. These pests had tagged along since Man-po, and they were thriving. Most of the men adopted a ritual of strip-ping down every day to pick lice off their bodies and from the folds of their filthy clothing, but it was impossible to eliminate them. Eventually the officers were allowed to form a sanitary detail to boil the clothing, but even this was problematic. The laundry detail would go to a shack, order all the men to strip, and take their clothes to boil them in two fifty-gallon barrels. Meanwhile, the men, left naked in an unheated room, either got very cold or procured old, ragged, padded uniforms from the guards; these togs were also infested and could not be washed at all. When the laundered fatigues were returned, still wet, the unruly pile of pants and shirts was up for grabs. Anyone who got his own clothing back was considered lucky, especially if he was a good lice picker.

When they weren't grappling with illness, grossness, immorality, and general misery, the men faced monotony. Not much happened day to day, but occasionally some special event occurred. On the eighth of February, the lunar New Year and a Korean holiday, the prisoners feasted on nearly twenty-five pounds of pork. Divided among the hundreds still living, it wasn't much, but it was meat, and it was better than the dog meat that many of them had refused to eat in fatter times. When a pig was butchered in camp, men lined up with their cups to drink the blood.

School was also intermittently in session. A couple of North Kore-an instructors and an interpreter visited the camp to deliver lectures in-tended to indoctrinate the Americans in the Communist way. Ramrod, as the prisoners called the assistant commander, lectured the officers about the evils of capitalism. Doc deemed the lectures absurd, so fantas-tically ridiculous that the listeners had to swallow their guffaws. Mostly the men just listened and kept any comments to themselves. At first a few of the bolder prisoners attempted to argue, but it soon became clear that the speakers were parroting the party line and helpless if they were forced to respond to challenges. They simply did not believe that individual Americans who were not the political elite owned cars and shopped in well-stocked grocery stores.

On various occasions, each prisoner was ordered to fill out a POW questionnaire, which was surprisingly well-printed on high-quality glossy paper. It asked for names, addresses, and political, social, and financial information about immediate family, relatives, and friends. The prisoners learned early on to fill in the blanks to avoid further hassles and beatings, but bogus information was the rule. Some of the listed occupations included "nookie bookie," "boogie man," and "lamp lighter," and creativity was applauded. Officers cautioned their troops to remember what they wrote because they might be asked to fill out the same questionnaire days or weeks later. Oddly enough, however, no two questionnaires were ever alike.

On March 15, 1951, after the worst of winter had passed but before the warm breezes of spring had arrived, the prisoners decamped. Those able to walk marched west about four miles to a former Japanese compound surrounded by barbed wire, and their sick comrades were transported about two weeks later. This was cause for hope. Until they heard a bridge being bombed on March 31, the men were convinced that the war was over. In fact, although United Nations forces had secured the Inchon harbor and retaken Seoul about two weeks earlier, the fourth time the city had changed hands, the fighting raged on. The Chinese had suffered half a million casualties since November.

The prisoners' new home boasted some amenities, including a library building that housed no books but contained publications and a piano. There was a well, a building that became the hospital, and a storeroom that became a barbershop for shaves and haircuts. Most of the men were quartered in the main building's five large rooms, which were heated with large furnaces. Food was served in a mess hall with enough tables and benches for about two hundred prisoners. As spring became summer, the winter-weary men hatched plans and began constructing under-floor heating systems in the mess hall and one smaller building, but the work was never finished. September would find them on the move again.

In April, three English-speaking North Korean field grade officers arrived in the camp to organize a Peace Committee. Doc attended only one of their lectures, which was laden with propaganda about America's eighteen million unemployed, starving masses, and the "handful" of elitists living in luxury. The GIs in the audience chortled and yelled corrections, but they were ignored. The camp commander ordered Major Dunn to form the committee, but he refused and ordered his officers to do the same. Undeterred, the North Koreans called a meeting in the library to select committee members themselves. All prisoners were required to attend. The "election" was rigged. Most of the twelve men, a group led by Capt. Ambrose Nugent and thereafter known, along with other "progressives," as the Red Star Boys, had been preselected as "nominees." One man refused his nomination, which caused some consternation among the guards, but another was quickly chosen to replace him.

The next order of business was signing a peace appeal, which contained derogatory remarks about the United States. Dunn ordered the men not to sign it, despite the fact that the North Koreans had threatened to withhold all food as punishment. Dunn figured they could hold out for about three days, which would have meant death for several of the weaker men, but he nevertheless held his ground. After much negotiation, the captors agreed to remove the most offensive remarks. Each man signed a blank piece of paper. No one ever found out what happened to the petition after that.

Meanwhile, the Red Star Boys were promised better living conditions, more food, and written passes allowing them in and out of the gate. Some of these men took advantage of the perks and were ostracized by their peers. Others used their membership as access to inside information that they reported back to Dunn. In May, Nugent and one other man left with their captors and did not return; it was rumored that they had joined what was called Traitors' Row in Pyongyang.

By July, when the first cease-fire discussions were taking place, living conditions in the camp had improved. The men were each issued one pair of cotton overalls, and soybeans were added to their diet. They had also become proficient at stealing food from the countryside while out on wood details; treks through cornfields yielded great bounty that the guards often shared in exchange for looking the other way. One day an officer stopped the wood detail on its way out of the gate. He explained that one of the cornfields along their designated path belonged to a woman with children whose husband had been killed in the war. That field remained untouched.

On another day, an unsympathetic guard who caught a soldier stealing corn proceeded to punish him by taking thirty-six ripe ears of corn from him and breaking them over his head. Wiping juicy kernels from his hair, the soldier returned to quarters, where, out of sight of the guards, he reached into his pants and pulled out more corn. "At least they didn't find the other eighteen ears!" he exclaimed to his delighted roommates.

As the men began eating more, they started thinking about other things besides food. One soldier fell madly in love with one of the civilian prisoners, a seventeen-year-old Turkish girl. Prison life severely limited romantic opportunities, but the gossip surrounding the ongoing "relationship" became as addictive as a soap opera.

The summer's sense of well-being did not last. The prisoners had no news sources but occasionally saw jets, which meant that the war went on. In mid-September, the U.S. Army's 23rd Infantry, along with the French Battalion attached to it, attempted to take Heartbreak Ridge, which ran north and south for seven miles, perpendicular to another, called Bloody Ridge. For twenty-seven days they charged up hill after hill, only to reach the top and get knocked back down in brutal, bloody battles with waves of North Koreans. It wasn't until tanks flanked the ridge in mid-October that they were able to secure it. Peace talks resumed in Panmunjom on October 25.

As camp food supplies dwindled that fall, vitamin deficiency symptoms such as the swollen feet, face, and wrists of beriberi and the diarrhea, dermatitis, and dementia of pellagra proliferated. One man's testicles swelled to the size of grapefruits and hung to his knees. Another soldier's balls were even larger; he carried them in a basket. Morale plummeted as hours of sunlight waned, and despair once again clawed at its victims. Men dined on the burnt crust that collected on the bottoms of cooking pots and behaved like ravening wolves. To pass the time, they talked about food, devising menus, recalling favorite family dishes, creating recipes, planning repatriation feasts in vivid detail. Food was all they could think about.

Hundreds of prisoners had died since the Death March. Only fourteen of the twenty-three officers remained. On October 9, 1951, the prison group was divided into two: sick and well. The well prisoners, clothed in patched rags and wearing an assortment of shoes, some resembling boots, others made of straw, set off to march west in pouring rain for several miles along the Yalu River. There they boarded barges and huddled together to ward off the cold drizzle. The sick group followed a few days later.

Dirty and arrogant, calloused by death, indifferent to threats from the guards, these Tiger Survivors, as Doc and the others would forever call themselves, arrived in what was by then known as Camp 3. The American prisoners already housed there, wary and suspicious, refused to speak to them. But each of the new arrivals was immediately given a blanket and an overcoat. Within an hour, two dozen men had shared fifteen gallons of rice, which they ate along with a bowl of soup. For the first time since they had been captured, they could peer through the grimy slats of despair and spot faint rays of deliverance. Of the 738 prisoners who marched under the Tiger's command, according to Doc's count, only 275 had survived. The North Koreans had now turned them over to the Chinese, and they would live.

# 18

# San Antonio, Texas

## 1964

"This will be your room. Look at all the windows!" said my mother, her arms too full of sheets and towels to point them out. "Next week we can go shopping and find you a bedspread and some curtains that match!"

"That would be nice," I said, although shopping made me tired and queasy, and I could not imagine what colors or patterns we might choose. I had never had matching decor before. I liked the windows, which were tall and wide on two sides of my corner room at the top of the stairs across from the bathroom. My old room in Rockville had only one narrow, horizontal window, too high to see out of, like a prison cell perhaps.

Now that my father was a lieutenant colonel, we qualified for military housing at Fort Sam Houston. Our stucco house at 546 Graham Road seemed like a mansion, complete with maid's quarters (a small room and bathroom just off the kitchen) and four-season porches upstairs and down. Outside we had tall hedges, two huge trees in the backyard, and a garage on the alley. Parallel to the alley and across the main road were parade grounds, majestic in their grassy expanse and emptiness, stretching for more than a mile along the center of the post, like a spine with Brooke Army Hospital at the head. From the back of the house we watched horses from the post stables gallop by, their riders erect on English saddles.

The movers had already deposited the boxes marked "Cathy's Room" in black marker. I was reluctant to open them, to see what I had not missed during the travel weeks we spent visiting my grandparents in Maryland and driving down to Texas, camping along the way. My mother insisted that I "pare down" and take only what "really mattered" on these moves that were becoming routine. But what really mattered? More than once, I had carefully wrapped some precious object in newspaper and placed it in the box where it would not shift or get crushed by something heavy. But weeks or months or years later, I would find it broken anyway. Or it would be more worn and tattered than I remembered, more suited to a former life than the one I was about to create. Preserving nostalgia, I had discovered, was hard to do.

I could hear my father banging around in the hallway, trying to install the Fedders air conditioner in the window at the top of the stairs. Texas summers were stifling, over one hundred degrees during the day and hardly cooling off at night. He didn't seem to mind the sweat soaking his T-shirt and dripping down his nose. He was handy with tools and cheery when puttering. He was also happier now that he and my mother had decided life was too short to give up simple pleasures like smoking. They had switched to low-tar, low-nicotine Carltons, although she said smoking them was like sucking straws, and he admitted to smoking twice as many.

"Punky, would you hand me that wrench, please?"

"Sure, Pop," I said, handing it to him and watching as he worked with tapered fingers. My mother said working on car engines was too risky for surgeon fingers, but most home repairs he could handle. When no cigarette dangled from his lips, his tongue took over, back and forth, up and down, following his fingers' progress as if it could help pound a nail or turn a screw. I liked being near him when he was preoccupied. It was unlikely he would spot my flaws or perceive any disrespect, so I felt safe. It was a way, perhaps my only way, of feeling close.

"Better get busy," he said, noting my gaze. He didn't cotton to lolly-gagging. On move-in days, no matter how exhausted we were from unpacking as many boxes as possible, he insisted that no one sleep until the beds were made, the pictures were hung, and the stereo was working. We all followed the rules without complaint.

Moving had its upsides, such as hearing my mother laugh out loud when we found the salt shaker and the pepper shaker—and the teaspoon of salt and the teaspoon of pepper that had been in them—each wrapped neatly in a whole piece of wrapping paper. Eating take-out pizza and burgers on upside-down boxes was fun. Leaving friends still hurt, but I had learned not to say good-bye because they often showed up again in new places. A new place meant I could be a new person, better than the old one. With a new, better bedroom.

"What about your curtains?" my father asked, poking his head in my door after the air conditioner whirred into action.

"Mom is going to buy me new ones. Tomorrow."

"You need curtains today," he said, and went to fetch my mother to rig sheets over the windows. *The enemy must be out there, looking in.*

That night I fell asleep in my own bed in the sheeted dark, with strains of Frank Sinatra songs and low-tar smoke drifting up from the living room.

School that year was Robert G. Cole Junior–Senior High, located on the outskirts of the post, too far to walk. It was an all-military school, so making friends was easier than in Rockville. Someone I met at the officers' club swimming pool suggested that I sign up for the drill team, which performed precision-marching routines at football games in cowboy hats, white gloves, and green wool uniforms that were nearly unbearable in the Texas heat. There I met fellow sophomore Angie Lordello, a smart, sassy, quick-witted, frizzy-haired (in humid weather) future cheerleader. She always had a line of boys trailing her. One of them was Mark Curtis, a senior who lived in a house like mine one street over. It was at a late winter party at Mark's house that Joey Nash, my shy classmate and Mark's best friend, kissed me. At school the next week, Joey stopped by my locker.

"Want to go to the school dance with me?" he asked.

"I have to ask my parents," I said, praying that they did not have a cocktail party scheduled, in which case I would have to babysit. "But I'd like to go." I smiled up at him, afraid I might be blushing.

Joey smelled good. Or maybe it was his black, lightweight jacket that smelled so fresh. It hung off his shoulders while his hands hooked into his jean pockets. Slender with very long legs and curly, sand-colored hair, he smiled more than he talked, and his eyes were kind. I didn't know if he could dance, but I liked kissing him very much.

"Well, let me know. Mark's going to drive. We can triple with Angie and Kirk."

"OK. I'll ask tonight and let you know tomorrow."

Riding home on the bus that afternoon, I plotted my strategy. The default answer was still no, although in Rockville I had wrangled permission to go to a movie with a shy, short boy with big cow eyes and long eyelashes. He was very polite but said little as we sat in the backseat while his mother drove, swiveling at red lights to ask me about my favorite subjects. We had held hands with sweaty, popcorn-salted palms through what had to be the most boring movie I had ever seen, some historical drama. Afterward he had walked me to my front step, where I mumbled thank-you under the porch light and darted inside. That had been my only date so far.

My best bet was to catch my mother alone and busy in the kitchen, where she could see the big-block wall calendar on which she carefully printed all of our appointments. If the date was open, I might convince her to say yes before the pot roast came out of the oven. If she committed, my father wasn't likely to overrule her, or at least he wouldn't win without a fight.

"By the way," I said in a mock-casual tone as I dug silverware out of the drawer that evening, "I was wondering if I could go to the dance with Joey a week from Friday. There's nothing on the calendar."

She glanced at the wall.

"You have that competition the next day, and you have to leave early in the morning. We better talk about it at supper."

The Saturday after the dance was the day of the state scholastic meet in Kingsville, 160 miles away. I had won at the regional level in a peculiar math category I had discovered: completing complex calculations such as long sums, fractions, and percentages without using pencil and paper except to write the answer. This competition was goofy but fun as long as I wasn't tired, hungry, or distracted and could visualize the numbers in my head. Ironically enough in a football-fanatic state, these multisubject academic competitions carried social cachet. I was proud to be the only girl on our school's team, even though it meant needing a female chaperone for the night at a motel after the competition was over.

My stomach roiled as I spread the tablecloth. Setting each napkin to the left of each fork, I analyzed. Mark was driving, a negative, but he was not wild and freaky, a positive. He lived nearby, positive. My parents knew his parents, positive; never mind that it was in their living room, while they were gone, that Joey and I had smooched. (Deduct a point for bad parenting if my father had known.) I rehearsed my offers: I would wear a modest dress (with a full slip, because nice girls wore slips, and a girdle because, according to my mother, no girl with a butt the size of mine should appear in public without one). I would do the dishes before I left, finish my homework early, clean my room, and come home on time.

When dinner was ready we sat down, put our napkins on our laps, passed dishes, dolloped butter, shook salt. I pasted a smile on my face and glanced at my father. He was chewing.

"I was wondering if I could maybe go to the school dance next week. There isn't anything on the calendar." I did not say "please" because it might sound like begging. Caring too much would set his imagination spinning.

"With who?" He put down his fork and clamped his lips into a pink line. Oops. Imagination: off and running. His eyes accused me.

"With Mark and Angie and Joey and Kirk and Sue."

Mark was dating Sue, a lanky, freckled sophomore and championship swimmer with an irresistibly dark sense of humor. Angie's boyfriend of the moment was Kirk Delgado, also a sophomore, handsome and suave as a politician. Again I rehearsed my points in silence. Safety in numbers. Big car. (The four-door Oldsmobile's bench front seat made backseat lap-sitting unnecessary. Better not bring that up, though.)

"Who's driving?"

"Mark. Curtis." My father wasn't good at remembering names. "You know. He lives in that house." I pointed.

"I don't think it's a good idea," he said, picking up his fork again.

"Why not? I'll be really careful, and Mark's a good driver." I made that last part up; I had never ridden with Mark. I looked at my mother, whose lips were also threatening to disappear. *Speak, Mom, please.*

"It's just a school dance," she said. "There will be chaperones." She dug into her mashed potatoes.

He set his chin and looked away, his face working as if pestered by a buzzing bee. I saw the irritation I caused, but I was seated too far from him to be slapped away. He pursed his lips and cleared his throat.

"What time is the dance over?" More throat clearing.

"Eleven thirty."

"Then you are to be home at eleven forty-five. And you are not to go anywhere else. Go to the dance and come straight home. No stopping."

"But I'm not the one driving. What if they want to go to the Frontier for a Coke?" The Frontier was a popular drive-in just off the main highway leading from the army post into town. Servers on roller skates delivered burgers, fries, and root beer on trays that hooked on to a partially rolled-down car window. It was the only place to go for after-hours food, and indeed the food was good enough, and the small sit-down area clean and shiny enough, that my mother often took us there for dinner when my father was out of town. She liked the onion rings.

"I said come straight home."

"OK."

I got the message, along with butterflies. How would I manage this? I was the baby on this triple date, scared I would say or do the wrong thing, too shy and inept to tell a senior what to do. I was a nerd with glasses, dorky pleated skirts, and laced-up shoes from the PX instead of Thom McAnn. How could I force my restrictions on everyone else?

While I contemplated, the Lecture unrolled at the head of the table. How in battle, the survivors were men of honor. They had high standards. They earned trust. They had integrity. They kept their word and they didn't rationalize. I had heard it so often I tuned it out, paying more attention to the fact that the meat, starch, and vegetable dividing my plate into thirds tasted like identical cardboard. At least he wasn't quizzing me about democracy.

The following Friday, Joey was right on time. When the doorbell rang, I was ready, wearing a dress that made (I hoped) my butt look small, my waist look thin, and my breasts look present. Dirk answered the door.

"It's him! For you!" he yelled up at me.

I waited upstairs, counting slowly to twenty before joining Joey in the center hallway. My mother came out from the kitchen. My father, still seated at the dining room table, wiped his mouth with his napkin before standing up and shaking Joey's hand. He looked gruff and tried to smile at the same time. "Come straight home," he said. Joey and I nodded.

"Have fun, kids," my mother said.

As we started down the sidewalk, Dirk grabbed me from behind and attempted to demonstrate the judo throw he had just learned. I stumbled but managed to keep my balance. He and Eric danced around us, giggling.

"You know when my sister walks, her butt looks like this!" Dirk said, demonstrating my wobble with a football. Eric thought this was hilarious. Joey politely refrained from guffawing.

"Be home on time," my father ordered from the doorway.

As we walked to Mark's house I explained my curfew: be home precisely fifteen minutes after the dance ended, no side trips. Joey didn't think it would be a problem. Mark was indeed a good driver, and we got to the school gym quickly. Inside, "Wipe Out" blared, and outside, boys in shirttails hunched in small circles to smoke. For the next two hours, the six of us danced nearly every dance, shoes off, doing the Twist, the Monkey, the Swim, stopping only to go to the bathroom or drink from the water fountain. Everyone wanted a Coke, which in the South meant any carbonated beverage, but the single vending machine was broken.

"I'm really thirsty. Let's go to the Frontier," Mark suggested. I looked at Joey, hoping he remembered what I had told him. I didn't want to say anything because girls were not supposed to run the show.

"She has to be home right after the dance," Joey told Mark.

"Well, then we'll leave early so we have time."

"I'm really supposed to go straight home," I explained.

"But there's nothing to drink here. We're just getting a Coke. We'll get you home on time," Mark said. He didn't seem worried. But my butterflies, which the dancing had chased away, were back in full flutter.

Somewhere around 10:30, Mark rounded us all up and we headed for the Frontier. In the backseat I sat silent, staring straight ahead. Joey held my sweaty hand. At the drive-in, the lights were bright and the skaters busy, hustling among the cars that pulled in and out of the long parking lot. At least I wouldn't run into any of my parents' friends there; they would all be home drinking cocktails. I ordered root beer in a tall mug. In between sips I checked my watch.

"Are you OK?" Joey asked. He was squeezed against the door and I was crushed in next to him, so we could fit four in the backseat. He reached his arm up, crooking it behind my neck so he could get his hand on my shoulder. I could feel his heart beating fast.

"Yes, as long as we hurry."

"Want an onion ring?"

"No, thanks."

I was too nervous to eat. I felt my cheeks flush as I nestled under his arm. Despite the sweaty dancing, he still smelled good, like sheets hung on a clothesline all day. I wanted to kiss him. He smiled at me as if he knew.

Next to me was Kirk, or rather Kirk's back; he was turned toward Angie, whispering something that made her laugh. In the front seat, Mark and Sue were tickling each other and shooting the papers off their straws, trying to hit the empty cup on the tray parked on the window. Angie wanted another Coke. She was bubbly and funny, flirty and warm, and she got what she wanted. Mark reached out to press the buzzer.

I worried. We still had time to get home, but we needed to leave soon. Joey read my face.

"As soon as we get our order, I think we better leave," he said to Mark.

Mark threw his arms up without turning around and said, "OK."

More cars were arriving, their occupants calling out to each other as we pulled out of our space. I loved the energy of this place, the late-evening laughter that signaled the end of the school week. I felt sad to go, guilty that I had caused our departure, helpless that I had no other option. But I looked forward to kissing Joey.

The highway lights were green, and we got home in ten minutes. Mark turned left onto our street. But a block before my house, he took a right and drove two more blocks to an empty line of parking spaces that bordered a grove of trees. No streetlights penetrated here. It took me a minute, but I got it: we were going parking. Where we could make out in the car. Kissing with company.

The other couples wasted no time. I heard limbs adjusting, clothes rustling, breathing growing heavy.

"I can't," I whispered to Joey.

"I'll take her home and see you tomorrow," he whispered over the seat to Mark, who did not respond. Joey opened the door and we got out. He closed it as quietly as he could.

My watch said I had five minutes until curfew. I took off, running down the middle of the street. Joey followed a few steps behind; I could hear him puffing. I was back on that junior high field in Rockville, racing for first place, hoping there were not any holes. If my ankle hurt as I sprinted diagonally across the grass to the front door, I didn't notice. I had reached our front door on time. I stood still under a light so bright I had to squint. Joey was laughing as he took his place in front of me. He put his arms around my waist. I put my hands on his shoulders. We kissed.

The door jolted open with a shriek of hinges. A hand reached out, grabbed my right arm, and yanked so hard that I almost fell.

"You get in here!" my father shouted.

Joey's eyes opened wide. He looked at my father, then took off across the yard, toward his house. I heard his footsteps hit the pavement. He was fast.

I was inside then, pulled into the middle of the dark living room. My father was sputtering, furious. Saliva coated his lips. His glasses were askew. He stood there, shaking, in a grayed T-shirt with holes and baggy jeans ripped at the knees. My mother stood next to him, looking smaller than her five feet eight inches, her face drawn tight across high cheekbones. I was afraid. So was she, I could tell.

"Where the hell have you been?" he shouted.

Catapulted into a hostile universe I did not understand no matter how often I landed there, I was trapped, unable to escape injury and avoid pain. Inside my head, I scanned frantically, looking for explanations. Certainly there had been a misunderstanding. Nothing bad had happened. Certainly this would all go away. But I knew better.

"Tell me! Now! Where the hell were you?" He was spitting on me.

"You know where I was. I was at the dance." My voice was low. My breathing may have quickened, but I seldom yelled back. I had learned to counter loud with quiet, aggression with defense, authority with deference.

"You knew what time you had to be home!" Still shouting.

"Yes, and I was home on time." I held up my wrist with the watch. It said 11:50. The clock on the mantle said 11:53.

"You were late!"

I was not going to win this one. He had been watching the clock. His clock.

"Well, only five minutes. And we were on the steps for a while."

"Where. Were. You."

"At the dance."

Louder: "Don't lie to me! Where! Were! You!"

I didn't know what to say. I didn't want to step deeper into that hole.

"You went to that place, didn't you." He was breathing hard now, looking down on me from towering ire. His lips had disappeared.

"You. Tell. Me. Now." He thrust his forefinger against my breastbone with every word. His eyes bulged. My mother stood at his elbow, wanting to grab it, I thought, perhaps afraid. I never saw him hurt her physically but I knew that he could, if he really blew.

I said nothing.

"Goddamn you, you went to that place. It's a whorehouse, people pick up whores there, and if you go there you're just like all the other whores."

"Oh, Pete. Stop." My mother's voice caught. A tear rolled down her cheek. She was wringing her hands, now standing apart from him as if there were an invisible wall between them, one she could not get over or through.

I couldn't breathe. The lump in my throat felt like a baseball. My knees shook. I didn't know what to say even if I could have spoken. I didn't know which sin was more unforgivable, going where I was forbidden to go or lying about it to protect myself.

The fist caught me square in the mouth and knocked my glasses to the floor. I bent over, picked them up, and put them back on. With my tongue, I felt along the insides of my teeth. All still there. But warm wetness was spreading from my lower lip down toward my chin. Slowly, carefully, I spread my top lip over the area and sucked back the blood without breaking eye contact.

My mother reached out with her hands, but it was as if she did not know whom to touch. She was agitated, shifting from foot to foot, arms in the air, cheeks wet. She pleaded again for my father to stop. He seemed calmer as he took deep breaths, in and out.

"We're going to stand here until you tell me the truth," he said, leaning down into my face.

And so we stood. For minutes, an hour, more. He yelled, lectured, yelled again.

"Who do you think you are? Are you going to be a goddamn slut like the rest of them? Hanging out in places like that, when you have been strictly forbidden?"

I did not answer.

"What you do reflects on me, you know. It affects my job. It affects this family. It affects my promotions, our future. I am being watched, you know. That means they're watching you, too. You're a soldier in this man's army, and you better damn well behave like one."

"But I'm not."

"Don't kid yourself, young lady! You most certainly are. When you disobey, when you do something so stupid, it says something important about you. About all of us. And when you lie, you're the lowest of the low. Scum of the earth. No worse sin in this world. How do you expect to survive in battle? There is no excuse for it. None. Ever. It's unforgivable."

He glared at me. Shook his head.

"Where do you think I'd be if my buddies acted like you? If I couldn't trust them to tell me the truth at all times? Those men had character. There are plenty of despicable people in this world, and I saw many of them in action, betraying their fellow man, stealing, lying, pissing on principles. I will not tolerate it. Not in this house."

I didn't interrupt. He said the same things, over and over, re-arranging sentences. There were silences, every so often. He coughed. My mother begged him to go to bed. The clock ticked. It was nearly 2:00 a.m. I noticed how dark the living room was, lighted only by a lamp in the adjoining sunporch. Also how my cheek was going numb, and my bottom lip was swelling up under my top one. I had to leave at 6:00 a.m. for the math competition. I thought about how much I wanted to win and considered my options. I waited a few more beats, listening to my heart pound.

"OK," I said finally. "I went to the Frontier for a Coke, because the machine at school was broken. But we were only there for a few minutes, and we even left the dance early so I could get home on time."

"I don't care. I gave you an order!" he yelled. "You disobeyed! And you didn't tell the truth!"

"I just did."

"Quit rationalizing!"

The tirade didn't end there, but the energy waned. The crisis had passed. He had won, taking with his victory the pleasure I had been savoring from fun, friends, and kissing in the light night air. I was dismissed, and I climbed the stairs to my room, my feet heavy with the dread of the coming day.

When the alarm went off, my eyes burned behind their lids and my head and mouth hurt. I was dressed and ready when Miss Callander, my chaperone, rang the doorbell. I could feel her eyes on my face as I greeted her, but I avoided meeting them, even though she kept sneaking looks when she thought I wouldn't notice. As we drove for hours across the bleak Texas terrain, I stared out the window at the scrub pines and made halting conversation that sounded hollow and absurd. I heard myself as if I were riding in the backseat, wondering who this passenger was and why she was here, now, carrying a secret so onerous it bowed her shoulders and constricted her throat so that sometimes she could not talk at all.

We got to the school where the event was being held, and I found my room, my pencil, my test paper. I slid into an empty desk and ignored the competitors surrounding me. I wrote my ID number on the top of the page and began when the signal was given. My head felt thick and my eyes gritty. My lip throbbed. The numbers I usually saw so clearly in my mind blurred and disappeared before I could finish calculating. I did not do as well as I knew I could.

That night our team stayed in a motel with a swimming pool. I had brought my new bathing suit, a becoming two-piece with white lace over blue backing. I had looked forward to flirting with the boys alone, with no bubbly cheerleaders around to distract them. Heady with postcompetition highs, we could play Marco Polo and do backflips off the board—I had been practicing. Instead I sat on the pool's edge and watched. My suit stayed dry. I hoped the boys would not look at me or see the shame I wore.

Eventually the lip healed and the bruises cleared, but no one ever mentioned them. In the math meet, I came in fourth. I had let my team down by not placing in the top three, and that hurt. Letting myself down by failing to do my best hurt more.

As spring became summer, the tension in our house heated up along with the weather. Gone were the few happy times when my father would whisk an LP album out of its cover, his long fingers spanning from edge to middle hole without touching the grooves. He would blow the dust off, then place it on the turntable and drop the needle precisely, so it would not scratch. Sometimes it was a symphony but more often a musical, like *Oklahoma!*, *The Music Man*, or *My Fair Lady*. He would crank up the volume until the windows rattled and, eyes closed, dance in circles while conducting an invisible orchestra with his hands. I tried to dance along and catch his eye. My brothers cavorted. My mother came in from the kitchen and stood holding the dish towel, smiling approval. He might swing her around if she let him, although she usually rebuffed wild romantic gestures. She confided that he was a good ballroom dancer when he wanted to be, which did not happen often. Neither did these episodes, though they created, for me at least, a lifelong passion for dancing in the living room.

Dinner times ceased to be question-and-answer sessions; the lecture series continued instead. Other parents had been sharing stories, often about my old friend from Germany, Tommy Wilson, who led various creative missions after sneaking out in the middle of the night: joyriding carts across golf courses, swimming across all nine military swimming pools, escaping through a hole in the post fence to pool-hop at nearby apartment complexes. No doubt he and his cronies were also responsible for draping huge trees in white toilet paper. My parents watched me closely as they disclosed the awful details, which I found hilarious, but the truth was that I had not participated; I had not even been invited.

My father blamed me anyway. His rants about how easy it was to lose trust made sense to me, but sometimes he blew up for no reason, railing at people who weren't there to defend themselves. When he accused me of being one of the evildoers, all I could do was shake my head and say I wasn't. I could tell he did not believe me. He did not believe most people.

At night, lying on my bed watching the moon through the filmy pink curtains that matched my floral bedspread, I was angry about the unfairness of it all. My classmates razzed me about being a big chicken, so scared to do anything risky that I'd earned the nickname Goody

Goody Two Shoes, or Two Shoes for short. I figured that as long as my parents presumed I was guilty anyway, maybe I should give these pre-dawn forays a try. I needed to grow up and be bold.

The next day, I proposed to Angie, Joey, Sue, and Mark that we all sneak out and meet somewhere. We set a day, time, and place. On the appointed night, I set my alarm for 3:00 a.m. and put it under my pillow, but I was awake before it went off. I was too nervous to sleep. I got dressed and put on my gym sneakers, the quietest shoes I had. I stood on the landing at the top of the stairs, ready to duck into the bathroom if necessary. Slowly, I placed one foot on each step, waiting to make sure there was no creak, until I was down the stairs. I listened for stirring. All was quiet. I was glad we no longer had a dog.

I unlocked the door, went out, and pulled it closed. Stars lit the night; the moon was only half there. I crossed the street and sat on the curb. A few minutes later, Angie showed up and sat down next to me. No one else came. We whispered for nearly an hour before deciding that no one else was coming and we should go back to bed. I crept up the stairs and climbed in under the covers.

Now I was properly guilty. I fell asleep.

# 19

# Camp 2, P'anjung-ni, North Korea

## NOVEMBER 1951

On his first morning in the new camp, Doc stood back, watching the hungry men fight for position in the food line, and shook his head. *Pathetic,* he thought. Then one of the Chinese guards, or "instructors," as they preferred to be known, called for attention.

"You don't have to push," the man proclaimed in a loud but modulated voice. "There is plenty of food for all." No one believed this. The men scoffed and hurled obscenities at their new guards, figuring that psychological torture, Chinese Communist–style, had taken a cruel new turn. Then the cooks started handing out the first pieces of bread the newcomers had seen in sixteen months.

This performance was repeated at the next mealtime: angry jostling, calming announcement, enough food. There really was plenty to eat. It was crude and unsavory but delicious to starving men. For days afterward, however, those men suffered what Doc elegantly called *abdominal discomfort.* At least they were able to nurse their sore tummies in relatively comfortable mud huts, and the Chinese proved more reasonable and efficient captors than their predecessors. Two doctors were available to handle sick call, and one spoke fairly good English. He befriended Doc immediately but must have been reprimanded, because he turned cold and aloof the next day.

Doc's stay in this camp lasted only a month. On November 10, 1951, the officers were separated from the enlisted men and moved to Camp 2, near a small town, P'anjung-ni, about ten miles northeast of Pyoktong. Camp 2 housed about 350 officers—English, Australian, and Turkish as well as American—and 200 Chinese guards. During the move, Doc and Major Dunn were searched, and the death records they had so carefully kept throughout their ordeal were confiscated. Before they left, they had made five copies and distributed them to selected enlisted men for safekeeping, but those were eventually lost as well.

(Fortunately, PFC Johnnie Johnson had printed his own list with a pencil stub on scraps of wallpaper and discarded cigarette packages. He hid two copies, one in the wall of his mud hut, the other in the dirt floor. The guards who found the wall copy beat him, but he dug up the other copy and smuggled it back to America in an empty toothpaste tube. Known as Johnson's list, it contains 496 names.)

Enclosed by a fence made of saplings, the new camp consisted of a schoolhouse that became living quarters, a separate building that housed the kitchen, and two other shacks that served as hospital and dispensary. A Chinese doctor, his elderly assistant, a pharmacist, and two nurses, Lee and "Florence Nightmare," lived as well as worked in the dispensary.

The doctor, known as Dirty Hands, practiced medicine by listening subjectively to complaints, then treating whichever complaint he chose. Someone who had pneumonia as well as severe diarrhea could not be treated for both. Doc could do little about this except counsel the men to mention only their most serious malady, if indeed they could figure out which one it was.

Day to day, there was not much to do. Mornings and afternoons were spent sitting on the floor, uncomfortably cross-legged, in the cold, miserable library, listening to Chinese instructors and American prisoners read propaganda treatises. Doc was convinced the American readers were not sympathizers; they were merely the unlucky selected. Several became quite facile with ad-libbed humor, much to the amusement of bored listeners and the consternation of intent captors. It didn't take the Chinese long to recognize that this group approach was a profound failure. They changed strategies, adopting one-on-one and small-group instruction instead. But even that didn't work. In the evening, back in their individual units, the men were asked to discuss and answer a list of questions. Instead, they assigned one representative to complete the task, in as irrelevant a flight of fancy as he could muster, while the rest returned to interminable bridge tournaments and rounds of charades.

Winter came and went. Despite the various illnesses that continued to plague them, no one died. In May 1952, a large red cross was placed just outside the camp. The following October, the Chinese reorganized the camp and moved the Camp 2 company, which included about 140 U.S. Army officers and Air Force sergeants, to another camp they had built for prisoners about three-quarters of a mile away. The red cross went along, too.

This new camp consisted of three straw and mud buildings built on wooden frameworks, plus some scattered mud huts located behind them in an area the prisoners dubbed Snob Hill, which housed both POWs and Chinese. The main building, fronted by a courtyard, was a typical Japanese schoolhouse with seven large rooms. One room was used as a library and lecture hall. The rest were divided in half and used as living quarters by a dozen platoons. The buildings were heated by kangs, crude systems of elevated platforms built over rocks and mud. Every day, small fires were built along the kang, one every twenty or thirty feet or so. Flues from the fireboxes ran through and heated the rocks under the platforms. The platforms got very hot, so each man was issued a bamboo mat to sleep on, with a space about six feet long and eighteen to twenty-two inches wide to call his own.

The second building was the kitchen, and the third was a typical latrine, where men squatted over holes in the ground. Local villagers removed the waste daily to nearby fields, a task prisoners were rarely asked to do. Instead, they did what they could to spruce up their toilet, which an Air Force lieutenant colonel christened Club Hemorrhoid. It boasted an electric light and magazines to read. Fly swatters hung near the holes, and a sign was posted: "Swat while you squat." This certainly beat the arrangement in some of the officers' previous camps, where no latrine had been available and both prisoners and guards urinated in a corner of the yard. In winter, the frozen urine had piled high, and the prisoners were ordered to chip it away, chunks flying into their eyes and mouths, and transport buckets of pee ice to nearby fields.

The Chinese also built a bathhouse with two large tubs made of concrete, mud, and stone. Inside one of the tubs was an iron pot for heating water so the men could dip basins into the hot water to wash themselves. Work details had to fetch the water from a local well or stream, but the prisoners could bathe daily if they wanted to, without incessant harassment from the guards. *No jabbering—finally,* Doc noted with approval.

Relatively speaking, life in this camp was a pleasure. Each man had his own spoon, cup, and bowl. Each got two sets of summer uniforms—blue cotton pants, jacket and hat, and white shirt and underwear—as well as two pairs of canvas and rubber shoes. One winter uniform—padded quilted pants and jacket, hat, mittens, one or two pairs of underwear—was also provided. Sometimes the men got socks, though often several sizes too small. They also got face towels and soap, a blanket, a comforter, and a quilted overcoat. And at long last, toothbrushes and toothpaste. By that time, many men had lost teeth. Some broke due to the pebbles mixed in with the grain they ate; one of the captive doctors used forceps to pull others. Some prisoners pulled their own teeth, as many as a dozen at a time, using pliers or rigging simple wire or string systems like second-graders anxious for a visit from the tooth fairy. They had learned early on that ignoring an infected tooth presented grislier problems than yanking it—one man lost his whole cheek and part of his lip before succumbing to the grim reaper.

Each room had an unexpected luxury: a lightbulb. Prisoners could use the drop cord to turn it on, but the guards who controlled the main switch doused the lights an hour or two after dusk, or earlier if the prisoners misbehaved. The rooms also had hollow walls that housed rat nests. The rats scampered across the men while they slept. To retaliate, the men baited them with food scraps in the cracks between wall and floor, then attempted to capture and dismember them with the crude knives they had made.

Although physical conditions in this camp were better than in the last, the Tiger survivors faced new challenges. They were outsiders, having joined a recently captured group that had experienced only Chinese rule. Shortly after they arrived, they were warned to watch what they said, because informers might be listening. The Tiger survivors had not encountered such betrayal before, nor had they contended with such a complete absence of military discipline. Here, the men called each other by their first names and fended for themselves, without any unifying goals or structure. No one pulled rank; no orders were issued or followed. Doc found this behavior detrimental to group well-being, but not as downright disgusting as the constant presence of "canaries," progressives who had become informers. No one knew exactly who the tattletales were. But when even the most casual conversations worked their way into the "confessions" that prisoners were forced to read months later, it was obvious that someone had been writing down details and handing them over to the guards. Trust became increasingly rare, and the handful of men Doc trusted became lifelong friends.

The Chinese used every aspect of captivity to their advantage. "Be kind to the American prisoners, share what you have with them, pretend that you are their friends, don't threaten them, but use deception," declared one document, swiped, hidden, and turned over after the truce.

The captors dispensed edible treats on American holidays: chicken, beef, apples, candy, peanuts, beer, wine, soda pop. They issued tobacco and—after too many pages from the *People's Daily*, a Communist newspaper, disappeared—paper to roll it in. Improved food stocks included soybeans, pork, and once every ten days or so, a cup of white sugar for each man. Some of the men had been eating a staple grain, *kaoliang*, otherwise known as sorghum (and, in America, used as mule feed), which was supposed to alleviate the nocturia associated with rice. But sorghum smelled like kerosene, turned feces purple, and caused stomach cramps and diarrhea, not to mention weight loss.

One of the prisoners, Lt. Bill Funchess, kept track of his weight by circling his leg just above the knee with his fingertips. They had been as close as an inch apart. Now they were about an inch and a half apart, so he was doing better. He figured out how to hang from the hook of the sorghum scale to test his weight: 105 pounds. Most of the prisoners had weighed less during the worst days of captivity.

The dreaded sorghum eventually disappeared, replaced by rice, potatoes, and flour. Local vegetables were plentiful in summer, but winter nutrition always suffered. Officers appointed to the "daily life committee" were told they could order whatever food they wanted, which they did: oysters on the half shell, filet mignon, lobster, fine wine. They knew full well that nothing would change. While he marveled at ingenious GI cooks who tried their best to make bread, cookies, pie, and french fries as well as find new ways to bake, fry, and liquefy the same old ingredients, Doc fostered no illusions. The food was terrible.

It was, however, sustaining. The prisoners began to pad their bones with flesh, and to value daily treks outside the camp to scavenge wood for winter fires. Sympathetic guards showed them where to find *chop chop* (food) that tasted good *(ding how)*, weeds like lamb's-quarter and wild onion. They learned how to look under rocks for snakes, which they skinned and cooked. They ate mulberries full of worms. Someone figured out how to trap chickens with a loop of string pushed through a gap in the barbed wire, then smuggle them inside a shirt to be plucked, cooked, and eaten.

Doc was relieved to see healthier minds result from healthier bodies. Conversation was refreshing now that men were using words no one had heard for months. The prisoners still had health problems, of course. Doc drained abscesses with a knife made from the arch support of a combat boot—without anesthesia, because there was none. He sewed up lacerations with an ordinary needle and thread, sterilizing the needle when someone had a match to run it through. He was unable to correct the riboflavin deficiency that caused sore, bleeding mouths and gums or supply the vitamin A that could have prevented night blindness, which was becoming a severe problem.

At least sixty men suffered varying degrees of this malady, which they first reported as seeing spots before their eyes. The spots were easy to see; Doc could map them out by passing a lighted cigarette back and forth in front of the patient's eye. In some patients, especially later on, the main visual field went black, with light creeping in only at the periphery. The scope of this problem called for some creativity. Around eight thirty every night, a man who could still see announced that a train was leaving for all points. The blinder men formed a human chain to make their last trip to the latrine before bed. Jokes abounded as they snaked their way through the darkness.

Humor had returned along with sufficient calories, although it had never gone missing entirely. The guards proved to be excellent joke targets. They were christened with nicknames, like Dirty Pictures Wong, so called because, according to some, he blamed the Americans' initial high death rate on dirty pictures the men carried in their wallets or, according to others, because he collected pornography. One commandant searched the entire camp for a blanket he had hung out to air, but by the time he noticed it was missing, a few men already sported new, crudely woven socks. Another commandant's pet black rabbit supplied the prisoners with much-needed protein. When the Chinese kept stealing the prisoners' drinking water, which had to be hauled from a considerable distance, a wily prisoner began replacing it with rice paddy water. The guards scratched their heads over the rampant diarrhea they suffered. Of course having the runs made them thirsty, so they drank more water . . . and so it went.

One officer on a wood detail became so irritated by the actions of a young guard that he calmly took the rifle out of the guard's hand, laid it on the ground, kneeled down, put the guard over his knee, and spanked him. When he finished, he handed the rifle back to its owner, who ran, crying, back to the camp.

At night the platoons would "pass" songs back and forth across the compound, much to the frustration of the guards. If they could not identify the prisoner who initiated the song, they appointed someone in his place as a target for their threats and lectures. One night the singing continued until midnight, and then a prisoner yelled out a code. The entire camp turned out, saying they had to pee, which meant that all the guards had to be awakened to stand watch at the latrine. On that night, no punishment ensued, but sometimes the pranks backfired. When the antique dinner bell used to call the men to propaganda sessions wound up at the bottom of the well, the designated perpetrator went to solitary confinement for weeks.

A prisoner was put in the "pokey" or the "hole" to "examine his conscience" for various reasons, from exhibiting a hostile attitude to organizing his fellow men. Left wet, cold, hungry, and cramped, unable to stand or lie down in a four-foot-square hole in the ground for days or weeks, the alleged offender was supposed to confess his sins. If he refused, he was kept in the hole. Sometimes other methods were applied to secure a proper confession, like forcing him to stand at attention for hours in the frigid outdoors. Making him kneel, then kneeing him in the chin. Pouring water down his nose until he was dazed. Tying his thumbs to a beam rigged so that only his toes touched the floor. Making him face a firing squad. The camp commander, Snake Eye Ding, was the most sadistic, *a master of these fine arts who enjoyed his hobby,* Doc concluded.

The prisoners soon learned to write confessions for minor infractions, such as calling their captors "yellow bastards," so they could stay above ground. Eventually the self-confessions became a source of entertainment for the prisoners and embarrassment for their captors, especially when the culprits were forced to read their crimes aloud. After a few days in solitary confinement, one prisoner confessed his misdeed and professed, with conviction, "I will not be caught stealing chickens again."

Five men read elaborate confessions in which they admitted stealing a total of thirty-six pictures of leading Communists from the library wall. Everyone knew that there were only eighteen pictures, and only about six of them had been stolen before the Chinese removed the remaining ones. The prisoners gleefully pointed this out. Eventually the guards got tired of being needled and discontinued the public performances.

The men found hilarity wherever they could, and guard baiting was one of their favorite pastimes. When American B-52s flew over and dropped pieces of foil intended to scramble radar signals, the Chinese were convinced they had been bombarded by deadly viruses, germ warfare meant to spread across the countryside. Using twigs as chopsticks, they meticulously picked up the pieces and placed them in a can. Meanwhile, the prisoners were conducting their own inspection, holding the pieces up to the light, then putting them in their mouths and pretending to chew them. The guards were beside themselves. On another occasion, the prisoners found a dead rat, attached him to a parachute harness, and draped him over the front gate.

For the first time since being captured, Doc had physician colleagues. Capt. Clarence Anderson, Capt. Sidney Esensten, Capt. Gene Lam, and Capt. William Shadish had arrived from other camps, one known as Death Valley, and had their own horror stories. One camp held as many as three thousand prisoners, and death rates were as high as twenty-eight a day. Typhus and infectious hepatitis epidemics had swept their camps, the latter caused by an immunization program that used a single shared needle, "cleaned" by an alcohol wipe between injections. Shadish reported that of 100 to 150 men in his camp who got pneumonia, only six lived. They spoke of bizarre Chinese remedies, like inserting chicken livers under the patients' skin (which didn't seem to do much harm but didn't help either) or inoculating them with pig bile. They had learned to eat cat (tastes like squirrel), dog (like strong beef), rat (wild flavor), trichinous pork, and maggots. They had witnessed what became known as give-up-itis, the propensity for young soldiers in particular—even those with no egregious medical problems, at least no worse than anyone else—to announce that they would be gone tomorrow, then simply lie down and die. They, too, had learned to force-feed and bully in order to save those they could.

But only Doc had survived the Tiger.

# 20
# Atlanta, Georgia
## 1965

School was out and we were moving again, this time to Fort McPherson in Atlanta. I had never been to Georgia, but Jenny Morris, my friend from Landstuhl who now lived two blocks away in San Antonio, said her friends the Whitaker twins liked it there. In fact, she got permission to ride with us so she could visit them. Having her along would make the trip fun. Otherwise, I would be consigned to playing endless games of Twenty Questions and arguing with my brothers over who had to sit in the middle.

As usual, moving was bittersweet. Adventure lay ahead while best friends stayed behind. Joey had remained scarce since his midnight run, but Mark and I had a brief romance, mostly imaginary, conducted via telephone. When my father wasn't around to enforce my five-minute phone limit, I huddled on the floor by the phone alcove in the downstairs hallway, whispering into the receiver. But Mark moved before I did. He called me long-distance once, and we wrote letters, but our correspondence quickly dwindled to nothing.

I purged and packed. The movers came. Before dawn one stifling morning, we loaded our suitcases and ourselves into the blue Ford station wagon and set off across the massive state of Texas, headed for the Deep South.

"Got the map?" my father asked.

"I do," said my mother. She sent for maps from AAA and followed them religiously, paying close attention to construction zones and motel recommendations. She was good at navigating, and my father never questioned her. Driving, especially in cities, made him so tense it scared us silent. If anyone in the backseat happened to speak, he blew up, stomped on the brake, and threatened to leave the offender behind on the roadside.

"Don't you think we should turn on the air?" she added. He liked to rest his left elbow on the open windowsill while guiding the wheel with his fingertips. But my mother knew that after one day of driving, his pale arm would be so bright red he would have to wrap a T-shirt around it, and after we reached our destination, his skin would peel in sheets, leaving discarded shreds all over the furniture.

"I suppose," he said with a small groan, rolling up the window.

When we stopped for lunch, my mother checked guidebooks for AAA motels with pools. Sometime around three or four, whenever my father said he was tired, we played I Spy to find vacancy signs. After we found one and checked in, the kids raced for the pool while the grown-ups stayed behind in the room, drinking martinis from their portable bar. Afterward, we ate in the nearest diner, usually ordering hamburgers or fried chicken with fries, and ice cream for dessert. My mother wasn't too persnickety about vegetables on road trips.

We had been on the road a couple of days when we stopped somewhere in Mississippi for gas. Like most of the small towns we had passed through, this one looked dingy, as if life there had worn it down and out. I tried to imagine moving there. Even on Main Street, house roofs were partly torn off or caved in, and porches sagged. Blackened boards were nailed haphazardly across broken windows where tattered curtains sometimes fluttered out the gaps. Broken furniture and old tires were strewn in weedy lawns. Residents sat smoking on stoops or leaned against the posts that held up the roofs.

The gas station looked all right. Its pumps and windows seemed clean; only a few scraps of newspaper and crushed Dixie cups had blown into the corners against the curb. I wondered if my father would let me have a Dr. Pepper out of the big red cooler sitting out in front, the kind where you slid the bottle along a little track until you could pull it out of the icy water. The sun was hot on my side of the car, and I was thirsty. I also had to pee. I had been holding it for a long time.

My father pulled up to the pump, and we all got out. I looked for the restrooms, usually located somewhere on an outside wall. Small-town gas stations were simple: no convenience stores or keys for the ladies' room, just pumps and a soda machine and room inside for shelves of basic supplies like gas caps and fan belts. I looked along the front of the building, then went around to the side. No luck. I climbed a well-worn path up a mud-packed rise and peeked around back. There it was, its door slightly ajar.

I had never seen such a filthy bathroom. The floor was sticky brown muck, lumpy in places. Feces-stained paper was half in, half out of the toilet bowl. The seat was broken, and there was no lid, just a bare, sweaty tank streaked with yellow. I couldn't close the door because it was the only source of light, and the stench was so bad I was afraid I would gag. *But I am not a snob.* I held my breath as I unzipped my shorts and squatted over the seat without sitting down, the way my mother taught me. I would have to drip dry because there wasn't any paper, just shreds on the cardboard tube. I tried to flush but the handle produced only a gurgle. The single faucet in the small, rusted sink spun freely; no water to wash my hands.

As I made my way back down the hill, wondering what the others would say—where were they, anyway?—I sensed eyes watching me. Lots of eyes. The pump attendant stared right at me. Across the street, two men had gotten up off the stoop and were looking in my direction. A woman ambling down the sidewalk with a squeaky cart slowed and watched me before looking away. I checked to see if I had zipped my zipper and made sure my shirt wasn't messed up somehow. Everything seemed OK, except for the feeling. I wiped my hands on the back of my shorts.

"Can I have a Dr. Pepper?" I asked my father. He shook his head.

"Just get in the car," he said. I didn't think he was mad at me because he wasn't looking at me, but he sounded mad in that mysterious way he had sometimes, as if you could hear the volcano rumble but had missed the steam. I noticed that everyone else was already in the car, and Jenny had an odd look on her face.

He started up the Ford with a roar and pulled away from the pump, faster than usual. It didn't take long to drive out of the town, back into the fields. Everyone was quiet.

"What's the matter? Was something wrong?" I asked finally.

"You used the colored bathroom," he said, tossing clipped words over the back of his seat in my direction. "The white one was inside."

On Fort Mac, as everyone called the post, our quarters weren't ready. This was not unusual. Before we moved into quarters in San Antonio, we had spent nearly two months in a cramped, sparsely furnished apartment in a sprawling complex of mostly concrete. I used the time to teach Dirk and Eric how to dive off the small pool's diving board while my mother, who was afraid of water, sat white-knuckled in a plastic chair nearby, tempting us to quit with a Fresca from the vending machine. In Atlanta we had only a week or two to wait, so we dropped Jenny off at the Whitakers' house and dragged our suitcases up the stairs in the bachelor officer quarters (BOQ), drab, soulless barracks located behind the much grander officers' row. Unlike officers' row—huge old frame houses that sat tall, boasting sprawling porches, on spacious lots facing the parade grounds—BOQ housing was basic: rooms with a bed, desk, chair, and lamp. In our case, rooms were linked to make an apartment of sorts, with a living room and kitchenette, plus one bedroom for adults and one for kids.

"It's just temporary," my mother assured us.

Jenny called to invite me to the teen club's Saturday excursion to Lake Allatoona, where we could swim, water-ski, and dance to records after a picnic dinner. I needed a permission slip from my parents. I asked how many chaperones would be on the bus, how far away Lake Allatoona was, what time we would leave and get home, whether I could get a ride back to the BOQ from the bus stop. She called back with the answers, and to my surprise, my parents said yes.

Saturday dawned steamy and bright. I had studied a map and walked the few blocks to the bus stop the day before to make sure I knew where I was going. This morning the old army bus was there, waiting. I climbed on board, too shy to take my eyes off the rolled towels under the arms of laughing strangers, but soon Jenny and the Whitaker twins were including me in the jokes bouncing back and forth across the aisle. By the time we reached the lake ninety minutes later, I felt accepted.

The day flew by in a festive splash of water polo and dunking contests, volleyball games, and hamburgers from the concession stand. Anyone who was eighteen could rent a motorboat and take three other people water-skiing for an hour. I watched wistfully until late afternoon, when a trim guy with dark hair named Mark invited me to be number four in his boat. I gave him my $5 share of the cost and climbed in. I knew how to water-ski but, self-conscious with these new friends, I asked to be the spotter instead. I was the first to see my boat mate's bikini bottoms fall to her knees as she made it up on her skis, only to toss the tow rope and plunge back into the warm water as guffaws rumbled across the lake.

As dusk fell someone plugged in the record player, set the speakers on the corners of the shelter's concrete slab, and piled a stack of 45s on the picnic table. We danced to "Wooly Bully" and "You Were on My Mind." Mark asked me to dance often, even to the slow songs. "You've Lost That Lovin' Feeling" felt good in his arms, close but not too tight. We smiled at each other.

Going home on the bus, Mark sat next to me. We talked the whole way, stopping only to join in on "100 Bottles of Beer on the Wall," which got boring by 92 and drifted into quiet somewhere in the 80s. It seemed rude to turn around, but I was sure people were making out behind me.

"Would you like to go to the movies with me on Friday?" Mark asked as the guard saluted us through the post gates.

"I think so. It depends." I had already asked him every question my father might ask—about his work, education, background, living arrangements, parents' occupations—and he answered them all readily. I tried to archive every detail in my brain, which was tired but still buzzing from the day of sun and fun. He drove me home in his polished maroon car, dropping me off at the BOQ with a warm handshake and a promise to call. The next afternoon, he called to tell me which movie we would go to, when he would pick me up, and when he would bring me home.

"Who was that?" my father asked when I hung up the phone. He was sitting in a chair reading the newspaper.

"Mark," I said. "I met him at the lake. He's really nice, and he asked me to go to the movies on Friday. Can I? Please?"

My mother, who had stretched out on the couch with a paperback, looked at me and then at my father. She didn't say anything. I wished I had been able to ask her first, but that was impossible with all of us hanging out in this small place.

"Does he drive?" my father asked. I nodded. I conveyed every detail I could remember, including how polite he was, how responsible and nice, how well he treated me.

"How old is he?"

"Twenty-one."

"Absolutely not."

My mother's eyebrows went up. My father wasn't shouting, but she knew better than to interrupt.

"That's only six years older than me. It's not like it's my first date," I said.

"No."

"We're going to the movie at the post theater, and we'll come home right after, I promise."

"No. You are not going anywhere with him."

"It's only a movie! And it's not a school night."

"I said no!" Then, with half a sneer, "So how did you meet this guy?"

"At the lake. He knows everybody in the teen club. You can ask the chaperones; they know him, too. We rode together on the bus, and he gave me a ride home."

He squinted at me. "So what did he do, feel you up? Stick his tongue in your mouth?"

"What's that supposed to mean?"

"It means men are animals, and so is this one. He's too old for you. You're not going, and I don't want to hear another word about it. Go to your room."

I thought I heard my mother sigh, but when I looked at her, she was looking down at her book. She was not going to help me. I was furious at my father for assuming the worst, for keeping me prisoner in this place, for refusing to give me a chance. For the first time I just wanted to go home, back to San Antonio. I needed to talk to Angie.

I eyed the black telephone on the side table. I knew her number. But I couldn't call because I didn't want to be heard. I went into the bedroom, pulled out the notepaper and pen I had stashed in my suitcase, and sat down at the desk.

I pushed my pen with vengeance across the page. I didn't use the line guide that fit under each piece of notepaper. I didn't care if the lines slanted down as I went, or if the "y" tails crashed into the "h" posts on the next line. I wrote about how mean my father was, how he never trusted me, and how nice Mark was, and how all I wanted to do was go to the movies with him, nothing special. He had nice clothes and a clean car, and he didn't make any moves so why not, even if he was older than me. He *liked* me. Wasn't that good enough? Then I went on about our trip and our cramped quarters and what the weather was like and how the lake was fun but I was afraid to water-ski. I wrote so many pages that when I folded them and stuffed them in the envelope, I thought I had better put two stamps on.

"I'm going to mail this," I mumbled as I walked through the living room, heading for the door. I had noticed a mailbox on the corner.

"You're going to mail what?" my father asked. His voice was strained and hollow, like someone was standing on his chest.

"It's just a letter." I opened the door. "I'll be right back."

"You are not going anywhere. Get back in here, young lady." I hated *young lady*. It meant *bad girl*. I closed the door.

"Did you just write that?"

"Yes, sir."

"Who is it to?"

"Angie."

"What did you tell her?"

"Oh, just about what's going on. About the trip and the teen club. Nothing important." I tried to keep my voice even. My mother was watching both of us, her jaw clenched. The line etched between her eyebrows deepened.

"Then read it to me," he said.

My mouth fell open, but I closed it in a hurry. He had never asked me to do anything like this before. The things I had written about him were true, but they weren't nice. I hated him while I was writing, but writing helped me hate him less. It didn't matter. I was trapped.

"No," I murmured.

"Don't you tell me no! Read it!"

"But it's private. I didn't write it to you, I wrote it to Angie. She's the only one who is supposed to read it." I knew talking back was a major offense. But opening someone else's mail was a major offense, too, and reading it was even worse. I pleaded with my eyes.

He was having none of it.

"Read it, dammit!"

"But I already sealed the envelope . . ."

Now he was shouting. I stood in the middle of the room, wishing I didn't feel half-naked in my shorts and sandals, exposed and unprotected. My hands shook. I slit open the envelope with my forefinger, pulled out the wad of paper, unfolded it, and began to read. I could hear my voice, flat with defeat, as if I were hovering up under the eaves. I read fast, dismissively. I glanced at him over the tops of the pages, watched him fold his face in and sink into the chair as if he had been pushed. When I finished, he was silent. Pain painted my mother's face. No one spoke.

I shifted my weight from one foot to the other and back again. Waited.

"How could you do this?" His voice like a drowning man's.

"I was just mad," I said. "I'm sorry. I didn't really mean it." I did really mean it, but maybe I had gone too far, broken something I could not fix. This time I wasn't afraid that he might hurt me. He seemed like a little boy instead of a raging giant, like someone who needed a hug.

"How could you?" he asked again, with a small gasp for breath. "Don't you know? Don't you see? What do you think I was thinking about on the worst night of my life, far away in a foreign country, at war, wondering if I was going to die? How do you think I got through that? All I could see in my mind was a picture, like a photograph, of this baby girl I had left behind, the one with all the black hair who giggled when I threw her up in the air. All I wanted to do was to get home to that little girl. That was you. And this is what you do to me. How could you?"

"I don't know," I whispered. He hadn't talked like this before. I didn't know what he was talking about, exactly. I was afraid he might cry. My mother had a Kleenex in her hand; family crying belonged to her. I hung my head and waited.

"May I please be excused now?" I said finally. He nodded.

"Give me that," he said, holding his hand out for the letter. I handed it over and returned to the bedroom as he crumpled it in his fist and threw it on the floor. Tomorrow I would write another letter, with a different story, but I would be more careful and not get caught.

We moved into a brick duplex on Murphy Circle, across the street from a picturesque albeit manufactured lake on the post golf course. I got the small bedroom, a third the size of my last one, at the end of the upstairs hall, next to the bathroom. The room that mirrored it on the other end of the hall was my father's study. There were also two larger bedrooms, one for my parents and the other for my brothers, just big enough to hold the L-shaped bunk beds my father had built, with space-saving shelves and drawers underneath.

Every day after breakfast dishes, I went out the kitchen's side door, across the patio, and across Wetzel Drive to the officers' swimming pool. Teen boys were the lifeguards, and they gathered daily with friends to play Marco Polo or water volleyball and swim laps. I learned their names from the 25-mile chart, where they kept track. In the grassy area under the trees they also kept a table or two of bridge going, rotating in and out. I figured out how to play by watching over their shoulders, but I was too unsure of myself to accept their generous offers to take a turn. I also avoided adding my name to the laps chart, but I started swimming a quarter mile daily after breakfast and kept track at home. After lunch, I went back to the pool to eavesdrop, work on my tan, and bleach my hair.

I was still proud of my long hair, which had not yet turned mousy brown. Instead, sun, chlorine, and lemon juice rinse had streaked it white blonde. "Great highlights," said my mother's stylist, who was surprised that I used no professional products. Natural blondes were unusual here in the South, and I was determined to keep it pure. I liked shaking my head *no* when people asked if I was a bottle blonde.

Hair remained important in our family. Not so much for boys; my mother bought clippers and gave my father and brothers buzz cuts while they squirmed on the red kitchen stool. But my father kept a dusty picture of my mother from her nursing school days in his workshop, less well hidden than the *Playboy* foldout of Marilyn Monroe posing nude against red cloth that matched her lipstick. I knew when I saw it that he still preferred long hair, even though my mother's Lauren Bacall locks, so luxurious in her wedding picture, had long since been shorn. But now that I was turning sixteen, old enough to refuse the home perms my mother had given me since junior high, something had changed.

"Did you just wash your hair?" he asked one night at the dinner table, a few weeks after school had started.

"Yes. Why? Do you like it?"

"When was the last time you washed it?"

"I don't know. A couple of days ago."

"Once a week is plenty."

"Why? It gets greasy."

"It's not necessary. Believe me, you can go a long time without washing your hair. Besides, when you wash out the natural oils, your body will just make more. So the more often you wash it, the faster it gets dirty." He cut a bite of pork chop. "It's a vicious cycle."

"But ..."

"I don't want to hear any more about it. Once a week is enough. You could go months without washing it if you had to." He peered at me through the smeared lenses of his glasses, then went back to eating and changed the subject.

I took to calculating on my fingers as I lay in bed at night. Which day did I really need clean hair? Friday, when I was going to the movies? Or Monday, when I had a test and wanted to feel confident? I wanted clean hair when I wore my favorite outfit, blue hip-hugger bellbottoms and a blue-and-yellow checked top, which was fashionable and fit well. My father exploded when he saw it and told me to return the clothes to the store. My mother let me keep them as long as I promised to wear them only when he wasn't home.

In between washings, my hair turned dark with oil, stringy and smelly in the Georgia heat and humidity. "How come your hair's all wet?" the kids on the school bus taunted me. "It isn't," I said in a low voice as I slid into a seat with my head down, trying to hide behind the seat back in front of me. They were not mean, just observant.

To look good twice in the same week, I tried everything I could think of: sprinkling my head with talcum powder and brushing it through, using cream rinse meant for extra oily hair, wearing wide headbands that hid as much as possible. Once I crept into the bathroom after midnight, when the lights were off and I thought everyone was asleep. I got down on my knees in the tub, turned the faucet on to a trickle, and stuck my head under it. My father came roaring into the bathroom, furious. He yanked my head out from under the faucet.

"What did I tell you?" he yelled.

I knew what he told me, and I had disobeyed, so I didn't argue. I put the towel around my hair and went back to my room. I wondered how he remembered that this was not the seventh day. Apparently we were fighting a war of sorts. The more I cared about my appearance, the stronger a stand he took.

"Can I get contact lenses?" I asked one evening. My government-issue spectacles were not attractive. I had spent many minutes looking in the bathroom mirror, holding my glasses sideways in order to see half my face glasses-free. That side looked so much better. I took Dorothy Parker at her word, that boys didn't makes passes at girls with glasses.

"No," he said. "Absolutely not."

"But why not?"

"They're bad for your eyes."

"My friends wear them, and they do just fine." I didn't share how often they lost the hard lenses that seemed to pop out at will.

"They won't be doing just fine when they go blind."

My mother explained that he had already called his ophthalmologist friend, who agreed that contacts were too newfangled to consider and that it would take another generation to judge long-term effects.

"Wear your glasses. I don't want to see you without them. Period," my father added. "How you look is not important. How you see is."

I developed a peculiar ritual, leaving the house wearing my glasses but as soon as I was out of sight, jamming them in my purse. At parties I smiled at everyone at first because I could not recognize individuals. Eventually I learned who stood straight but cocked their head, who leaned slightly to the right, who put a hand on one hip when they talked. I studied walking patterns to figure out where the bathroom was. But good-night kisses on the front step were unavoidably awkward. As soon as my date kissed me, I turned my back on him so I could shove my glasses back on my nose as I opened the door.

By Christmas, I had a regular boyfriend who lived up the street. Russ had been one of the pool lifeguards as well as a respected bridge player who didn't mind me studying the game over his shoulder. His rumbling voice, aw-shucks manner, and funny but compassionate sense of humor attracted a large circle of friends, and my parents seemed to like him. Most of our dates consisted of strolling on the golf course in the moonlight and finding our own bench while our friends sat on a green and smoked cigarettes. Or we would meet at the Whitakers' duplex. Even when twins Kathy and Diane weren't home, their mother, Alice, welcomed the friends who crowded around the dining room table. She would feed us, listen to our troubles, offer advice if we wanted it, and put us to work matching socks and chopping vegetables.

Although we occasionally made out in the front seat of his Chevy Malibu, Russ did not seem like an animal. He was shy and careful with me, and while I could tell that he wanted what my father warned me all men want, he never went further than I wanted to go. After he left for Virginia Military Institute, where freshmen had shaved heads and restricted phone privileges, he wrote me newsy, wistful letters on VMI stationery and sent me a VMI necklace. Wearing it meant something like being pinned to a frat boy, but not quite. I guessed we were going steady, sort of. I longed to see him at Christmas, although his holiday vacation was very short.

Christmas turned my father into a curmudgeon, crankier than usual. I would have attributed this to his bad luck at being born on Christmas Day, meaning he got stuck with joint birthday and Christmas gifts instead of raking in loot twice a year like the rest of us, but he seldom cared about presents. Something else seemed to preoccupy him during the holidays, making me wary and casting a pall that lifted inexplicably when we returned to our normal routines.

Like most families, we had rituals. On Christmas Eve, we ate our traditional oyster stew, hung stockings, and left cookies and milk for Santa even after we knew Santa was a pseudonym. On Christmas morning, we opened presents. On Christmas night we ate my father's traditional birthday dinner, which he always dubbed *chop chop, ding how*.

Nothing much happened on Christmas afternoon. My mother cooked. My father went to his workshop or fiddled with his ham radio. My brothers played with their new toys while I read my new books. So Christmas afternoon seemed like the best time for Russ to come over to exchange presents, especially since he had to leave early the following morning for school. But I needed permission to invite him.

I decided to be creative. If I asked my father straight out and caught him in a bad mood, he would yell no, and that would be that. So I wrote a letter as sweet as I could make it. "Dear Santa," I began, "Please grant me this one wish. It would be the best present of all." I explained why Christmas afternoon would be the only time Russ and I could see each other, and I promised not to let it interfere with family time, because I understood how important family time was. I signed it "Love, Punky." I put the letter on the mantle before I went to bed, nestling it among the evergreen boughs but making it obvious so that whoever ate Santa's cookies would see it. I was sure it would work.

It was cold and unusually dark that Christmas Eve, the sky layered with ominous clouds. I had planned to walk my brothers to the post chapel for a special Christmas Eve service for their Sunday school class, but the weather was so threatening that my father drove us. We all got out of the car. As the boys hurried into the small building that served all denominations, my father stopped just outside the front door and leaned against the wall.

"Aren't you going in?" I asked.

"No. Go on in. I'll wait out here."

"Don't you like to go to church at Christmas?"

"No." He stared out over my head. He hadn't shaved that morning, and white whiskers sprouted on his chin.

"How come?"

His sigh rattled deep.

"Because all I can think about is one Christmas I spent very far away, when I wasn't sure there was a God because he didn't seem to be there."

"In Korea?"

He moved his chin down and back up, once, and looked straight at me, as if I were somehow to blame for sending him back there in his memory, for causing him shame. I was ashamed of myself for asking. I had violated the pact of silence that seemed to exist. I did not know what to say to make it better. I looked away.

"Go on in," he said. I did as I was told.

The next morning I woke early, listening for Christmas sounds. Dirk and Eric whispered as they waited for permission to go downstairs and see what Santa had left under the tree. When I heard my parents rumbling around in their bedroom, I put on my slippers and bathrobe and joined my brothers. But as soon as we clambered down the stairs, I sensed that something was wrong.

My letter was propped approximately where I had left it. Certainly they had read it, but no one mentioned it. My parents were quieter than usual, hunkered in. They watched us open our presents. We weren't big on presents; we got one from each other, plus one from Santa. Sometimes my parents exchanged gifts, sometimes not. My father kept shifting in his chair and got up for water more than once.

After presents, breakfast. After breakfast, reading the newspaper and sitting in the living room. My parents drank their coffee and smoked their cigarettes. My brothers took their presents upstairs. I tidied up, saving the bows in a pile for next year. Then silence. My mother went into the kitchen; it was already past our usual lunchtime. I needed to call Russ, and I was getting nervous.

"Did you read my letter?" I asked at last.

My father lowered his head and looked at me from under his eyebrows. He put his hands on the arms of his chair and pushed himself up. Limping slightly, as he did sometimes when his feet hurt, he went over to the mantle, grabbed the letter, and threw it at me.

"Don't ever do that again," he bellowed. I felt more than heard my mother's footsteps. She had stopped in the doorway to see what would happen next.

"But why? Why can't Russ come over, just for a few minutes? He just wants to give me my present, and this is the only time he can come." OK, I was whining. "We won't bother you. Nothing is going on anyway."

"NO. It's Christmas. Family time. You know that." He sat back down. He was done with me. My tongue went numb. I had so much to say, about wanting him to understand what it is like to be in love (although I wasn't sure that was quite accurate), about granting special favors for loved ones, about being practical and trying to work with someone else's schedule. Calm, cool things that made sense and heated emotional things that made my breath catch. But I had already written those things in the letter, and I could not repeat them now.

My throat hurt from holding it all in, words I couldn't form. I picked up the letter and trudged up the stairs. I read what "Santa" wrote on the back of my letter, mostly philosophical jargon but some things I understood. "Materialism is so insignificant its discussion is distastefully mundane.... Happiness to me is selfishness, if it makes someone else unhappy.... This is Christmas, not today alone, but every day you have the privilege of living."

I put the letter away and went into my parents' bedroom, where the phone was. I turned the alarm clock so I could watch my allotted five minutes tick by, and called Russ. We made a plan. I would leave his present by the front door, and he would put mine in the mailbox. Back in my room, I sat by the window and watched for him until my mother called me to help with dinner.

# 21

# Camp 2, P'anjung-ni, North Korea

## JANUARY 1953

It had been two and a half years. Now that they had more food, more clothes, and less abuse, the prisoners' biggest common enemy, other than communism, was monotony. To combat this, they not only told jokes but also taught classes: foreign languages, elementary mathematics, calculus, electronics, shorthand, philosophy, and history. Those who could accumulate enough paper and pencil lead wrote their own textbooks, including a book on electricity written by Lt. Col. Paul Liles and his associates. They also read from a well-stocked library that included, alongside Communist propaganda and outdated periodicals, classics ranging from *Les Misérables* and *David Copperfield* to *Of Mice and Men* and *The Grapes of Wrath*. One group developed a set of logarithms the old-fashioned way by doing long multiplication. An English officer wrote and produced a three-act murder mystery that Doc thought was excellent. Another re-created Shakespeare's *Merchant of Venice* from memory. The Chinese supplied cloth for costumes, wigs, and makeup for what became quite elaborate performances. A quartet and a choir often held concerts. But even entertainment invited intervention. The guards once stopped the performance of "You'll Never Walk Alone," a sentimental favorite, because they deemed the song political. The prisoners walked out.

They had chores. Every time it snowed, those who were able were ordered outside to "conquer nature." They used tree branches, brooms, and whatever utensils they could find to remove every trace of snow from the center of the compound, where PT was still held daily. Meanwhile, snow drifted to six or eight feet outside this area and remained there until the spring thaw.

They hauled logs to build a new annex. Some were as long as twenty feet, and the men had to carry them on their shoulders for at least two miles. It was hot, dirty work, but they appreciated the opportunity to sneak away from the group and forage food. One prisoner discovered tobacco seeds drying near a shack by the road and stole a few. He germinated them on a piece of tin, mixed them with topsoil and human manure from the latrine, and with his buddies' help transplanted the seedlings to the south slope in front of the schoolhouse. When the plants were three or four feet high, the enterprising growers cured the leaves in the cookhouse loft and shared the "not too bad" tobacco with their fellow prisoners.

Church was a welcome diversion, albeit a political quagmire. Catholic and Protestant services were held every Sunday, complete with carved crosses, an altar, and other artifacts supplied by resourceful prisoners. The Chinese loudly proclaimed their belief in religious freedom, which made for good propaganda. Yet the services were censored and reported on. And when the prisoners requested permission to have a special service, it was denied.

"This is not religious freedom!" the American chaplain insisted.

"Yes, it is," the guards told him. "We have given permission for everyone to pray individually."

"But we don't need permission for that. You can't stop a man for thinking what he wants to think."

"That's not the point. You have permission to think about religion if you like, because we gave you that permission, but once you do more than think about it, you are disobeying. You do not have permission for services."

*Religious freedom Communist-style. A mockery.*

As the men regained strength, they also regained a taste for athletic competition. They constructed softball, volleyball, and basketball courts in the courtyard and played soccer as well. But softball was the hands-down winner. Even some of the English cricket players were heard to say that softball was the better game. One of the prisoners made softball gloves, and a commission ran three leagues—Dawn, Sunrise, and Sunset, with Sunset considered the majors—complete with umpires and official scorekeepers who posted box scores. Players were hired and fired. Money changed hands. Doc declared that the $500 to $1,000 that rode on each game did much to boost camp morale, but where the money actually came from was a mystery. Perhaps those who had not marched with the Tiger had managed to hang on to their wallets.

In November 1952, as Dwight D. Eisenhower was being elected president back home, athletic teams from Camps 2 and 5 competed in the Intern Camp Olympics held in Pyoktong. The Camp 2 officers, understanding that these Olympics were designed to advance the Chinese propaganda agenda, debated the wisdom of participating but finally decided that the physical and psychological benefits outweighed the political risks and sent a team. (The Chinese would use highlights of the event to illustrate an elaborate brochure. In order to save face in the international community, particularly if the war ended soon, they wanted to ensure that the prisoners appeared well fed and cared for.) Two Camp 2 companies were preparing to launch another matchup on a smaller scale during the summer months.

Even more fun, at least for the nonathletically inclined, was Crazy Week, or Hell Week, as some called it. It was a protest of sorts, as goofy a guard torture as they could muster. On the first morning before dawn, when the guards opened the door to one shack and shouted "Get up!" as usual, fifteen to twenty prisoners burst through the door and lined up with precision, saluting West Point–style. The guards were delighted, of course; these men were coming around. But when they stuck their heads in the door and shouted "Get up!" again the following morning, the shack was empty.

One afternoon the men formed conga lines, performing what the South African POWs called the Zulu war dance. "I zickie zoomba, zoomba, I zickie zoomba zay," they chanted as they snaked around the camp, each man's hands on the hips of the man in front of him.

At random times, Air Force pilots simulated aircraft, zooming around in formation with their arms outstretched, practicing aircraft carrier takeoffs. Small groups pretended to play cards with no cards, sew clothes with no needle or thread, and polish boots with no boots or polish. One American claimed he was celebrating the Indian Holiday of His Ancestors and could speak only Indian, while one of his buddies served as his interpreter. Another pretended to be plowing, following his mule everywhere and shouting "giddy up," "gee," "haw," and "whoa" as necessary. Others barked instead of talking, limped instead of walking, or raised a ruckus by continually pointing out imaginary objects.

John "Rotorhead" Thornton, a former helicopter pilot with a rubber face and rollicking wit, rode an imaginary motorcycle everywhere. When roll was called every morning, he revved it up, climbed aboard, and circled the group before parking it next to the main building and joining his company. After roll call was over, he retrieved the bike and rode away. This happened daily.

Exasperated, the guards finally confronted him. "It's against camp rules to have a motorcycle!" they insisted. Thornton burst into tears, moaning in despair. Rumor had it that a group of his buddies later formed a team and met with the guards, demanding that the motorcycle be returned to its rightful owner.

For the third time since Doc had lost his freedom, spring began to show itself in small ways: earlier dawns, later sunsets, rivulets of melt trickling out from under hard packs of snow. The soft tinkle of ice as pieces rubbed against each other on the riverbank. On occasion, when the air was still at midday, slight warmth from the sun.

Letters began to arrive on a regular basis, although they were restricted to one per person at mail call. Doc yearned for newsy letters in my mother's sloping longhand and an occasional picture of the two of us. He was devastated once when the letter addressed to him was written by another wife, asking what he knew about the whereabouts of her missing husband.

In April 1953, news of "Little Switch" arrived at the camp. During the peace talks being held at Panmunjom, the two sides had agreed to exchange the sick and wounded prisoners. But voluntary repatriation, particularly for Communist prisoners, had been a major sticking point in the talks. As many as half of the North Korean and Chinese prisoners held by UN forces reportedly did not want to return to their homelands. "Big Switch," the final prisoner exchange, would have to wait until the adversaries agreed on what to do with them.

The news of a limited release caused much consternation among the senior officers at Camp 2. Who would stay and who would go? They compiled a list of those they thought should be the first to leave and considered whether to present it to the Chinese. But Doc and others thought that making such a demand might be unwise. They did not trust their captors. Were they bluffing? Would they follow through, even if an agreement were negotiated? Or would the proposal merely cause more problems and delay the process? What if the Chinese became suspicious of the men on the list and jeopardized their exchange? If the Chinese suspected trouble, all they had to do was move the troublemakers out of the camp; their fellow prisoners would never know what became of them.

The officers finally decided to keep the list to themselves, to wait and hope instead. Eventually the Chinese chose three men to leave the camp, one amputee and two others who had been sick, although not as sick as some of the men the officers had listed. In fact, one of them, Maj. Marin (Pappy) Green, spent weeks learning to fake terminal cancer symptoms so that he would be first out. When he was released, his mission was to provide truthful information about prison conditions and assist the military in establishing repatriation protocols. The amputee was detained in Pyoktong, they learned later, but the others were repatriated as promised. Unfortunately, U.S. military officials suspected Green of collaborating with the enemy, so his carefully rehearsed efforts to set the record straight were disregarded.

On July 27, 1953, after two years of peace talks, the commander-in-chief of the United Nations Command, the supreme commander of the Korean People's Army, and the commander of the Chinese People's Volunteers signed the Korean War Armistice Agreement in Panmunjom. A cease-fire was declared.

Earlier that day, the camp commander ordered the men to fall out in formation in order to hear some of their fellow prisoners being sentenced to prison terms ranging from months to years. No one knew what this meant. Later that afternoon the group was reassembled, but this time American jazz was playing on the PA system. Outsiders had set up movie cameras in discreet locations. Excited guards milled about. Chinese officials grinned as they anticipated effusive thanks from their captives as soon as peace was announced.

The prisoners, however, had planned carefully for this moment. When the announcement came, they stood quiet, sullen, and disgusted, with their hats down over their eyes and their arms folded behind their backs. Slowly, without a word, they did an about-face and retreated to their shacks. The Chinese officials were confused. Eventually they turned off the music, sent the press home, and left the camp.

Then all hell broke loose—this time, in the best way possible.

# 22

# Atlanta, Georgia

## 1966

"Why is your door closed? What are you doing in there?" my father roared from the upstairs hallway one Sunday afternoon in September of my senior year. I was stretched out on my bed trying to decipher my government class notes for Monday's quiz, hoping no one would bother me. Increasingly I sought solitude in my room, hiding out in a safe place where I would not be teased about my hair or my clothes or my body, which was finally, slowly, developing breasts. I knew the rule about no closed doors but hoped it would not be enforced.

"Studying!" I yelled back as he threw the door open with half a crooked smile on his face. I went back to my notes, trying to ignore him.

"That's good." He continued on down the stairs.

Later that night, I was standing under the shower washing my hair when the bathroom door burst open, blowing the curtain into my legs. I had not locked the door, of course. It was a shared bathroom, and my mother and I, both fans of long bubble baths, were accustomed to male visitors who needed to use the toilet. I had tried to choose my time carefully, when my brothers were asleep, my mother was in the living room sipping Gallo sherry with ice, and my father was fiddling with resistors in his study. I didn't peek out to see who had come in. I assumed whoever it was would do their business and leave.

"What are you doing in there?" my father boomed.

"Taking a shower!"

I calculated frantically. I was sure I had waited long enough to wash my hair this time. He grabbed the curtain and swung it aside, the metal rings grating on the rod. I turned to look. He was smiling at me, playful. He grabbed my nipple and pulled hard. I screeched. He laughed.

"Why did you do that?" My voice caught.

"Because that's what men do. You better get used to it."

He did not sound mean or mad or malicious. I wanted to laugh along with him at his little joke, to please him, but I didn't think it was funny. It was humiliating. And my nipple really hurt. I pulled the curtain shut, turned the hot water up, and stood under it. He peed, washed his hands, walked out, and closed the door behind him.

Men are brutes, disgusting, brazen, vile. Occasionally, on the rare evenings when I sat with my parents in the living room's smoky haze, he made these proclamations from the depths of the green chair, refusing to let me go to bed until he was done. He also issued challenges.

"What do you do when a man gets a hard-on?"

"Nothing. What should I do?"

"Just take your hand and go like this," he passed his hand across his zipper, "and they'll ejaculate. Then they'll leave you alone."

"That's disgusting," my mother said, rescuing me.

She could shout him down when she wanted to, although if he was in full battle mode, she seldom had the stamina it took to win. In high school, she pointed out, she had boy friends—two words—who never touched her or asked to. They sat beside her at soda fountains, rode beside her on hayrides, and asked her out even though her strict mother, who made no bones about disliking men, did not allow her to date.

"Maybe they had lust in their hearts, but they were civil and respectful. A boy can be a perfectly fine friend. They do not all act like animals."

"Bullshit." My father's voice went flat, his eyes squinty. "They want only one thing. She's better off knowing the truth."

"Can't you both be right?" I asked once when this argument replayed. But my father stood firm. By this time we all knew our places: my father to bark the blazing truth according to him, which was, bottom line, that only virgins achieve marital bliss; my mother to either confront him or utter a long sigh and go back to her book; and me to listen in silence, because being shouted down made me feel like a bowl of Jell-O on a hotplate, oozing into vapid liquid. My truth was evident: Trust eluded my father. So did compromise.

Now that I was a senior, my name was on the Georgia Tech fraternity guest list, which allowed me to join carloads of girls invited to parties so the frat boys would have someone to dance with. Parents received an official letter describing this procedure and inviting them to meet the young men who picked us up and returned us promptly at the designated hour. I liked this group approach because, increasingly, real dates made my knees wobble. My anxiety had little to do with my date; I just never knew what my father would do.

On real dates, I was always ready when the doorbell rang. I would rush downstairs to open the door and invite the boy in to greet my parents. Sometimes my father would hop up and shake his hand. He would ask questions and make funny remarks and tell us to have a good time. I would let out the breath I had been holding and hurry us out before the mood changed.

Occasionally he seemed to want us to hang around. He acted lonely. He would engage us in animated conversation about current fashion (he disapproved), politics (politicians are idiots), or whatever else followed his jocular greeting: "So how's your liver?" (I once asked why he chose this, and he explained that the liver is our most important organ.) My date, if polite, would be torn: leave and piss off the old man, or stay and indulge him while I scowled my anxiety from the corner. "The colonel" apparently was gaining a legendary reputation among my friends not only for oppressive house rules but also for such antics as interrogating visitors at length and charging out into the street to yell at passing cars to slow down. I considered it my job to navigate the minefield on my escort's behalf.

That year I dated two Jacks, the college Jack who made my heart race and the high school Jack who did not. Craggy and slender with white-blonde hair and a wide grin, the high school Jack was everything I thought my father might find appealing: polite, personable, part of the army brat crowd, fond of basketball and cigarettes. He opened the door for me. He didn't swear in the house. He got me home on time. On the one occasion he invited me to a school dance, my father took our picture. Jack, wearing a suit and a crinkled smile, is handsome. I am wearing the blue velvet A-line gown my mother sewed and cried over when she had to redo a seam and left telltale holes in the fabric. I'm also wearing makeup. My clean hair is curled in a shoulder-length flip, and my glasses are invisible in my hand behind a fold of the dress.

Most of our dates, however, consisted of driving to McDonald's, located just outside the post gate on Campbellton Road, two minutes away. We sat in bucket seats, listened to the radio, drank Cokes, and ate fries. I wore my glasses so I could see who else was there. He told lame jokes that only he found funny. He would light a cigarette, take a few drags, start the joke, blow the smoke out the window, and, way too late, deliver the punch line. He giggled a lot, especially at his punch lines. We waved at people we knew who would sometimes lean in our window so he could tell his jokes all over again. Eventually he would drive me home, walk me to the door, peck me on the cheek, and leave.

That was the extent of our intimacy. So I never knew why, when Jack picked me up on one such occasion, my father jammed his cigarette into the beanbag ashtray, cleared his throat, and leaped out of his chair. He stuck his face into Jack's. Jack, as tall as my father, didn't back up.

"Where are you going?" my father shouted, hoarse as a drill sergeant, spewing saliva. Jack stopped chewing his gum.

"To McDonald's," he said, his voice rising slightly.

"What are you planning to do there? When are you coming back?" Jack didn't get a chance to answer. Faster than I had ever seen him move, my father threw up his forearm and pinned Jack against the nearest wall. Jack's eyes bulged, but he didn't look away. He yelled back. *Asshole! Bastard! Son of a bitch!* I lost track of who was shouting what.

My mother came running, but both of us stood there in the doorway, tongue-tied. She was probably praying, but I just waited. Out of words, Jack stopped talking and stared straight ahead. My father kept sputtering but turned away, grabbed his cigarettes and lighter, and stomped up the stairs to his office. Jack grabbed my arm and we left. He did not come back to my house after that.

Whatever he thought of Jack, my father did not trust me. It didn't seem to matter what I did or didn't do; I was evil waiting to happen. The house rules were getting tougher. No one could call after 10:00 p.m. I could see the same boy only once a week. I couldn't call boys because nice girls didn't do that. Waiting for the right boy to call first, and hoping he would pick my free night, was agony. I never figured out how to win this game.

One quiet evening, I had just finished getting my brothers into bed when the phone rang.

"Can you talk?" asked my friend Carolyn, who knew the rules. She had heard my father shout at me to get off the phone, and she had also been on the other end of the line when he grabbed the receiver from my hand and slammed it down.

"Yes! They're gone. They just left about an hour ago, so I have some time."

I was babysitting three or four nights a week. As the hospital's commanding officer, my father had a full social schedule. My parents attended frequent cocktail parties, usually at the officers' club. At least once a year we hosted a couple hundred people at our house, in one-hour shifts. They drank from small champagne glasses we stored in cardboard boxes and ate hors d'oeuvres, including the steak cubes and mushrooms I sautéed in garlic butter, from my mother's vast array of silver and china.

"Guess where I am," said Carolyn.

"At the Taylors'?"

"Yep. The kids are asleep. Let's sit out back."

The Taylors, for whom I also babysat, lived across Murphy Circle in another of the four duplexes spaced around the perimeter. Each unit's patio adjoined the grassy area in the center, which was devoted to clotheslines, swing sets, and sandboxes cluttered with toys.

I checked on Dirk and Eric, both asleep already, and headed out the kitchen door. Carolyn waved from one of the swings. Hugged by rubber swings meant for smaller hips, we sat, swaying as we talked about school, homework, boyfriends. Crickets chirped as the last sunlight faded into the golf course pond across the street. Cool had crept into the air. Nearly time to go in.

Behind us, the neighbor's Chihuahua started yapping. We turned to see what he was seeing. A team of military police, gleaming rifles in their white-gloved hands, were striding around the corner of my house. Four of them. Two hung back near the patio while the other two marched right up to us, very official.

"What are your names?" the leader asked. We struggled out of our swings and stood up.

"Cathy Boysen, sir," I said. Carolyn told him her name. He said she could go and faced me.

"You are to return to your home immediately."

Had someone died? Heart attack? Car accident? My heart was pounding so loud I was sure he could hear. Then time stopped. The malaria!

About two weeks earlier, I had come home from school to find my father in bed, moaning and thrashing, talking but making no sense. A pile of soaked sheets sat at the top of the stairs, and my mother was just coming upstairs with a clean set. She was shaking her head.

"He soaks through them in about fifteen minutes," she said.

"What's wrong?"

"It's the malaria."

"What malaria?"

"He's had it for a long time. He gets a high fever and sweats a lot, then it goes away after a while."

She was an RN, but I wasn't sure that she was telling me the truth. I was scared. I knew that he had a heart problem—he sometimes mentioned ventricular fibrillation as if to warn us not to provoke him— though I had never seen evidence of it. But malaria? I wondered if it was another leftover from Korea, like his rotten teeth and the discolored splotches on his ankle. Something new to add to the list of questions I was afraid to ask.

I could not imagine life without my father. He had power the rest of us lacked, even my mother, as capable as she was. He could lift us up or smash us down with a force that often caught me by surprise. Yet he was the magnet that bound us to each other, whether we hid in fear or basked in fun times. Our lives revolved around him, sick or well, sane or crazy.

The MPs escorted me to my back door and told me to go inside and wait there. Within a couple of minutes, another police car screamed around the corner and pulled up behind the first. The door opened and my father bolted out, his eyes on fire.

"Where the hell were you?" he yelled.

"Out back, talking to Carolyn."

Louder: "Where are your brothers?"

"Upstairs, sleeping." I was shaking.

"What makes you so sure? When did you check on them?"

"I don't know. Maybe fifteen minutes ago? They were asleep. I just put them to bed a little while ago."

"No, you didn't. You weren't even here fifteen minutes ago."

"But I was." My mind raced. The clock. I had looked at it before I went out, but now I couldn't remember. Was it 7:15? 7:20? 7:30?

"Don't lie to me, young lady. I called fifteen minutes ago and no one answered the phone. You had a job to do and you didn't do it."

"But I was just . . ."

"Don't. You. Ever. Do. This. Again." Foam at the corners of his mouth. His hands agitated, clutching at his sides. "Go to your room, and don't come out."

He had called the MPs, left the party, come home in a police car from the officers' club, a five-minute walk away. I did not think he would pull my pants down and spank me this time, but I knew I would be punished for breaking the "no one in, no one out" babysitting rule. And I was. No phone calls. No dates. No friends over. In the vernacular of the day, I was on restriction. For a month.

Stuck home alone, at least I got my homework done. Senior year was hectic. I got a small part in the class play. Karen Rogers and I coedited the yearbook, spending evenings on the floor at one of our houses, using a primitive orange plastic contraption to size pictures to fit our layouts. Sometimes we would work until nearly midnight, when she would go home and I would pretend to go to bed. Instead I would stay up to write the ten-page paper due every other Friday, checking for light coming in under the door to make sure I would not get caught. Or I would set the alarm and rise before dawn, when the typewriter's clacking was less likely to wake anyone. I had a perpetual sore throat and aching fatigue, but I wanted to be the class valedictorian. I was up against smarter kids, one of whom got perfect scores on his SATs. Mine were nowhere close.

To appease my father and fill my dateless weekends, I thought I might try photography. I gathered the courage to visit his basement workshop one evening when his mood seemed mellow. He was perched on a gray metal stool, tinkering with something on the workbench made from an old door. A hanging bare bulb provided scant light.

"Hi, Pop," I said, shy with intimacy as I stood at his elbow. I waited.

"Hi," he said finally, without looking up. Screwdriver in hand, he was squinting at an electronic part.

"I was wondering if . . . well, maybe we might . . . um, could you teach me photography? I want to learn to use a good camera." Like his Leica, or his Rolleiflex, not the Brownie box camera I had used since elementary school, I was afraid to say.

He didn't say no. He slid off his stool and peered at the shelves along the wall, where books sat forlorn, spines ragged and discolored, leaning into each other. He hesitated, his finger raised. Then he plucked one out and smacked it down on the workbench.

"Read that," he said. He slammed another on top of the first. "And that. And that. And that." The dust made me sneeze. I opened a couple. These weren't books of beautiful photographs but of technical information, in dense type. I picked up the stack, now tall enough to just fit under my chin. It was heavy.

"Read all of them, and then we'll talk," he said as he sat back down and picked up his screwdriver. I think he knew that I would lug them upstairs, page through them, then eventually creep back down and return them to their places. And that I wouldn't ask again.

One night that fall my father announced at the dinner table that we would be moving again after school was out in the spring. I wasn't surprised. He had been unusually preoccupied, hidden away in the den or basement or brooding in his chair. My mother had been brooding, too. I felt guilty that I couldn't make her happy. She said she would love for me to invite my friends over, not just Karen and Carolyn but several of them—maybe have a party. She offered to fix little hot dogs and chips or whatever I wanted. The yearning in her voice made me sad. I told her I would think about it, but I didn't have to; I could not risk my father blowing up in front of everybody.

This move was different because it would split our family. My mother and brothers were going to move back to San Antonio and rent a house off-post. My father would drive us to Texas, wait for the moving van to arrive, and then fly to Vietnam. I would be going off to college in the fall.

There was another war on, and he wanted to go. He treated the wounded soldiers who made it back to his small hospital at Fort Mac, but it bothered him that they got sent to Nam while he stayed home. As an army officer, being close to the front was his job, he insisted. He had to get special dispensation from President Lyndon B. Johnson to go back to the Far Eastern Theater, he told us, because the Communists still had his name on a list and were out to get him. But he promised my mother he would be careful. I could see she wasn't convinced.

Along with this announcement came the promise of something rare: a family vacation! Cross-country moves had replaced vacations since we had left Europe, and we had sold our camping trailer long ago. We drove to Florida a week later on a school day and checked into a weather-beaten motel on the beach, across the street from a shoddy diner that served runny eggs and thin, dry hamburgers on soggy buns. On our first day we all played on the beach, laughing together like TV families. My mother slathered suntan lotion on everyone except my father, who said he didn't need any. After my brothers splashed in the water and built sand castles, he suggested that we all walk down to a point jutting out in the distance.

"That's too far," my mother said.

"No, it's not," he said, and started off. Of course we all followed. We trudged through the sand, my brothers carrying their pails and shovels, for about twenty minutes, but the point seemed just as far off as when we started. We walked for another twenty minutes and the same thing happened. We walked some more. Finally my mother convinced him to turn around and go back, which made him grumpy, but he pepped up at dinner.

The next morning dawned cloudy and bleak. I smelled salt in the air, along with the pungent fish entrails we had seen tangled in seaweed. I propped myself up on my elbow on the foldaway cot and peered out the window. The beach was vacant.

My mother was already up, digging through her suitcase, which was odd because she liked to sleep in. My father was always the first one up—he refused to let us kids sleep late on weekends—but he was lying on their bed in his boxers and T-shirt, his head propped so he could read the newspaper. His skin was bright red.

"What's going on?" I asked.

"Nothing. You don't have to get up yet. Go back to sleep if you want," she said.

"But something's wrong. I can tell."

"Your father can't walk." She didn't want to talk about it.

"Why not?"

"Shin splints," he said.

"He walked too far yesterday. Especially when he's not used to it." She gave him a dirty look.

"I guess your mother was right," he added.

My mother pressed her lips together. She didn't gloat, though it wasn't like him to admit someone else was right or to accept help. He was the colonel, the surgeon, the god in our lives. It was our duty to obey and accommodate.

He spent the day in bed. When he had to go to the toilet, he called my mother and she called me. We lined up on either side of him, so he could throw his arms over our shoulders as we walked him to and from the bathroom. I could tell from his groaning that it really hurt him to put weight on his feet. For meals, my mother went across the street and brought back cold burgers in brown paper bags with grease spots. The sun hid behind thick clouds. My brothers played board games while I read *Doctor Zhivago*.

The next day my father could limp to the bathroom by himself, but it started to rain. The wind made a high-pitched howl, whistling through the windows where the glass and frames were misaligned. I read with a pillow over my head. When I went across the street to pick up lunch, I noticed that few cars remained at our motel. Ours sat forlorn in its parking space. By afternoon, the sky had turned from light to dark gray, threatening black. The wind turned colder and started to roar. The windows didn't break but sounded as if they might. Rain poured at a slant. Water seeped in beneath the sliding glass doors to the balcony. My mother tried to call the front desk but no one answered. The power went out. There must have been hurricane warnings somewhere in Florida, but my father wasn't one to run from a storm.

That night my father still couldn't walk well enough to help, so my brothers and I gathered up all the towels to plug leaks and mop the puddles forming by the windows. My mother stationed herself by the bathtub, where we brought her batch after batch of dripping towels to twist dry and hand back to us. We took breaks to rummage in our bags for leftover snacks because the restaurant had closed and the street had become a stream. Our arms ached, but no one complained. My father stared out the window at the roiling ocean. Finally we gave up and went to bed, tiptoeing across the squishy carpet.

By the next morning the air had grown calm. My father thought he could make it across the street where an *Open* sign hung crooked in the dirty front window. We were the only customers.

"Look," my mother said, holding out her hands. I saw that her wedding ring was bent and her knuckles were so red and swollen she could hardly hold the menu. I felt bad, but no one else seemed to care.

After a breakfast of fruit and dry cereal, we packed up and went home early. As we pulled out of the parking lot, the sun came out.

It was afternoon on Christmas Eve, our last in Atlanta. I lay on my bed, watching the sodden sky out the window, wondering how I could feel so bad without being sick. I wanted this Christmas to be better than last year's, so I told my friends not to call because I would be spending time with my family. The heaviness in the air, thick and invisible, made it hard to breathe. I wondered if Dirk and Eric could feel it. I heard them rustling around in their room, but they weren't making noise and jumping around like they usually did. They had brought me their presents to wrap for Mom and Dad. I wanted to help but I could not get up.

I pressed my face in the pillow and thought about my recent sleepover with Amy, a friend from the Governor's Honors Program we attended in Macon the previous summer. We went to the football game and dance at her school. The next morning, she was driving me home on the rain-slicked freeway when she lost control and the car swerved sharply to the left. It hit the median divider. Her hands flew up in the air. She screamed. I screamed. The car spun around, back and forth across four lanes, as brakes screeched and horns wailed behind us. With a final jolt we came to a stop, sideways but safe, on the shoulder.

"My parents!" I yelled into the stunned silence. Amy dropped her hands in her lap and looked at me, her mouth open.

"What?!" she said.

"My parents," I repeated, quieter this time.

"Why'd you say that?"

"Because they would kill me!"

"Weird," she said, shaking her head.

Why did I say that? I wondered as I smelled my pillow. How could I explain what came into my head at that moment? Of course I didn't think they would literally kill me, but they might be angry if I were hurt. Would they be happier if I were dead? Or if I had never been born? Possibly, but that wasn't the issue. I caused them so much trouble. The burdens they bore at Christmas were already so heavy. My father's deep plunge into morose silence. My mother's diligent efforts to lighten the pall and maintain the traditions. My job was not only to stay alive but also to spare them further agony. I had to protect them. A car accident was unacceptable.

The light outside the window was dimming. I rolled off the bed onto the floor and dug presents and wrapping paper from their hiding place. I had finished all but one when I ran out of Scotch tape and went into the study to look for more.

The smell of stale tobacco permeated the house, but this was its epicenter. To stand there, inhaling, was to acknowledge invasion of an inner chamber fraught with unseen perils, not guard dogs or bear traps but mind weapons, stockpiled and waiting. My father was here, towering, even when he wasn't. On this day, old smoke competed with a new scent: mustiness, trapped air from a moldy attic or basement. I was surprised to find open boxes scattered about. Boxes usually didn't appear until a week or two before the moving van arrived, and our move was months away.

I held my breath and rummaged. Mostly I found old faded books, threadbare at the edges, medical textbooks with thin pages of tiny type, electronics manuals. But at the bottom of one box I spotted something I had never seen before: a thick scrapbook with a gold squiggly design framing its brown cover. It was scuffed and tattered, its corners worn through.

How could I have missed this? I loved scrapbooks and picture albums. We had moved from Martinsburg to San Antonio to Kaiserslautern to Landstuhl to Rockville to San Antonio to here. I remembered all of those moves except the first. I had packed and unpacked boxes, made lists of contents, sorted and organized. Where had this been hiding? The scrapbook was nearly square and overstuffed. It couldn't have gotten lost among the bookcase books, which I knew by heart. I didn't think anyone else in our family kept scrapbooks, although I had started two of my own when I left my best friends behind and had trouble not crying.

I wasn't supposed to snoop, but I could not help myself. I sat cross-legged on the floor and opened the cover. On the first page was the Western Union telegram from July 26, 1950. I removed it from its envelope. "The Secretary of the Army has asked me to express his deep regret that your husband has been missing in action in Korea since 12 July 50," said the missive from Edward F. Witsell, the army's adjutant general.

I turned more pages and found more telegrams. My perfectionist mother had kept a meticulous record of my father's captivity in Korea. Letters from the War Department. Letters she wrote to my father early in his captivity that had been returned, marked "missing." Condolence notes. The picture from newspapers in Des Moines and Pittsburgh and South Bend—where relatives then lived—featuring the youthful, blond, lanky soldier, without his glasses but unmistakably my father, in the second row of troops.

A black-and-white *Life* magazine spread, grainy and bleak, is a long shot of riverside terrain dotted with men trekking uphill, guarded by other men with guns. The man in the first row on the left hangs his head down, his face hidden. His hair is thick and matted. His left hand is on his thigh, as if to help it gain the hill; his long fingers are splayed in a peculiar way that I recognize. On later pages are notes from friends and family around the country, including copies of the same picture with a note jotted in the margin: "Is this Pete?"

Turning the pages took my breath away. The volume was a treasure vault, feast for a starving heart, aloe for an open wound. Paging through such painstaking history was like finding the missing pieces of a blurry puzzle. I didn't remember my father being gone. My mother told me that when I was a baby he used to come home from work and toss me in the air, and indeed I had seen the pictures she kept of me, mischievous, grinning, squealing in his arms. But I didn't remember any of it.

Nervous about getting caught, I combed through as many pictures and envelopes as I dared. At some point, the letters my father wrote in prison camp had gotten through, but the salutations made no sense. "Dear Trish," some began. Who was Trish? Was my father confused? Had he had an affair? A previous wife? Lost his mind? I knew of no Trish in our family. No Patricia. My mother was Margaret Eleanor, Margy for short. Trish was not Meg, or Peg, or Peggy, or El or Ellie or any other version of my mother's name that I could think of. Who was Trish?

"Come set the table," my mother called up the stairs.

I startled. I had lost track of time. I didn't want to go downstairs. Of course we were having oyster stew, and my appetite for the slimy goobers had not improved. But the stew wasn't stewing yet, and the scent of fresh-baked angel food cake wafted up. I carefully replaced the scrapbook, desperate to recall its exact position, turned off the light, and made my way down the stairs.

High on my rich discovery, I floated into the tiny kitchen, which had three doorways and standing room for about two and a half people. I heard the oysters sizzling in butter. Serving dishes crowded the narrow counters. Tomorrow's cake, which had spent the afternoon suspended upside down over a bottle, had been removed from its pan and placed on the wind-up musical cake holder we used for birthdays.

My father was watching my mother as she bustled from counter to stove to sink. It was unusual to find both parents in the kitchen, and their togetherness made me feel cozy and welcome. My traditional holiday depression lifted a little as I basked in unexpected comfort. I opened the kitchen drawer to collect the silverware for the table.

"I have a question for you," I said to neither of them in particular. "I was looking at that Korea scrapbook up in Pop's room. How come those letters were written to Trish? Who's Trish?"

Instantly I knew I had made a mistake. My father, who had been gazing out the window, pivoted to face me. His face turned the color of the ash on the cigarette burning in the ashtray on the sill. His cheeks sucked hollow. Behind his glasses his eyes went beady, fixing me in their glare. His chin shook. Spittle bubbled. I froze. Even when his hand shot out and grabbed the cake plate and threw the cake against the wall, smashing it into an avalanche of sweet almond-flavored chunks, I did not move.

"Pete!" my mother cried. Her voice screamed more grief than anger. It was as if I left my body then, escaped into the corner of the ceiling, and watched. I saw that she, too, was stunned and helpless. She couldn't protect us, not really. So she simply steeled her face against his fury, turned her back and reached for the dishrag.

He faced me again, still shaking. I heard the air burning through his nostrils as he inhaled.

"Don't you ever, ever ask me anything like that again," he ordered, his voice taut, controlled. The colonel had spoken.

My mother baked another cake on Christmas Day. After the birthday dinner we ate it in silence, chewing with our mouths shut and resting our left hands politely on the napkins in our laps. After the holiday, we went back to school and work. In our spare time, we sorted through drawers and tossed what we didn't need. Every time we moved, I found fewer things that I cared about saving. I never asked again about Trish. The scrapbook disappeared. Whenever I was alone in the house I searched for it, but it wasn't to be found.

The acceptance letter from the University of Minnesota, my parents' alma mater, arrived while my parents were in Texas, looking for a house to rent for the year my father would be gone. I told them the news when they called. Although I hadn't visited Minneapolis since I was eight years old, I knew the choice would please them, and I could spend holidays with my relatives up north in Bemidji. Minnesota also had one of the country's best journalism schools. My mother insisted that I needed a trade to fall back on in case something unexpected happened to the husband I would no doubt have. Journalism was the only trade I could think of.

When I got off the school bus the next day, a tall package, addressed to me, was waiting on the doorstep. Inside were a dozen red roses and a note in some florist's handwriting: "Congratulations and good luck, Punky. We are proud of you. Minnesota should be another step to living. Much love, Daddy." I was taken aback, since a college acceptance letter seemed like military orders for the next move—in other words, nothing special. Red roses were my father's favorite gift, but he had only sent them to my mother in the past. I didn't deserve them.

I still wanted to be valedictorian, but three of us were tied academically. The faculty decided that we should each write a speech and audition it on stage before a committee who would make the final choice. "United we stand, divided we fall" was the theme of my speech, based on political solidarity and patriotic duty, which were among my father's favorite dinner table lecture themes. I did not question his views, nor did I write anything that examined my own thoughts or beliefs. Although antiwar sentiment was sweeping the country, loyalty plugged my ears. I wrote the speech for my father, through my father. The committee liked it best.

I wondered whether he would attend graduation. He hated crowds. He didn't go to kids' things, at least not often. He didn't play catch with my brothers or attend their baseball games. He didn't come to the senior class play, *The Mouse That Roared,* in which I had a minor role, stomping grapes, dressed in a Women's Army Corps uniform. When I was named second runner-up in our Miss Therrell High School spring pageant, wearing the blue velvet gown my mother had cried over, I stood on the stage scanning faces as people applauded. I could only make out those in the front row because I wasn't wearing my glasses, but I found out later that no one in my family had attended.

May 25, 1967, dawned hot and humid, sticky with dread. By midday my mouth was parched from nerves and speech rehearsals. I rolled bits of dried spit off my lips. I wondered where the podium stood in the huge convention center. I worried that I would trip over my long white gown. Or over my too heavy feet. My mother said I sounded like an elephant when I walked.

I rode downtown with friends and watched, awed by the yawning massiveness of the hall, as the graduation scheduled before ours ended. When it was our turn, we filed onto the stage, gowns swishing, and climbed the stairs to our risers. My riser was about halfway up, my place at the end of the row. My heart pounded through the processional and the invocation. When my name was called, I climbed carefully back down to the podium and set my sweaty paper on it. I looked out at the audience. I wore my glasses but couldn't see much because the lights were too bright and the people too many and too far away.

"Lord, let us stand for something, lest we fall for anything," I began. "Exposure to reality is often harsh, cold, and premature." I recited from memory, hearing the quaver in my voice as it bounced back through the speakers. At first, I ran out of breath before reaching the end of some of my sentences, but I got stronger as I went along.

*Many protests have been heard against our involvement in Vietnam.*

*Why are we there? Perhaps these dissenters do not realize that we are fighting to protect the very freedom which gives them the right to protest! Yes, we must stand for something. Many fall under the spell of communism, which suppresses the individual and attempts to manufacture a human machine in its place. We must not let ourselves fall.*

I invoked the Lord once more, and my speech was over. Shaking and drained, I climbed slowly back to my place.

When the ceremony ended and we filed out, friends shouted and hugged in a spirited swirl of released tension. I stood aside, trying to peer over everyone's head, aware that my intense, distracted, down-turned-mouth expression might make people think something was wrong when it wasn't. I just wanted to find my family.

There was my father, half a head above everyone else. My mother was with him, and my brothers, too. I let out the breath I hadn't realized I was holding and waved. They made their way toward me. My mother hugged me. My father looked down at me, not smiling. He had that anxious look he gets when he wants to be somewhere else.

"Did I do OK?" I asked. He nodded. Not a big nod, but good enough. We stood there for a few minutes but didn't say much.

"I guess we'll be going now. Don't forget your curfew," my mother said. "We leave for Texas before dawn."

"I won't forget. I'll be home by 2:00 a.m." I watched them snake back through the crowd and disappear.

Tonight was my last date with the college Jack, who took me to his favorite place across town and shared his beer as he set up his chemistry notebooks and studied for the next day's exam. I felt grown-up, sitting beside him on a tall stool in the bar's dim light, but also sad and bored. After we ate our hamburgers, he signed my yearbook: "I'll never forget you; love you forever."

We took the long way home, swinging by the all-night graduation party so I could hug my friends good-bye. We didn't stay long. My yearbook was already full of have-a-good-summer, raise-hell notes, and they were busy making plans for tomorrow's picnic and next week's dates and next fall's reunions. It was as if I had already left; they knew I would not be coming back this way.

Jack drove me back to the BOQ, where our family had taken up residence for one last night. He pulled into the parking lot and turned off the ignition. He put his arms around me and kissed me, long and slow, but we both kept glancing up at the lighted window, wondering whether my father was watching. We said good-bye, knowing that we might never see each other again, or maybe we would, depending. He walked me to the door and kissed me again, quickly this time. I watched him get in his car and pull away. Inside, the light was on but no one had waited up. I set my graduation cap and yearbook on my suitcase and lay back on the bed, still clothed, to wait for the alarm and consider all that had happened in Atlanta, where the door would soon shut. New doors would open in the next place, maybe to better times, maybe not. Tears came into my eyes, but I blinked them out and rubbed hard at my temples, trying not to sniffle so I wouldn't wake up my brothers in the next bed.

When the alarm rang, we got up and carried our suitcases to the car in the dark. The dampness in the still night air was cool and clammy. No one said anything except "ssshhh." We climbed into the car and tried not to slam the doors too loudly. My father backed it out of the parking lot. Three right turns, and we were off the post, going west, into our next life.

# 23

# Homeward Bound

## SEPTEMBER 1953

Once the armistice news had been digested and the celebratory cheering, crying, and dancing had subsided, no one could guess what would come next. Tension had eased, but confidence remained elusive. The prisoners dared not hope for much because they distrusted their captors. It wasn't long, however, before change was evident. More food arrived. So did mirrors, safety razors, and various Red Cross supplies that should have been distributed months before but were relatively useless now that POW life was almost over. The Chinese stayed in the game, matching America item for item whenever possible. Every time the guards handed out a carton of Camels with one hand, they handed out a carton of Chinese cigarettes with the other.

Doc continued to shake his head in frustration with what he considered lame excuses and circular reasoning. Finally armed with a copy of the armistice agreement, the officers confronted their guards. Why hadn't Red Cross teams been allowed to visit the camp, as the agreement had stipulated? They got no satisfactory answers—only conversations rigged to avoid embarrassing questions. *Sincere lies,* Doc called them. He considered negotiations with the Communists a complete waste of time. One day they would promise the cooks one hundred eggs. The next day they would deliver half that many. If anyone objected, they would say they'd agreed to fifty, not one hundred. *You can never win, so why bother trying?*

One morning soon after the anti-celebration, trucks rumbled into camp. A neutral team arrived to monitor the transfer, but its members were not allowed to converse with the men. The first contingent of prisoners, ragged but elated, climbed aboard for the ride to Manpo, where they boarded boxcars to make the trip to Kaesong. Massive war damage, including an entire field of destroyed trains, decorated their route. They took up residence in a tent city in Kaesong, eight men to a squad tent, all luxuriating in the roominess of their new quarters. They ate in a mess hall with tables and benches. They had hoped for good grub but didn't get it; the tasteless fare still disappointed. They sunbathed and killed time with games of bridge and volleyball.

Every day for about a month, some men left the camp. Every day, Doc waited for his turn. Finally, on September 5, 1953, the last day of repatriation, Doc climbed aboard the truck for a ride to the exchange point and Freedom Village. His first glimpse of the Stars and Stripes thrilled him.

Doc was evacuated through medical channels from Inchon to the 121st Evacuation Hospital in Yong Dong Po, just west of Seoul. He had lost four teeth and was infested with worms but apparently was otherwise physically healthy. In their last months of captivity under the Chinese Communists, who were eager to prove themselves compassionate captors, most of the survivors had regained some of the weight they had lost, although they still suffered from vitamin deficiencies.

From Korea, Doc was airlifted to Tokyo, where he visited friends and spent nine days easing back into society. But easing back wasn't easy. Like his buddies, he was plagued with worries. Did most Americans believe he and the other survivors were now Reds? Would the military try to re-indoctrinate him? What would he do if some interrogator accused him of being Red—take it or hit him? Was his wife bitter toward the Korean War and the army when he felt the opposite? Had she innocently joined some front organization or sent a letter to a senator "to bring her poor boy home"? What would happen—how would he react—if someone called the Korean War a foolish war? Or just a police action?

He decided that while he felt a strong allegiance to his country and the army, he was indeed bitter about a few things. Number one: Communists. Number two: the deplorable actions of many of his fellow prisoners, those who lied and stole, those who defied officers' orders, those who sold out their countrymen. He was hurt that the British soldiers, for example, displayed more unity and discipline than the Americans. And he thought the American military should have kept the returning prisoners longer, letting them tell their stories and reconnect with their buddies one last time for support and affirmation. They all obviously needed psychological help, but none of them got it.

His judgment during this time was perverted, he admitted later. Relatively minor things took on major importance. He thought it strange to be treated like an American, with rights and expectations. He watched men hardened by prison life break down and cry when a nurse performed a procedure as routine as taking a temperature or blood pressure reading. He took hours, even days, to work up the courage to ask for an aspirin because he didn't want to impose. He was afraid to leave the hospital for fear that he would do something wrong—what, he didn't know. If someone invited him to go somewhere, anxiety washed over him. What if he said something he shouldn't say? What if he wasn't accepted as an American? What if someone called him a traitor?

While Doc waited for medical clearance in Tokyo, my mother waited at home with me. I was about to turn four years old. By then, she must have become very used to waiting and not hoping for much because she had so often been disappointed. WEPM, the local radio station, sent her their Associated Press wire copy of the prisoner list as a memento. The army sent her a telegram saying Doc had been returned to U.S. control. Then she received a telegram from him, posted September 7, 1953:

DEAR TRISH AM ON MY WAY HOME HEALTH OK LOVE.

Three days later, she received another:

SUGGEST CATHY REMAIN EAST YOU COME WEST CALL TOKYO YOUR CONVENIENCE.

Yet another telegram from the army said he would need further treatment in an overseas hospital. She had read that seriously ill or injured prisoners were held in Japan. "Are you all right?" she asked over and over when the Tokyo call went through, using more than half their allotted minutes. He told her to stay put and wait; he would be home soon.

A letter arrived, written after the phone call. "A free man is writing a letter with his own pen, his own hand, and his own mind," Doc wrote, along with advice to avoid newspaper reporters and not cry over spilled milk. "My story of Korea—let it rest there. . . . I imagine I have changed but do not know how nor have any inclinations of such," he added, and signed off, above his name, "Your soldier husband and a hell of a proud American."

Local newspapers documented her news, and strangers helped when they could. The phone bill for $85.83, which included the $24 call to Tokyo, arrived in her mailbox marked "paid." The post office delivered one letter addressed simply to, "Mrs. Boysen, Martensburg [*sic*], West Virginia."

On September 18, a telegram arrived with news that Doc was flying into San Francisco; an earlier post had said he would arrive by boat. Mitzi and Jackie helped my mother pack me up with my things, and we made the three-hour drive to my aunt and uncle's farm in Pennsylvania, where I would stay, at my father's request, while my parents were reunited. "Our daughter is a stranger to me," he had written, "yet I don't want to hurt her."

My mother returned the next day to Martinsburg, where the phone was ringing as she unlocked the door. My father's plans had changed again, and he would be home earlier than expected. In fact, he was in Chicago, about to board his flight to Washington, D.C. She threw some clothes in her suitcase and drove two hours to National Airport. White-knuckled and dry-mouthed, she drove in circles around the parking lot, searching for an elusive empty spot. After finally finding one, she ran into the terminal and trotted down the concourse in her high heels, scanning the faces of tall, thin men in uniform.

"Hey, do you remember me?" asked a familiar voice behind her. She had sped right past the place where Doc stood, patiently waiting. How ironic, she thought, that after all the years she had spent waiting for him to come home, he was the one who ended up waiting for her.

They headed for the Lord Baltimore Hotel in Baltimore, where they had spent their honeymoon six years before, almost to the day. Six years married, three years apart. Neither was sure exactly where the hotel was—they prided themselves on the fact that they weren't citified—but they found it and checked in. After two days they checked out and drove to Pennsylvania, where they found me nursing stitches in my gashed eyebrow and not remembering the skinny man with worms and missing teeth who was my father.

"Oh, how blessed we were," my mother wrote, decades later.

After thirty-eight months and twelve days as a prisoner of war, Doc was home.

# 24

# Minneapolis, Minnesota

## 1970

Leaving home for college didn't mean leaving behind my father's stern admonitions. The sexual revolution was in full swing, but at the University of Minnesota, where I was majoring in international relations with a minor in Japanese, it had passed me by. In spring of my sophomore year, I fell in love with Jim, a premed student from International Falls, Minnesota, a paper-milling town near the Canadian border. His courting was earnest and respectful, and his bad puns made me laugh.

"He's smart, gentle, and kind, and he starts med school in the fall. I think he might be the one for me," I told my mother the day after I returned home from college that June. We were sitting across the table from each other in the dining room of an aging duplex perched on a bluff in Yokohama, where my family now lived in former navy housing. I was smoking a cigarette from the pack I had bought in the barracks at Travis Air Force Base in San Francisco. I had spent three days and nights queuing up for every departing troop flight, hoping to secure an open seat.

She seemed pleased, both by my announcement and by the fact that I had adopted her bad habit. Smoke curled up lazily from the ashtray she set between us. She took a puff and raised her eyebrows.

"Did you tell your father yet?"

"I will. I know he would like Jim. I can't not tell him—he'll be mailing my letters."

All our mail went through the APO address, in care of my father. For the past year he had been commanding officer at Kishine Barracks, where choppers landed several times daily to deliver wounded Vietnam vets to the one-thousand-bed hospital. I had a summer job in the steno pool there, typing mess hall menus on long, smelly mimeograph pages. He had undoubtedly pulled strings on my behalf. He and I drove to and from work in the compact Japanese family car, conversing about random subjects, often philosophical, seldom personal. He mostly talked, and I mostly listened.

Our routine rarely varied. After supper and dishes, I jogged, traversing the steep hills near our house, once falling and gouging my knee so deeply I had to quit running for a week. I read library books, listened to vintage radio shows, and wrote to everyone I knew. I wrote Jim at least weekly, neat cursive on page after page of pale pastel onionskin stationery. Jim wrote often, too, detailing his summer job at the paper mill and reporting considerable despair over my absence.

Every day at lunch, I peeked into my father's office to see whether a letter had arrived.

"Not today," he would sometimes tell me, looking crestfallen and watching my face. Then he would pull out a familiar blue envelope and wave it in the air with a grin.

Sex and virginity consumed my thoughts that summer. Literary sex scenes made me ache with longing. When our family and friends climbed Mount Fuji and spent the night with strangers in a one-room shelter near the summit, I couldn't take my eyes off a well-traveled Scandinavian couple about my age who were clearly sleeping together. I so envied them. But so far, the fear of breaking my father's rules had outweighed my urges. I was still a good girl.

Jim had graciously accepted my haughty insistence on keeping my legs together, as my father put it, as if to shock me with his crassness. Instead of falling into bed when I returned to college in the fall, we got secretly engaged. In October we celebrated with a dinner we couldn't afford at Charlie's, a venerable restaurant where most locals, including my parents, toasted special occasions. Even then I held onto my resolve. But on Thanksgiving, after his roommates vacated the apartment and we cooked a modest dinner and shared a bottle of Mateus, neither of us could hold out any longer.

The next day, we hovered in the drugstore aisles, giggling as he rehearsed asking the pharmacist for condoms. Now that we had started doing it, we did not plan to stop. When the student health service reopened the following Monday, I called to get my name on the long list for birth control appointments.

I sat on the cold steel examining table in a stifling room in the student health center. Sticky inside the paper gown, I held the drape across my lap and dangled my feet, waiting for the doctor to knock on the door. Outside it was March 1970, still cold enough for parkas and boots, hats and mittens, and here I sat, sweating like August. My stomach churned. I'd had to wait four months to get a diaphragm, taking my turn in a long line of unmarried women seeking birth control services, a new student offering in these feminist times.

A quick rap on the door and the knob turned. With two medical students trailing, the doctor strode in, white coat flapping, brusque with efficiency. He had short dark hair and square black-framed glasses perched precipitously on his small nose. He didn't smile.

"Feet up and push back," he said, pulling out the stirrups. I did as I was told.

"How are you feeling?"

"OK. I was having some stomach problems a while back, but I've been fine lately."

I had, in fact, visited the health service more than once since Thanksgiving, since throwing up suddenly after eating my roommate's revered chili. Something was not right. I could not stand the smell of Gain detergent, and fatigue wiped me out at night, long before bedtime. I had gotten used to the depression that set in before Christmas and held me captive during the long nights of winter, but this was different.

"Could I maybe be pregnant?" I had asked during that first visit.

"No." The doctor was emphatic. I had been seen the previous year for amenorrhea and had been warned that getting pregnant would be difficult.

"Couldn't we at least do a test?"

"Not necessary."

Instead, he sent me to X-ray. I spent most of a morning choking down barium, gagging, and trying not to vomit while the technicians checked out my upper digestive tract. They found nothing and sent me home. When I returned with the same complaints a few weeks later, the doctor, sure that upcoming finals were creating stress, referred me to the psychiatric clinic. Eventually the symptoms eased on their own.

Now here I was again.

"Ouch!" The gynecologist's fingers were probing so deep I squirmed in pain.

His fingers still inside me, he laughed in my face.

"So what was it you came in for?"

"A diaphragm. I guess."

"Well, you're not going to be needing that anytime soon," he said, still chuckling as he turned toward the students, who smiled uncertainly.

"Why not?"

"Because you're, oh, about three months pregnant."

"Oh." I could not breathe or look at him. My mouth was so dry my lips stuck together.

"I'll send the nurse in," he said as he ushered the students out the door. I lay on the table, staring at the ceiling squares, shocked into new being. Somehow I had known all along. I was scared. Also excited. And relieved. At least I wasn't crazy.

"How did it go?" Jim asked as I climbed into his car an hour later, after I had gotten dressed, sat gingerly on a straight-backed chair while the nurse delivered endless instructions I didn't hear, and found a pay phone to call him.

"You better put September fifteenth on your calendar."

"What?"

"Put September fifteenth on your calendar."

"You mean you can't get birth control until then?"

"No. September fifteenth. It's the due date."

His face went pale as he understood. He pulled over, and we hugged in numb silence.

My numbness wore off quickly, as if there were no time to waste in ushering in My Life, Next Phase. In an odd way I was deliriously happy. I loved Jim. I had always wanted kids and was afraid I couldn't have them. Now I would, even though the timing was horrid. He had three years of medical school left after this one. I had one more year of college, expensive because I was paying out-of-state tuition, and I was considering Columbia University for grad school. We had been arguing about wedding dates. He had wanted to get married next year, but I had wanted to wait until my parents moved back to the States, probably two years off. At least that was settled; it would have to be soon. We told our friends, who seemed happy for us and not surprised. Jim's parents were upset and disappointed. His aunts, however, hosted a baby shower for the extended family, explaining that everyone knows that second babies take nine months to arrive, but first babies come whenever they please.

I wrote my parents a letter, agonizing over the wording on a practice pad before penning the real thing. I stamped and sealed the envelope, then pictured my father receiving it at work. I grabbed the pen again and wrote on the back: "Please sit down before you read this."

Then we waited. The mail would take days to reach Yokohama through APO San Francisco. I didn't want to think about it because thinking about it gave me a stomachache. I had been feeling much better. I was feeling great, in fact, sleeping well and enjoying guilt-free sex. The phone rang one evening while I was scrubbing macaroni and cheese from a stubborn pan. The apartment was quiet, windows closed to the still-freezing dark. My roommates were studying on their beds in their bedrooms down the hall. I picked up.

"We got your news." My mother's voice was cold, pained. I could tell she had been crying. "Your father wants to talk to you."

I could hear the signal whooshing soft, then loud, coming in on ocean waves. Transoceanic phone calls were expensive and rare. Since moving to Japan, my parents had never called me.

"Who was it?" My father spit words like tacks. "Some guy you picked up at a party on Saturday night?"

"Of course not. It's Jim. You know all about him and how we feel about each other. What are you talking about?"

He didn't answer. I pictured him thrusting the phone at my mother. She took it and issued the orders. The wedding would happen as soon as possible, and we would invite only close friends and Bemidji family. There would be no invitations, only announcements engraved from plates the old-fashioned, expensive way, not offset type in the current style. She would come early to help me shop for a dress. In the meantime, I should watch my mailbox for a letter. Or two, as it turned out.

The first letter arrived a few days later, three typewritten pages of anguished prose that returned often to "hard, cold facts" and the "hard, cold reality" of my selfish act.

"You have to sit down and realize that the jig is up for you," my father wrote. "Education of yourself has been sacrificed, and it would be foolish to sacrifice the education of your husband, but all of this falls upon the shoulders of the two of you. . . . Income from us is against our principles and therefore out of the question." I could, however, keep the money I had already received for spring quarter tuition as well as a small savings account intended for graduation.

And the wedding could not be procrastinated.

"You may not agree with the timing of getting married, the way it is accomplished and many other factors . . . but it is now your turn to listen so that no more damage is accomplished. The damage is not to you, but to others, to your father, your mother, and your brothers."

The "quiet" wedding was to be on Saturday, March 28, during spring break. If we couldn't make that work for some reason, I was supposed to call. The letter also contained pledges of love and support, flowery, God-bless pledges that I read but could not feel. Around the margins my mother had penned further instructions: get a license, check on blood tests, find a minister.

The next letter, written two days later, was also from my father, "the last letter written to my daughter for she should soon become someone else's wife." I must have asked for his forgiveness earlier, because he said it wasn't about him forgiving me, but about me forgiving him.

"I have to ask you to understand the problems and tribulations of your father," he wrote. "I am sure you realize that it is my conviction that there is little lower that a man can do to a person such as you than your future husband has done. It reveals a lack of character that is despised by the lowest sailor, the raunchiest soldier, and the finest physician and officer that the world has known."

In his eyes, I had chosen the animal he feared, but Jim was nothing like the animal he described. I knew my father was wrong, yet his criticism tore at my soul.

He explained how I had destroyed my mother's trust, hope, and expectations, but I should keep my chin up nevertheless, no matter how hard and difficult my life would be. He insisted that I felt bitterness and remorse, despite my claim that I did not feel those things.

"Don't kid yourself, my love," he wrote, "you have and you will, and at times life will look awful black to you because of it."

But black hardly described my life. The tips of jonquils were starting to push through the earth in sun-warmed garden beds, and at night I lay in Jim's arms, our fingers playing lightly over my softening abdomen, wondering when we would feel the first stirring. Boy or girl? Either would thrill us. I longed to visit the baby section of Dayton's department store, to drool over the onesies and little socks, but knew it was bad luck this soon. Something could go wrong. I wanted nothing to go wrong.

At Dayton's the following Saturday, Jim and I paged through sample books in the stationery department. The patient saleswoman tried to convince us to spend substantially less on offset printing, challenging us to detect the difference between that and engraving, but I didn't dare commit another sin. She shook her head at my stubbornness. Jim set his lips but remained silent.

At J. B. Hudson's we bought gold wedding bands, $25 for his and only $15 for mine, because the fourth finger of my left hand was very slender. The ring looked beautiful on it.

We also visited the Fort Snelling Officers' Club. The stone fireplace and expansive Minnesota River valley view created a lovely venue for a traditional wedding reception, but ours was shotgun, and the rental fee was high. Instead we scheduled the chapel at the Naval Air Station, where we liked the affable chaplain but suspected he didn't often, or ever, do weddings. He had us fill out questionnaires and insisted on premarital counseling sessions, which we dutifully attended without sharing our secret. He predicted a good match.

Three days before the wedding, we drove to the airport and parked in the (cheaper) long-term lot. Already I was tracking every cent we spent in a small black notebook with red binding and blue-lined pages. We had visited the university's financial aid office to apply for loans, but we didn't qualify because both sets of parents could afford to pay. That they declined to do so made no difference. Even if we were careful, I would have to drop out for a year until I qualified as a state resident. We planned to work odd jobs during vacations and summers.

My stomach somersaulted as we headed down the concourse to the gate. My mother's plane was on time. We watched it pull in and roll to a stop. I brushed my hair out of my eyes with the little brush I brought in my coat pocket. Jim waited somewhere behind me as I leaned forward, scanning the line of passengers beginning to emerge.

There she was, in a tailored wool coat, striding purposefully up the ramp, her face sharp and taut under her tight cap of permanent-set curls.

"Mom!" I called. "Welcome!" I ran to her with my arms open but stopped short. She wasn't in a hugging mood. She looked not at my face but down at my stomach, visible under my unzipped coat but still flat, revealing no sin. Then she looked at Jim, who was trying to introduce himself. She looked away in disgust. Now I wanted to vomit. Without a word, she set off toward the baggage claim as we followed in punished silence.

The next morning I felt like a good-will ambassador, gushing about my splendid city, my treasured friends, our favorite places. This had been my mother's college town, but she wasn't interested in new retail, entertainment, and dining choices. She had never heard of Target, and she didn't care. We had serious shopping to do, and we would rely on old standbys, like Young Quinlan and Harold's, where she hoped we would find decent wedding apparel.

I had already helped Sandy, my maid of honor and roommate since freshman year, choose a pattern and fabric to sew her dress on a borrowed machine. I hadn't given much thought to mine. Growing up, I had gone to slumber parties where other girls aired their wedding dreams while rolling their hair on juice cans and slathering Pond's on their faces, but rollers hurt my head, I hated the smell of Pond's, and despite my best efforts, I couldn't think of anything to add to the gown discussion. I was more inclined to read the novel I had stuck in my pillowcase.

My mother and I left early to traipse through downtown stores through most of a day that quickly blurred into queasiness and failure. I was hungry—always hungry, desperately trying to heed her stern command to gain no more than ten pounds during the pregnancy—and unsteady when I stood too long. She searched racks of dresses while I searched for a place to sit. I had begun by taking her to the bridal shop on Nicollet Mall, but she refused to go in.

"No," she said, shaking her head. "You don't deserve to wear white."

*White*, I thought, *never looked good on me anyway.*

So I searched for colors I loved. I found a light blue beauty, its bodice fitting but modest, its skirt a forgiving drape of soft fabric. It was my size and not expensive. It made me feel like dancing. I held it up to my waist, twirled around and smiled at her.

"How much?" she said. I told her.

"Too cheap. And it's not right."

I put it back on the rack. *This wasn't my dress we were looking for*, I began to realize. It was ours. Not just hers and mine, but my father's too, because she harbored him behind her eyes, his disapproval hijacking any compassion she might have had. Searching became rote. We went to one rack, then the next, through one store, then another. I would show her something and if she said yes, I would try it on. We finally settled on a two-piece suit-type dress with an A-line skirt, mid-knee length, and buttoned long-sleeved jacket. It was a nice-enough light green, although I didn't particularly like green, and the brushed satin fabric spoke quality. Next, she said, I needed a hat, but she let me buy a feathered headband instead.

My wedding morning dawned crisp and sunny, precious spring light sneaking in under the apartment window shades. I poured a bowl of cold cereal and sat down to eat.

"Don't you have eggs?" My mother's voice was cold.

"Sure," I said, praying there were eggs in the refrigerator. "Want me to fix you one?"

"I'll do it."

I sat at the table, facing the window, listening to the kitchen and bathroom clatter, as my roommates snacked and showered and blow-dried their hair. I missed Jim, who had spent the night with his former roommates. But sitting there, watching the cars go by on University Avenue, I felt content, almost blissful, excited about the day and the new life it would launch. Last night we'd had the rehearsal dinner—although no rehearsal occurred—at Jax Café, my new favorite special-treat restaurant, which stamped our names on the matchbooks at each place. Our friends, including Corwin, the charming, wacky best man who had flown in from Arizona (and who was, coincidentally, the son of my father's favorite frat brother), made sure the occasion was festive, with much laughter and many toasts. I declined the alcohol, which tasted terrible, but finished everyone's chocolate pudding.

The phone rang. Sandy picked it up.

"It's for you," she said, handing it to my mother.

My mother took it but remained impassive. "Yes . . . Fine . . . We'll see." Then she motioned to me with the phone. "Do you want to talk to your father?"

I nodded and took the receiver, stretching the cord around the corner of the kitchen, where I could huddle in semiprivacy. He had stayed home in Japan, claiming that he wasn't allowed to leave, military orders, a war on.

"Hi, Pop." I heard the whoosh of the open line but nothing else. My hand shook. "Are you there?"

I thought I could hear him breathing but wasn't sure.

"It's a beautiful day. I wish you were here," I said. I was being honest. The ocean between us felt vast and cold, too deep to navigate.

He said nothing. I could hear my heart thumping. Cheerios swirled uneasily in my stomach.

"It's going to be OK, really," I tried again. Nothing.

I went back around the corner, my hand over the mouthpiece. "He won't talk to me," I told my mother. She took the phone, turned away, and murmured into it for a minute before she said good-bye and hung up. I went down the hall to take my turn in the bathroom.

The wedding was short and anticlimactic. My uncle from Bemidji walked me down the aisle as my cousin snapped black-and-white pictures. Jim and I "pledged thee our troth," stifling our giggles at such an odd word. We were late joining our guests for cake at the apartment afterward because I made him stop at the Dairy Queen for a Brazier burger. My mother left the following day after lecturing us about needing to find a new apartment. Dutifully, we found a tiny furnished place with a couch, desk, table, two chairs, chest of drawers, and bed. The living room was barely long enough to accommodate the couch against the wall, and anyone sitting on the couch could stretch their legs and reach the opposite wall with their feet. But I was proud to write home with our new address.

We got two letters back. In his one-page letter to Jim, my father said he was "more than willing to communicate and do everything in my power to make your life a success," but he also reiterated his credo: "Your standard of character is not mine, our definitions of love do not coincide, and your assessment of the impact inherent in your past decision fails to recognize the reality of the consequences that both of us must now face with courage." He accused Jim of not only hurting me, but also potentially destroying my father's career and adversely affecting assignments and promotions.

In a long, rambling letter to both of us, he gave instructions. I was not to write my name or return address on any letters we sent. By doing so, we would create serious problems with serious results. But we shouldn't shed tears over this.

These letters confused me. I grew up worshipping this giant man, the war hero, he of lofty language and long reach. I wanted to take his side and mostly I had, blindly and boldly belting out his arguments. But honor and obedience no longer felt right, especially when it meant I would inflict pain on someone else I loved and believed in. I couldn't reconcile this conflict, these two sets of high standards—in my mind, the same high standards—that somehow didn't match.

Six months later, in early September, the doorbell rang in our new apartment at 2600 Portland Avenue. I groaned. I had just lowered my aching loins into the warm water of the cramped bathtub. I knew I shouldn't be groaning because we were lucky to be here, lucky to find a place big enough for a real bedroom instead of an alcove behind a curtain, lucky to have reduced rent in exchange for managing the building's many apartments.

*Ding-dong, ding-dong.*

"I'm coming," I yelled through thin walls as I struggled into my postpartum paraphernalia and pants. Our precious Kristin, as pretty and perfect a baby as I had ever seen, had arrived two weeks early on a sunny Sunday morning, weighing exactly six pounds and interrupting

206 • THE WAR CAME HOME WITH HIM

Jim's best-ever day driving taxi. While I spent five days in the hospital with her after she developed jaundice, Jim's friends helped him pack and move. Boxes in random piles still cluttered the living room.

*Knock knock knock.*

"Yes! Just a minute!" I peeked at Kristin, asleep in a dresser drawer lined with towels. We didn't have a crib yet. Or a bed either. We slept spooned on an ancient green couch we had found at a garage sale, with a back that laid down flat, stuffing towels over the exposed springs and draping a sheet over us.

I opened the door slightly, reluctant to reveal the chaos or the baby. Two tall black men in their early twenties, one with a beard and baseball cap, the other with a stained shirt hanging down over baggy pants, stood there.

"We want to see the apartment for rent," said the one with the beard.

"OK, just let me get the key." I scanned the mess of dishes on the counter and books piled on the small table. The keys must be there somewhere. Feeling eyes on my back, I tried to hurry.

I found the keys and rental applications stashed in the silverware drawer. I skipped shoes—I couldn't remember where I'd left them—and went out into the hall barefoot, closing the door behind me. I led the men upstairs and waited while they looked around the empty apartment, hoping they wouldn't try the toilet in case it was one of the plugged ones. The bathroom was grimy and the living room carpet soiled. Our building was one of two on this corner, not in the best area of town; there had been a recent shooting in the other one. I wondered where our name ranked on the student housing waiting list at the university. Couples with babies got moved to the top, so we had called from the recovery room to announce our changed status.

"So if we decide we want it, then what?" asked the baggy pants man as we went back downstairs. I was supposed to have them come in and fill out an application, but I was so tired that all I could think about was climbing back into the warm bathwater, hoping it would soothe my sore bottom and nipples and maybe let me doze, head against the cold tile.

"Here, take these." I thrust the applications into their hands. "Fill them out, then slide them under my door, and we'll call you." Somehow I knew I wouldn't hear from them again.

Days blurred into nights and nights back into days as we took on life with child, attempting to merge our new responsibilities with apartment caretaking and medical school. Jim couldn't go back to driving cab because the shifts were too long, so he took a job mopping floors instead, extending his long days of labs and classes. He arrived home weary, the hollows under his eyes dark with sleep deprivation, and sighed as he read my list of tenant complaints. The phone rang often, interrupting naps and breastfeeding. I had declined the then-routine antilactation shot because we had no money for formula.

"How is she?" Jim asked, peering down into the drawer that night.

"Fine. Beautiful. Hungry. She's still eating every two hours or so."

"That's normal, I suppose, for a six-pounder. And how are you?"

"OK," I mumbled as I laid cheese slices on bread for dinner.

But I wasn't OK. I was biting my lip and trying to keep my voice even. I was exhausted and lonely, worried about being confined through the interminable Minnesota winter. My fingers were raw from wringing out diapers. Every day or two, I lugged the heavy, stinking diaper pail and a handful of quarters down to the basement laundry room, praying for an empty washer. When the diapers were clean I carried them out behind the building and hung them on a rusty clothesline. It was the only time I left the apartment, except for the mail runs. Jim must have been reading my mind.

"So what came in the mail?"

"Nothing. Nothing today." Or yesterday. Or the day before. No acknowledgment from my parents that Kristin had arrived safely, making us a family. Kristin was nearly a month old, a precious, beautiful grandchild, and we had heard nothing.

Every day after lunch, I listened for the mailman. The mailboxes were down a half flight of stairs at the other end of the building, but if I paid attention in the midafternoon quiet (we had no TV), I could hear the jangle of keys and metallic clunk of the mailbox face as it opened and closed. Every day, as I grabbed the key from its hook by the kitchen window and ran down to open our box, I was sure it would be there. A card with a pink envelope. A little gift, neatly wrapped in brown paper, that fit into the oblong space. A notice that the post office was holding a bigger package. But every day was like today. The box was empty.

Jim shook his head. I hung mine. We had used up our words on this subject. I poured a can of tomato soup into a pan and slid the sandwiches under the broiler.

The phone rang.

"Who would that be?" Jim asked. Another clogged toilet, I knew he was thinking.

"I have no idea."

He picked up the receiver. "Hello? Yes, this is he." He kept saying yes, nodding his head, and promised to call back as soon as possible. He hung up and smiled at me.

"You won't believe this," he said.

"What?"

"A place opened up in student housing."

"But they said it would be at least three months and probably more like six."

"I know. But they said they'd gone down through the list and everyone else had declined. Now we have to decide whether to take it and get back to them by tomorrow."

"By tomorrow? How can we possibly decide by tomorrow? We just took a caretaking job. We can't just leave."

"I know."

I smelled burning bread crusts and ran to rescue them. I had lost my appetite. We had a chance to move out of this place, with its annoying tenants and questionable neighborhood. Student housing would be cheap, $82 a month including utilities, with a free bus to campus and plenty of friends for Kristin to play with. I would have people to talk to. But how could we make this work?

We tossed and turned on the hard little couch that night. We decided that we could leave only if we found someone to take our place, so we made a list of friends who might know someone. Jim said he would beg for more time, given the circumstances.

Somehow, beyond all reason, the pieces fell into place. We felt bad, breaking the news to the owners, but they seemed pleased with our replacements.

A week later, on the day our friends arrived to help us move—again—I saw the whisper-thin letter leaning against the small window of our mail slot, its pale blue air mail tint distinctive and taunting. I didn't hurry to get the key. By now I had gotten the message without seeing it typed in my mother's italic font. It wasn't until the last box was sealed that I went to retrieve it. I sat on the hallway staircase and slit it open.

There were no congratulations. Just news of home, weather, and a few sentences expressing relief that it was finally over, the evil deed was done, and now we could all move on. Yes, I thought as I stuck it into my pocket like a knife into my too-sore heart, it's done. We're moving on, we three who love each other madly. Thank God.

The garden-level two-room student housing apartment was clean and ready. The green couch anchored one end of the main room, and a bookcase of scavenged bricks and boards separated it from the other, where a miniature fridge and stove, sink, and small square of countertop lined up to define kitchen. A weekend garage-sale run had yielded a $5 crib and a compact chest of drawers for $15. Along with the new bed we'd ordered with our wedding gift money, that was all the furniture that would fit into the tiny bedroom.

"Just wait a minute, honey!" the frowzy woman who sold us the crib had said as we struggled to collapse the sides and load it into the trunk of our blue Impala. She grabbed my arm. "Don't go yet." She ran back into her modest rambler, where I had inspected the baby decorations still adorning the nursery walls although her youngest was five. In a few minutes she was back, thrusting a long cardboard box, stenciled in blue, into my arms.

"I just want you to have this. Open it." She grinned at me.

I opened the box. Nestled in tissue paper folds were the carved wooden pieces of a Mother Goose mobile, hand-painted in pinks and blues, that revolved around a music box. It reminded me of the finely crafted ornaments I had admired in Germany.

"Wind it up," she said, taking the box so I could reach in. Lullaby notes lilted in the afternoon air as Kristin stirred in her pink plastic infant seat, purchased for $1.

"I can't take this," I said. "It's beautiful, but it seems very special. You'll want to give it to your kids someday, for their babies."

"No, no, you need to have it. I want you to. I know you'll take good care of it, and I just have a feeling it's meant to be yours." She pushed the box back into my arms.

"Are you sure?"

She nodded. "Oh, yes."

"Thank you," I said. "It will mean a lot to me."

She hugged me. Just for a second, I felt like her daughter.

# 25

# Lawton, Oklahoma

## JANUARY 1955

The last day of January dawned cool and drizzly in Fort Sill, although faint afternoon sun would warm the South Plains home of the U.S. Army Field Artillery School to more than sixty degrees. The wind blew fiercer than the day before, gusting to twenty-six miles per hour. Doc held onto his hat as he strode across the post to the building that housed the military courtroom. His legs were khaki in pressed uniform pants, his out-turned feet decisive as they drummed the pavement in well-polished shoes. His insignia gleamed. It was his turn to testify in the court-martial of a fellow prisoner accused of collaborating with the Communists.

The previous November, the army had charged Maj. Ambrose Nugent, now forty-four, with thirteen offenses. The veteran officer, a fellow Midwesterner from Merrill, Wisconsin, was thirteen years older than Doc and had twenty-four years of military service. He had joined the army at the age of nineteen and survived the D-Day landing in Normandy in World War II. He had volunteered to go to Korea with the first contingent of troops and, like Doc, was among the first prisoners captured in July 1950.

Things didn't look good for Nugent, the fifth army man to face a court-martial so far. Air force officials had declined to prosecute, due to duress and other extenuating circumstances, any of the eighty-three Korean War survivors whose cases they had investigated, but army commanders believed it "important to establish a principle that men who violated the military code while prisoners of war would face trial after release," as the *New York Times* put it. Letting offenders off easy, they feared, would also undermine the sacrifices of those who had refused to break under torture.

The previous February, PFC Rothwell Floyd, then twenty-eight, was put on trial at Fort Leavenworth, Kansas. The London, Kentucky, native had been taken into custody nearly four months earlier, on October 30, 1953, two days after his wedding. He faced six allegations, including hitting an officer who ordered him back into line when cigarettes were being issued (and who later died in prison camp), mistreating his fellow prisoners, larceny, and murder. In April 1954, he was acquitted of murder but convicted of striking an officer, mistreatment, and larceny. He was sentenced to forty years at hard labor.

In May that year, Corporal Edward Dickenson, twenty-three, from Cracker's Neck, Virginia, went on trial for collaborating with the enemy and informing on a fellow prisoner who planned to escape. The court-martial was held at Fort McNair in Washington, D.C., where the Army–McCarthy hearings were in session nearby. It prompted hundreds of letters from sympathetic citizens begging the army to pardon Dickenson despite the fact that he was one of the twenty-three "nonrepatriates" who initially opted to stay with the Communists instead of returning to America. Dickenson changed his mind and came home, as did all but two of the others. He was sentenced to ten years' imprisonment at hard labor.

In September, Corporal Claude Batchelor, twenty-two, from Kermit, Texas, went on trial at Fort Sam Houston. Also one of the nonrepatriates, he had been in custody since March and was charged with six allegations, including communicating with the enemy and informing on a fellow prisoner. He was found guilty and sentenced to life in prison.

The first officer to be court-martialed for collaboration was Lt. Col. Harry Fleming, who had been incarcerated in May 1954, and went on trial in August at Fort Sheridan, Illinois. He faced seven counts of "willfully, unlawfully and knowingly" collaborating with the Communists. Fleming, forty-six, who was born in Canada and hailed from Racine, Wisconsin, was accused of leading discussion groups, writing pamphlets, making propaganda broadcasts and the like, while he was the commanding officer at Camp 12, known as Traitors' Row. He was also accused of sitting on Corporal Robert Gorr's foot during a truck ride, and "got rude about it" when told to get off, Gorr testified.

Fleming had defended his participation in alleged collaborative activities. "What I did, I did for the benefit of all in camp. Many of those who came back alive, as well as some of my accusers, would be buried in a Korean hillside except for some of the policies I went through with," he told the court. After deliberating for eleven hours, they sentenced him to dismissal from the service and forfeiture of all pay and allowances—the equivalent, for enlisted men, of a dishonorable discharge. He vowed to clear his name and later appealed his case, but the sentence stood.

No doubt aware of all these proceedings, Doc was prepared to do his part. He had his own piece of the story to tell. For months he had returned home in San Antonio late at night, after rising before the sun and spending long hours in the operating room at Fort Sam Houston's Brooke Army Medical Center. He would eat the dinner my mother kept warm in the oven, scoop vanilla ice cream from the cardboard bucket, smother it in Hershey's syrup, and savor every spoonful as he mused on the task ahead. Page by page, he had typed his story on the Royal portable, thinking carefully before he wrote because it was too hard to correct the carbon copy, and calling out occasional words to my mother. He was a meticulous surgeon, but he couldn't spell. The finished document was sixty-nine pages, single-spaced, with final corrections noted in pencil in the margins and on the backs of the translucent onionskin paper. It began with my mother's distressed phone call. It ended with: "It was a fortunate opportunity to be a prisoner. I hope that I may someday repay the privilege of surviving."

Although no fan of the media, Doc had gotten a share of the attention. His homecoming had been documented in local and hometown newspapers, sometimes with pictures. His residency at Brooke was announced in the press. The previous June, he and four other medical officers—Maj. Clarence Anderson, Maj. Sidney Esensten, Capt. Gene Lam, and Capt. William Shadish—had presented a professional paper at the American Medical Association meeting in San Francisco that documented their POW experiences and attracted considerable national coverage. In medical terms, the survivors described the boiled weeds that served as food, the saltwater eyelid injections that the Chinese medics used to treat glaucoma, the short needles attached to spring vibrators that they used to cure headaches and back pain, and the peculiar practice of using bile from the gallbladders of butchered pigs to remedy vitamin deficiencies. In his part of the presentation, Doc assured the assembled group that virtually all the prison camp deaths were caused, either directly or indirectly, by starvation, exposure, or harassment.

Medical maltreatment was not the issue he expected to address today at Fort Sill. Communism was the subject at hand, and Doc loathed it. The enemy's attempts to indoctrinate U.S. prisoners—brainwashing— was much on the minds of their fellow Americans, especially now that the McCarthy hearings dominated the news. While Doc and most of his compatriots considered these prison camp efforts lame, even laughable, some of the prisoners had indeed cozied up to their captors. These Red Star Boys were despised by many.

Nugent's trial was beginning its second week, and counsel would be addressing count number five, accusing him of signing and circulating petitions at a peace rally at Camp 7 in May 1951. Doc was the trial's seventh witness. The week before, Sgt. Marvin Talbert had testified that Nugent had offered to help his captors when one of them pointed a pistol at his head and said "sayonara." Nugent's response, according to Talbert, was to plead: "Me a personnel officer. Me can help you. Me got wife and kids." Nugent, however, told reporters that he didn't remember Talbert.

Another witness, Sgt. Minford Stearns, had testified that Nugent told him it was OK to make propaganda speeches as long as he remembered to say later that his captors had made him do it. Master Sgt. Harvey Bailey had testified that Nugent and three noncommissioned officers had been threatened: if they didn't write a propaganda broadcast in the next ten minutes, sixty-three men would be shot. Nugent's actions saved those men, Bailey said, recounting Nugent's words: "Being the ranking officer, for the good of all I will write the article."

Doc was ushered into the military courtroom, where he faced nine officers on the court-martial board. He was sworn in. He sat in the witness chair, laced his deft fingers together in his lap, and answered the first questions.

"I was captured on 12 July 1950 near Chochiwon, South Korea. I was with the 21st Regiment, 24th Division. I was detailed as a battalion aid surgeon," he began. By now he had shared these details over and over, in formal statements, affidavits, and a deposition elicited in December by Nugent's defense counsel, Maj. Robert E. Hough.

Prompted by counsel, he explained that he met Nugent on or about July 25 and that they shared a room from then until May 1951. Nugent had been the camp supply officer and had generally performed his job well, given the circumstances.

"How many were in your group?"

"About seven hundred, sir."

"And how many survived that first winter?"

"About half. Sickness and death became the order of the day," Doc said, adding that deaths numbered about eight a day during that time. Of the thirty-seven officers, fourteen survived, including Nugent, commanding officer Dunn, and himself.

In cross-examination that a local newspaper reporter deemed the most scathing of the trial so far, Hough focused on the peace rally that took place in May 1951. It was held in a room that was mostly bare except for a few ramshackle chairs and banners with Red slogans on the walls. Committee leaders sat in front, and Korean officials sat in back. Prisoners sat on the floor. Doc explained that he was late for the meeting, and that when he arrived, Nugent was reading a letter from Kim Il-sung, president of the Republic of North Korea, which said the Koreans were happy to give permission for the rally. Nugent then read the petition that the soldiers were asked to sign, a petition that was "so derogatory to myself, my fellow soldiers, and my country," Doc said, that the prisoners roared in protest. The peace committee of twelve huddled to consider the matter.

"How were these men selected?"

"I do not know."

"Wasn't Colonel Dunn actually sitting on the podium at the front of the room between Lieutenant Zimmerman and Captain Green?" asked Hough.

"I don't think so, sir, but I might be wrong."

"Didn't Colonel Dunn read one of these peace petitions when you were in another POW camp at Pyongyang?"

"Not to my knowledge, sir."

"Your memory is hazy on that one, eh?"

Doc spoke in monotones, emotion withheld. He thought before he spoke, staring out over the shoulder of his questioner.

2

"I'm just asking you a question in plain Arkansas language, Doctor," Hough exclaimed after one such hesitation.

Doc delivered his answers as if he were dictating a medical chart, straightforward, no nonsense, upright, at attention. But he was unwilling to presume too much authority. "It was my opinion," he would begin. Or "My impression was . . ."

"Avoid general terms. State the facts as you remember them," Law Officer Lt. Col. Donald Manes reprimanded him.

"What part did Major Nugent play in the peace rally?" counsel asked.

"I felt that he was the motivating force."

Doc testified that Dunn had at first ordered the men not to sign this particular petition, but said he neither saw nor heard Nugent receive the order. And while resisting cooperation with the Reds was always the policy, the men were instructed to use their own judgment in individual cases. After the peace committee watered down the wording, they signed.

"Wasn't it just as bad for you to sign the petition as it was for the accused to read it?"

"I put my name on a blank piece of paper. That was my judgment then and it remains my judgment today."

"Don't you think the accused, Major Nugent, was just as hungry and just as skinny as you were?"

"Yes, sir," Doc said.

As the day went on, the testimony turned to disease and death. Trial counsel Maj. Thomas H. Reese objected to this line of questioning, but the defense argued that it was necessary to show the conditions of POW life. In testimony the previous week, defense counsel had asked one member of the court: "Do you believe that a period of starvation, malnutrition, disease, beating with rifle butts, pulling of fingernails by pliers, and lack of sleep for four or five days and nights—do you believe that these things render a man abnormal in his thoughts and in the motivation of his action?" The question had been ruled out.

Doc described the Thanksgiving dinner that consisted of one millet ball apiece and the soup, made from nine heads of cabbage and water, that fed 350 men. He told of inadequate or nonexistent medical supplies, of Nugent's sixty- to eighty-pound weight loss, of the effects of malnutrition and diseases such as beriberi and pellagra.

"Were Major Nugent's feet and legs swollen?"

"We all had swollen legs," Doc said. And at one point or another, all were threatened with being shot if they didn't cooperate. They had only two choices in a world that often seemed unreal: to try to escape, or to try to get along with fanatical captors. Each had to make his own decision.

"Some were apathetic and subsequently died because of their apathy," Doc added. Others succumbed to Communist attempts to break down their resistance by starving them, then enticing their collaboration by offering small rewards. Crumbs. Dog treats. In other words, reducing the virtue of a man to that of an animal.

"As Pavlov can condition animals, so they believe they can condition human beings," Doc said.

After six hours of often-grueling testimony, it was over. For Doc, at least. The trial lasted nearly seven weeks, with forty-seven witnesses offering more than a million words of testimony. The nine-member court-martial board, seven of whom were Korean War veterans, deliberated for two hours and fifteen minutes. On March 7, Maj. Ambrose Nugent was acquitted on all counts.

Approximately 35,000 Americans died in the Korean War. About 3,000 of the nearly 7,200 captured by the North Koreans died in captivity, most of starvation between November 1950 and April 1951. A dozen or more camps spread throughout North Korea accommodated the more than 4,000 survivors; many lived in more than one camp before being repatriated in 1953. In all, five officers and nine enlisted men were tried for war crimes, all but one of them for collaboration. Lt. Jeff Erwin and Sgt. John Tyler were acquitted. Lt. Col. Paul Liles was suspended in rank for twenty-four months. Sgt. James Gallagher, who was charged with ten counts, including three for murder, was sentenced to life at hard labor but was paroled after eleven years. Maj. Ronald Alley was sentenced to ten years and served five. Corporals Harold Dunn and Thomas Bayes were each incarcerated for two and a half years, and M.Sgt. William Olson for two years. Sgt. William Banghart, who pleaded guilty, received a fifteen-year sentence that was later reduced;

he spent only one year in prison. Corporal Claude Batchelor, who received a life sentence, was paroled after four and a half years. Corporal Edward Dickenson was paroled after three and a half years. PFC Rothwell Floyd served ten years of his forty-year sentence.

Doc went back home to San Antonio, to his first house, to his wife, daughter, and first baby boy, to a demanding surgical residency and refurbished military career. There were other investigations, other statements, other pieces of testimony related to men and matters that never made the news.

At some point, before I learned to read, my mother bundled up my father's typewritten preparation and official affidavit, onionskin pages marked by rusting staples, and packed them into a used Department of the Army manila envelope addressed to Capt. Alexander M. Bogson at Brooke Army Hospital, San Antonio. She corrected the spelling—BOYSEN—with a passionate pencil. She scrawled "The Whole Story!!" across the top, with two lines underneath. "Some of it confidential," she added below, underlined once. And then she put the envelope away.

# 26
# Athens, Georgia
## 1995

F riday afternoon was sunny and warm, the sweet southern air gentle and fragrant with still-blooming forsythia. We were on our way to Athens, where my parents moved nearly a decade ago into what my brothers and I called The Compound, four acres of pristine Georgia pine surrounded by a high chain-link fence built to contain the dog and discourage solicitors.

Rick, my mate for five of the nearly ten years since Jim left our marriage, steered the rental car onto the shoulder and slowed to a stop. He pointed to the fifth Boiled Peanuts sign we had seen since leaving the Atlanta airport.

"Have you ever tried boiled peanuts?" he asked.

"Not that I can remember."

"Then now is a good time."

He forked over $2 at the makeshift stand, climbed back in the car, and handed me a greasy brown bag. I ate a handful. They were awful, but he had bought me a few more minutes to think, to compose myself, to prepare for the unknown trials I would encounter at my mother's funeral.

On August 31, the day after Kristin turned twenty-five, my mother died from swift, voracious lung cancer. My parents had called me the previous Valentine's Day to disclose her diagnosis.

"I knew it would finally catch up with me," said my mother on that bleak February afternoon, her voice choked up but strong. She didn't have to explain her reference to the smoking habit she had indulged since third grade. On the extension, my father was quick to point out that my mother's cancer, non-small cell, was also common in nonsmokers.

I had suspected something was wrong when they visited us the previous summer, when the Tiger Survivors' reunion was held in Minneapolis. The former POWs met annually in various cities; my father resisted at first but, at my mother's insistence, now attended fairly regularly. They stayed at the reunion hotel but spent their free day at our house, where the extended family, including Eric, Dirk and his wife and two kids, and my daughters, had gathered. I was excited to show off the 1903 home Rick and I had bought recently, but when I heard the car doors slam, I realized my butterflies were back.

I met my mother in the expansive living room, with its beamed ceiling, fireplace, and precious old piano she had refinished for us. Smiling wide, I opened my arms.

"Phew," she said, frowning over my shoulder. "Smells like my grandmother's."

"Come see the kitchen," I said. "Are you hungry?" She had told me they would arrive after lunch, but I had assembled a spread of fruit, bread, cheese, and nuts just in case. She followed me into the kitchen.

"You call this lunch?"

I fixed them a proper sandwich, which they ate without comment, then suggested we all walk my niece and nephew to the playground. She was reluctant, which I attributed to concern about my father's recent lung surgery. But he was fine, fully recovered. She was the one who had to stop and rest on a bench after one block.

Something was clearly wrong, although I couldn't imagine what. I hoped dinner—grilled chicken, corn on the cob, homegrown tomatoes, favorites all—would redeem the day.

"How's dinner, Mom?" I asked halfway through. She wrinkled her nose with displeasure.

"Just pass the bread, I guess."

They hadn't visited often through the years, but their visits were often memorable. Once they drove from Bemidji, where my father ran the Bemidji State University health service after retiring from the army. We were living in a subsidized two-bedroom townhouse in St. Paul while Jim finished his internal medicine residency. Kristin was five and our second daughter, Erika, was almost two. I had stayed up past midnight scrubbing floors and laundering curtains in the coin-operated machines in the next building. I washed extra sheets in case they wanted to stay overnight. I cleared the counters, cleaned out the fridge, hid the baby toys behind the couch. I wanted everything to be perfect.

They arrived midafternoon, later than expected. The lunch I had fixed was nestled under plastic wrap. I spotted them coming up the walk.

"Welcome!" I threw open the door and hugged my mother. My father followed her into the small living room. We all stood awkwardly as Erika grabbed my knees.

"Have a seat," I said, motioning to the couch. My father turned a complete circle and sucked in his breath.

"Well," he said, "I see no reason to stay *here*." They used the bathroom, clucked over the kids for a few minutes, then left for the four-and-a-half-hour drive back home.

Years later, when we were living in Shoreview, a St. Paul suburb, they brought along their German shepherd, who promptly got into a fight with our golden retriever in the driveway. My father tried to pull them apart, his shouts joining their snarling cacophony. When the melee ended seconds later, his hand was in the air, blood pouring down his arm onto the pavement. The slash was bone-deep.

Fortunately, it was his left hand. He was right-handed.

"Get me a needle and some thread. Black," he said, heading for the dish soap. I rummaged in the sewing box while he scrubbed in the kitchen sink. He lit a match, ran the needle through it, and asked me to thread the needle and knot the thread. Then, glasses lowered so he could see close-up, he sewed up his hand.

After dinner that night, we sat by the fireplace. My mother sipped wine she'd brought in a gallon jug. Beside her on the wicker loveseat, my father held his hand, now puffy like a blown-up glove, in the air.

"Why don't you take some aspirin?" she asked.

He shook his head. We sat still, listening to the clock tick.

"You know, we should tell her about the code," he said.

"What code?" my mother asked.

"The code. For the papers."

"What papers?"

He looked exasperated. "The papers in the secret room."

"What secret room?" I asked.

They both looked at me.

"You don't know about the secret room?" my mother said.

I shook my head. My father threw up his hands and grimaced in pain. Then he explained about the hidden room he had built in the basement, a bunker to hide and protect valuables. *And people?* I wondered.

"The papers will be there, all the bank accounts and everything. But the numbers won't be correct. They will be scrambled with a simple military cipher, something easy to remember. You know what I'm talking about," he said, looking at me. But I didn't have a clue.

Peering sideways at him, my mother started giggling, as if she couldn't hold back any longer. She put her hand on his arm.

He shot her an angry look and pulled away. "What's the matter with you?"

"Oh, Pete," she said, not without affection. "I mean, really."

He explained how codes work—something I didn't know he knew—until he ran out of vehemence, unable to convince us of the evil he perceived, and stopped talking. He retreated to that other world, where we couldn't follow.

Rick turned off the highway just before the Georgia Square Mall, and we headed down a wooded country road. We turned left by the small pond. The road curved up and around, offering only occasional glimpses of houses as we made our way to the compound. My father, always seeking high ground, had built their house on a hill. At the end of the driveway I got out to open the gate, then walked up to the house. My father met us outside, his lean limbs familiar in their comfort suit, baggy jeans with torn knees and sweatshirt stained with paint and coffee spills. I reached up and started to put my arms around him. He stood at attention, arms holding his sides, eyes straight ahead. I stepped back as he removed the cigarette dangling from his lips.

"Want to sit?" he asked, pulling frayed webbed lawn chairs from the corner of the garage and setting them up on the asphalt. Rick unloaded the car while my father and I sat down. He had something important to say. I could hear it coming, loud, ragged, inside me somewhere, between my shoulder blades. But we only chatted, which felt like subterfuge. I waited until Rick went inside before I asked.

"So how are you, really?" I opened.

He closed with the weather. He faced away, lighting another cigarette. He claimed he had given up, or at least cut back on, smoking. But all that had changed was the location of the carton: high on the utility closet shelf instead of easily accessible on the kitchen desk. My mother was hard on him when I was there last, in March.

"You stink!" she had said when he came in from smoking outside, his concession to her illness. "You know, I never knew how bad cigarettes smelled until I quit smoking them," she told me, leaning across the table toward me as if I were an old friend. "I didn't really decide to quit. Why would I, since the harm was already done? But they just quit tasting good."

She had tried chemotherapy but stopped after two treatments because the odds were poor and it took her all day to do the crossword. She showed my father how to balance the checkbook and launder the clothes; he noted "jeans, towels—warm & cold, ¾ soap" on an index card. She cooked, packing the freezer with his favorite meals wrapped in foil, neatly labeled. Every morning she spent time typing answers to questions I had mailed her when I panicked over the gaps in my knowledge: her favorite color, her dreams, accomplishments that made her proud. Who knew that she had always wanted to be a singer, always wanted to visit the Grand Canyon, regretted not having a job? She wrote about my father's homecoming from Korea, noting this was the first time someone had requested her side of the story. She admitted that she had never understood, either, why Christmas upset him so much.

Only occasionally did she dip into the vitriol I had noticed the summer before. Once she sent me an Ann Landers clipping about etiquette. When I called to ask why, my father picked up his extension first. "Please, not today, not today," he begged. But by then she was on the phone, chastising me for how I had raised my daughters. We never got to the bottom of this, and it didn't surface again. When I visited, my father was her target. He had been haranguing me about something, probably my journalism career—he hated journalists—or my stint in advertising, which he loathed. (He made a show of punching the mute button on the TV remote whenever commercials came on.) He pounded his point on the table, then left for the grocery store.

"Your father," she said as the car rolled down the driveway, "is a male chauvinist pig!" Her spittle misted my face. I was so taken aback that I failed to ask her to elaborate. She had told me once that he never said, out loud, that he loved her. But certainly she loved him. Our hero. Colonel Surgeon Father God. All I could do was nod.

That night I lay in the twin bed in the guest room, listening to her cough and cough and cough, wracking, wrenching sounds that made my own chest hurt, in the master bedroom across the hall. After the coughing quieted for a few minutes, I heard a knock on my door and got up to open it. She was standing there, in her thin blue cotton night-gown, with tears in her eyes.

"He loves you, you know," she said, gesturing toward the living room, where he was sleeping on the floor and would startle when I woke him before dawn to say good-bye.

"I know, Mom." I put my arms around her. It was the last time I saw her.

As dusk fell and relatives trickled in, my father and I abandoned lawn chairs and unspoken grief and went inside. My father left his green chair vacant, perching on a kitchen chair or couch arm instead. Pots of coffee were made and consumed. My cousin and sister-in-law helped in the kitchen. I had inherited lady-of-the-house rights, but instead of the easy competence I usually wielded at home, I felt trampled by ancient fear. I was afraid of putting too much mayonnaise on the sandwiches, of choosing Swiss cheese when American was better, of making the coffee too strong or handing my father the wrong cup, which I did once (he batted it away). I watched the others cook and clean with deft, decisive movements, and I envied them.

The next morning, my father ordered my brothers and me to check on final arrangements at the funeral home.

"And go buy a pen," he said as we started out the door.

"What?" I asked.

"A pen. Go buy one."

"What for?"

"So people can sign the guestbook."

"They will have pens for the guestbook."

He stared at me, anger painting his face. "We will not use their pens. Their pens have the funeral home name on them." Oh. Advertising. We stopped at the mall to buy a pen.

That afternoon we set out sandwiches and welcomed guests. The phone rang and rang again. Once when it rang my father answered it and handed it to me.

"Talk to her," he said and walked away.

I carried the phone back into the bedroom, where I could hear and speak in private. The caller explained that she was my parents' friend and neighbor. I had heard her name but never met her. Her voice was kind and cheerful, her words straightforward. She told me how much she liked my mother, who had imparted instructions about what to do with her clothes.

"Oh, thanks," I said. "I hadn't really thought about that. Do you think we need to do it now? I'm flying home right after the funeral, but I'll be back."

"Your dad wants them taken care of before you go. And your mom was very clear about what she wanted. You're supposed to take what you want, then donate the rest to a women's shelter on Forsythe Road." She gave me directions and warned me about the shelter's sporadic receiving hours. If I could just bag the clothes, she or someone else would drop them off. I wanted to keep her on the phone because the warmth in her voice comforted me, but we hung up after a few minutes.

I laid the phone on the dresser and opened the top drawer, right side, my mother's underwear drawer for as long as I could remember. It was lined with clean shelf paper, precisely scored. Seven pairs of cotton briefs, no holes or frayed threads, were stacked there, each fold facing the same direction.

They were all neat, drawers of socks and belts and eleven pairs of gloves of different lengths and colors. In the closet, skirts and blouses hung motionless, in order by length. I wanted none of them. They didn't smell of her. She wasn't here in this room, among these things. Her spirit had gone; I wondered how long ago.

I felt it again, that inexplicable, menacing fear. I longed to be home, safe, and I picked up the phone to check on my airline reservation. I stood in the corner between the bed and the wall, on hold, gazing out the window at a white oak tree, its largest branch severed but hanging by a sheet of bark, the leaves wilted but still attached.

When I turned around, my father was standing behind me, at the foot of the bed, his blue eyes wide, reflecting the sky, his white whiskers failing to hide the deep creases that pulled his mouth into a frown. His arms hung down but alert, ready to rise, swing, thrust. His fists were clenched and shaking. My mouth went dry.

I heard the airline person come on the line, but I couldn't listen.

"Thanks, I'll call you back," I squeezed out. I held the phone out. "Did you want this?"

"What were you doing?" he barked. I ducked. Instinct. He had not raised a hand. I watched the spittle form tiny pools. His eyes bored into mine, their message unreadable.

"What were you doing?" he asked again, louder. His voice shook, his shoulders hunched. "This is my business, you know."

I had no idea what he meant.

"I was checking on my reservation," I said.

"I don't mean that. The other call."

"It was your friend. We had a nice conversation. She told me where Mom wanted me to donate her clothes. She gave me directions."

He said nothing. As silence stretched, his face went slack and his body seemed to shrink. I slid past him the way I slid through childhood, guilty but not sure why. He followed me to the kitchen and got out my mother's address book. He called her friend back, his tone accusatory, to verify the details I had related. In his commanding officer voice, he asked the same questions in different ways, probing for truth but gradually losing steam. He is grieving, I thought, and confused. I let it go.

A dozen relatives had gathered by then, and I tried to be a good hostess. When my father complained that the glasses were too dusty, I returned them to the cupboard and got out different ones. When he said I had placed the serving bowls and trays on the wrong end of the counter, I moved them to the other end.

"What are you doing with those?" he asked.

"I'm just setting them out for dinner. You know, like a buffet table. We have lasagna in the oven, and there's salad, garlic bread, veggies, and Bundt cake for dessert. I thought everyone could help themselves, then sit wherever they're comfortable." I motioned toward the living room end of the high-ceilinged great room, separated from the kitchen by a center island. Twelve of us were too many, I thought, to crowd around a kitchen table that seated only six comfortably. He started moving the kitchen chairs closer together and told me to get more from the basement. I obeyed.

Relatives squeezed in around the table with plates full of lasagna and salad. I moved the bread from the counter to the table and took drink orders. At last we were all seated, jostling elbows and knocking knees, and in good spirits despite the occasion. We ate. When we were finished, I set the Bundt cake on the table and started to hand out dessert plates.

"Don't do that!" my father hissed.

I stopped, plates in midair.

"These are just clean plates for the cake," I said.

"Don't you dare do that!"

"Why not? I don't want anyone to have to get up and get their own."

"We have plates already. These are fine." He indicated his dinner plate, coated with tomato sauce.

"Well, I'll just put them here on the table then, in case someone prefers a clean one." I reached to set the stack of plates down. His arm shot out at mine. Karate chop. Near miss. I jumped. The plates clattered.

Blood rushed through me, pounding my temples. I sat down, plates on my lap. My cousin stood up and served the cake on the dinner plates, nudging uneaten lasagna aside. Everyone picked up their forks and ate. No one spoke. My father wouldn't look at me.

After the cake was gone and the dishes were cleared, most of the visitors left to get some sleep before the morning funeral. I busied myself in the kitchen while my father went outside to say good-bye. I was wiping off the table when I heard the door slam.

He strode over to me and stuck his face into mine. His breath was hot, stagnant with tobacco.

"How dare you," he spit at me.

"What? What did I do?"

"You know."

"No, I don't."

"These are simple people, better than you. You, you are a snob."

He ranted for an hour or more, making points I couldn't follow, talking about prisoners and merchant sailors, men he knew and trusted, men who didn't put on airs. I recognized the POW names, but I didn't know their stories. I didn't know why I wasn't like them, why I could never be.

"There's nothing wrong with clean plates," I pleaded, wishing desperately for my mother. She would have offered not only clean plates but matching ones, maybe even the good china. She was classy; she knew how to do everything right and proper. She was an East Coast girl, but she had convinced my father that she eschewed elite society and was better suited to his world. She was a good army wife.

When I sat down finally, he bent over me, his hand on the back of my chair, and kept talking. Dirk and Eric hovered at a respectful distance, occasionally trying to placate my father or change the subject. My sister-in-law retreated to the farthest corner of the great room. I listened with blank eyes. I had nothing more to offer, and I knew my father had to run out of steam on his own.

The next morning I lay awake in the guest room as I had during much of the night, feeling as if pinned by a boulder, relentlessly pressing, precluding sleep. Like a shy child on the first day at a new school, I was afraid to get up, afraid to leave the house, afraid to face unforeseen blunders. Would my skirt be too short, my shoes too pointed? Since I didn't have a black outfit, would navy blue be good enough?

At the funeral home my father stood stony and stoic, distant and displaced. The gold pen we had bought stood in its holder next to the guest book. The single red rose he had ordered stood by the podium in the brushed silver vase we had brought from home. The reverend read the eulogy as my father sat listening, head tilted slightly to the side, in the front row. The service was short. Afterward, we stood in a receiving line. Not many people came through. Only when an acquaintance of my mother's, a fellow volunteer at the hospital, asked me for her wild rice casserole recipe did I cry.

After the funeral I went back to the house to collect my things and say good-bye. Rick had already left. Dirk, his wife, and I loaded our suitcases into the trunk and climbed into their rental car. Those who had later flights stood in the driveway as if waiting for a parade. My father stood at the head of the line. So tall. So haunted. In the backseat, I rolled down the side window.

"Good-bye," I said to him. "Take care."

I hesitated, reached out my hand.

His eyes desperate, he grabbed my arm with both of his hands. One last wrench of skin against bone, trying to hold on, hurting. Then he let go. I rolled up the window as we pulled away, watched him growing smaller through the back window as he followed and closed the gate behind us.

# Epilogue

In March 2002, a month after I visited my father in the Athens hospital, I called the hospice workers to see how he was doing. He had declined surgery to replace his heart valve, and I wanted to know whether I should reschedule the flight I had booked for the following week.

"Death is not imminent," they assured me.

"The colonel's command of the remote control is uncompromised," Eric, who was attending him, concurred. "CNN blares all day long and most of the night, too." Since his return from the hospital, my father was no longer firing off disgruntled (but funny) letters to Tom Brokaw and Ted Koppel, printed out on his dot matrix printer, but he remained in good voice, making his opinions known. We thought he would be with us for a while.

Three days later, I was up late watching the Oscars when the phone rang.

"He's gone," my brother said.

I was stunned.

The family gathered in Athens for a memorial service, making sure a plain pen was available for guests to sign the guestbook. My father's commanding officer in the prison camp, Colonel Dunn, arrived from Alabama and agreed to speak.

"I was behind him climbing that mountain, in that ice and snow," he spoke slowly into the microphone, his eyes distant. He was ninety and tended to ramble but made one point clear. "His feet were a mess. Torn. Skin hanging off. He left bloody footprints on the trail. I figured that if Doc could keep going with those awful feet of his, we all could. At least we could try."

I had known nothing of Doc's bloody feet.

Before he died, I had searched my disorganized shelves for music my father loved to make him a CD that would help him recover (I hoped).

I knew what the songs were: "The Whiffenpoof Song," "Que Sera, Sera," "Hi-Lili, Hi-Lo," "You'll Never Walk Alone," "Three Bells"—the ones that rang in the little valley town for Jimmy Brown—but, except for "Danny Boy," which he had e-mailed me about, I didn't know why he loved them. I knew only that they were important and that the lyrics and mournful melodies alone couldn't explain the immense sadness they created in me.

When Colonel Dunn finished speaking, Shorty Estabrook, the young POW who had tried to keep everyone laughing, took the podium. "I didn't come all the way from California to not say something," he said. "Doc inspired us. He took care of us when we were sick. He kept us going. He was a hero."

That part I knew. But too many details were missing. As the oldest sibling, and the only one alive during the Korean War, I was in charge of the legacy, the stories. After all this time, all I had were pieces.

One summer when my children were small, I had gone to the downtown library and gathered all the Korean War books on a long table. Only half a dozen or so referred to American prisoners. I checked them all out and took notes. The material contained many historical facts but shed little light on feelings or my father's experience. I did discover that he had two sets of captors.

"Which captors were worse?" I dared to ask during a visit that seemed more comfortable than most. Knowing how he abhorred communism, a word he would spit rather than say, I carefully and quietly added: "The Chinese, right?"

Shock seized his face, as if I had kicked him in the stomach, forced him to vomit evil memories onto the floor in front of him, then pushed him facedown into that rank, bitter sea.

The look passed as quickly as it appeared, replaced by disbelief of my ignorance.

"No," he said, fixing his stare over my shoulder. "The Koreans." He turned his back and walked away.

He decried the few published accounts that appeared, attacking them as self-serving, barefaced, evil-laced lies. I begged him to write his own account, or let me do it with his help, but he refused vehemently, stabbing his finger in the air at my audacity. When missionary Larry

Zellers's book, *In Enemy Hands,* was published in 1991, a copy arrived in my mailbox. The book described the experiences they shared in captivity, including detailed accounts of the Death March and the Tiger's murderous cruelty. My father wrote a short note on the flyleaf describing my demands, at age three, to know whether he existed, and if so, where he was. "This book accurately tells you where I was," he wrote. "Enjoy."

*Korea P.O.W., A Thousand Days of Torment* arrived in 1997. A hand-printed note explained that my father had paid for the book and asked that it be sent to me. "Thanks for your interest in the events," author Bill Funchess wrote on the flyleaf. "Your friend, Doc Boysen, was a hero to all of us."

Sometimes, on rare holidays when the family gathered, my brothers stayed up with him long past midnight, hoping to ease out stories in the predawn hours after my mother and I had long since gone to bed. She disapproved of these attempts, knowing that even a ten-minute glimpse of an old war movie on TV could elicit night after sleepless night of flashbacks. But I treasured every tidbit and regretted those I couldn't grab.

One night while I was still up, he sat deep in the green corduroy chair with his feet crossed on the ottoman, shoes on, stubbing out cigarettes in a brimming ashtray on the glass-ringed table beside him. Smoke swirled around his head.

"We called him Rotorhead," he began with no preface. "He always had a motorcycle." As he started to relate the story of Crazy Week, complete with sound effects, he started laughing and couldn't stop. His whole body shook until he was gasping for air. Tears ran in gullies down his face, dripping onto his torn T-shirt, until he couldn't talk anymore. The story ended there.

The advent of e-mail helped. I was Apple and he was PC, but our mutual affinity for technology allowed us to share what we seldom discussed, from weather and menus to politics and pets. Sometimes, always in the wee hours, he would write a short post—a paragraph, maybe two—about the war. I would print it out and save it. Sometimes he would write a positive comment, almost praise, about my work. I would save that, too. My mother envied this connection; she preferred the telephone but called only on special occasions. The few times my father picked up the extension, he said little and plunged the receiver into its cradle when he got bored.

After my mother died, my father and I talked even less. He called a few times to discuss a health matter in medical terms, calm and clinical, safe in the emotional chasm that surgeons cultivate. Twice a year, on Father's Day and on his Christmas birthday, I called him. It took hours to gather the courage, my stomach somersaulting from the moment I woke that morning until I dialed the phone. I rehearsed my lines. After we said goodbye I went limp in relief. Somehow I always expected to be blindsided by some catastrophe, although I never was. Perhaps mellowed by age, he was gracious and grateful, and nothing bad happened across the miles.

Now that he was gone, those miles between us stretched long and impassable. I no longer felt like dancing in the living room. I wrestled with him in my head. I had made a marriage, two children, and a career, but I hadn't made peace with my father. I didn't know who he was, not really, or who I was supposed to be, trailing in his shadow.

The day after the memorial service, my brothers and I set about clearing out the house, dividing up the items we wanted, setting aside the rest to give away or sell at auction. We started in the basement, which my father had insisted on building despite the fact that basements were uncommon in Georgia. That mostly empty cavern housed only his workbench, power tools, empty boxes, and paint cans on a wood shelf on the south wall. Eric reached behind a paint can and unlatched the hidden door, which swung open to reveal the secret room. We all knew about the room, but we found little secreted there except the house plans and, in a safe encased in concrete, a small envelope of government savings bonds.

Room by room we went, studiously avoiding the one none of us wanted to enter: his office. His spirit lingered in this musty shrine to his solitude, haunted with the stench of stale tobacco and cluttered with his eclectic collection of ham radio equipment and hemostats, screwdrivers and depleted pens, and disheveled heaps of books, papers, folders, and index cards. Not until the last day before our flights home did we dare go in.

We decided to go in together. At first, standing awkward and silent in the middle of the room, we didn't know where to begin. We started opening drawers, rifling through the jammed contents, closing them again. I went through desk drawers while someone else tackled the file cabinet. The bottom drawer, yanked too hard, fell out with a clatter.

"Oops," I heard. Then, "Wow. Look at this."

Beneath the cabinet, where the drawer had been, lay the fat, faded folder we had never seen. "The Whole Story!! (Some of it confidential)!"

We pulled out the contents, onionskin pages with single-spaced typing that detailed events we had always wondered about. We were afraid to breathe.

"I found the brown scrapbook once a long time ago," I said finally. "But then it disappeared and I never saw it again."

"I found it once, too," said Dirk. "Same thing happened."

"Me too," Eric admitted.

We had never discussed it with each other or our parents until a few years earlier, when one of my brothers took the plunge and brought it up.

"Isn't there some scrapbook about Korea? What ever happened to it?"

"It's right there in the cupboard under the bookshelves," my mother told him. "It's always been around. You can look at it any time you want."

Her guarded tone of voice suggested otherwise. My brothers and I exchanged glances and dropped the subject. Despite the occasional blurt, we had learned our silence lessons well.

As we probably suspected, our discoveries weren't complete. Dirk, in charge of clearing out the computer files, found a document: "Intention." Unbeknownst to us, my father had been writing his own story, although he hadn't gotten very far. In the preface, he complained that it was painfully difficult to recall the details, not because he didn't remember the incidents, but because he wasn't too sure he wanted to. His purpose, he explained, was not to try to recount the incidents of his captivity as such, but instead to put them in perspective, to use them to point out the fundamentals of survival. And "to leave some of me to my children, a part they really never knew."

We made copies of everything for everyone and packed them in our suitcases.

In August we gathered at Arlington Cemetery to inter my father's ashes along with my mother's, which he had kept on his closet shelf. The three of us sat in the front row, sweating in the one-hundred-degree heat, as the honor guard in full dress uniform presented arms, folded the flag with white-gloved hands, placed it in my lap, and marched away in military precision, one peeling off from the rest to signify the missing man.

Taps sounded. Memories surged. *Day is done . . . God is nigh.*

That same day, the Tiger Survivors saluted Doc in a champagne toast at their annual reunion.

A year later, I decided to go the reunion in King of Prussia, Pennsylvania. I had been only to the one in Minneapolis, where my father had choked up when his buddies gave him a plaque of appreciation and where he inexplicably ordered our family not to drink alcohol because we might offend someone. This time, I was determined to do it my way, to explain that I wanted to write a book, to interview survivors about their experiences. I had read the POW papers we found, but I still craved details.

Trying to keep my notebook inconspicuous in my palm, I walked into the hotel ballroom and squinted at name tags until I found a name I recognized: Eli Culbertson, who had been wired to my father as they marched right after their capture.

"I'm Doc's daughter," I said and told him what I was doing. He greeted me warmly. We chatted for a few minutes before I started in.

"What was the name of the guy who had the shrapnel in his eye?"

"Naville. Herman Naville."

"Did the Tiger have a name?"

"No. Not that anyone ever knew. I was scared to death of that man."

"What, exactly, did he look like?"

He looked at me, then away.

"He was small in stature, with stooped shoulders. Typical Korean head and face, small, came to a point. His mouth was set. He had an evil look about him." He mumbled something else about buckteeth, high boots, and britches.

Then he cut himself off and looked me in the eye, kind but firm.

"You know, for the first twenty-five years, I blocked all this out," he said. "Now, every day I'm alive, I'm lucky enough to forget a little bit more. Why would I want to remember?"

Our interview was over.

I tried again with another veteran whose name I didn't recognize. He sat next to me at dinner and, after I introduced myself, spent most of the time chatting amiably with the person on his other side.

"Do you happen to know anything about the appendectomy my dad performed in the camp?" I asked when I could get a word in. I knew only scraps of this story, and I was skeptical. He turned toward me, his expression morphing from live animation to blank wall.

"Sure do," he said. He maintained eye contact but remained silent, which made me nervous. I thought these men gathered annually to talk about their war experiences, but it was becoming clear that I was mistaken. They came together because they survived the Tiger, which made them family, and they talked about family things. He was patient with me because, despite being ignorant and perhaps rude, I was extended family.

"I heard that he did the surgery without any anesthesia. Is that true?"

"Yep." He still faced me, unblinking.

"How do you know?"

"Because I was one of the ones holding the guy down," he said, and turned back to his dinner.

I abandoned my interviewing but not my quest. I had to accept that some questions—like whether the kind guard my father encountered early in his captivity was named Pashir—might never be answered. Still, I searched. Deep in the boxes we had packed in Athens, I found my father's black leather A Line A Day five-year diary, with its gold-edged pages and inscription: "Presented to me on my fifteenth birthday, December 25, 1938, by the whole family." Tucked inside was a newspaper clipping about how to use a war ration book and account for purchased sugar. With a fountain pen in slanted script, he wrote descriptions of blizzards, boring classes, very sore throats. He hoed corn and went fishing. He sold birdhouses to buy a Boy Scout uniform. He hit a chicken with the car, but it wasn't his fault. He met a dark-haired, brown-eyed "damsal" from Perham named Jean and a "honey of a blond" named Ruby. He explained that blank pages meant that nothing happened worth writing about.

His childhood diary wasn't unlike my own. Neither of us made it all the way through the first year, although his diligence outlasted mine. In subsequent years he noted events that counted. On January 11, 1942, he went to see the Ballets Russes de Monte Carlo, starring Tamara Toumanova and accompanied by the Minneapolis Symphony: "It was very beautiful," he wrote.

Yes, he loved the ballet.

Combing through old cards, pictures, and military memorabilia, I found his ship's journal wrapped in heavy canvas and tied with a piece of rope. On the flyleaf he granted permission to read only the first page before, assuming his demise, turning the book over to "my parents, my wife, or my fiancée." In case of accident, he provided a home address for his parents and a dorm address for my mother. He also printed, in painstaking block letters, his version of the "Physician's Prayer" by Maimonides:

*All good! Thou has chosen me in thy grace, to watch over the life and death of thy creatures. I am about to go to my labour. Be with me in this great work, so that it may avail, for without thy help nothing succeeds, not even the smallest!*

Between September 1945 and November 1947, two months after their wedding, he wrote more than eighty pages of letters to my mother about his fraternity troubles, merchant seaman adventures, and commitment to finishing medical school. He shared thoughts and observations about men, women, love, marriage, religion—all of which he thought might be "valuable entertainment someday"—and implored her not to become a snob, like so many of her East Coast brethren.

Little by little I solved the mysteries I had wondered about for more than five decades. "Dearest Trish" first appeared on a letter written from Seattle on June 30, 1946. It wasn't code for another woman. It was just a name he thought up one night while thinking of her Irish temper, and he fell in love with it. He knew no one else with that name, he explained, so now he thought of her as "my own little Trish." My mother wasn't Irish and didn't have much of a temper that I remember. But in his mind, at least, he was her "li'l sailor" and she was his little Trish. They had private lives eclipsed by war, and that is what I came to know, in time.

My father called on a Saturday afternoon.

"When are you coming?"

"In a week, after I get back from California."

"Why are you going there?"

"To help Erika pick out her wedding dress. She's flying in to meet me." My daughter was getting married September 14, on my parents' anniversary.

He paused. I pictured him pursing his lips, mulling this over.

"She could wear a gunnysack," he said.

"I know," I said, finally. "But she wants a pretty dress."

No one spoke. I listened to the phone hum.

"You're a good girl, Punky," he said. "I love you."

"I love you, too, Pop."

He hung up. I held the phone against my chest and closed my eyes. It was the first time he had said those things and the last time we would talk. Eric called the next night to tell me our father was gone.

I found out later that he had quit taking his medications a week earlier. He wanted to die like his buddies in the prison camp, unpampered, hard and cold. I thought about how they had never left his side. And how he will never leave mine.

# Sources and Acknowledgments

As long as I can remember, I wanted to write my father's story, but I was never sure what that story was. Books had been written, but no one had gotten it right, according to him, and the random clues he dropped were not enough, no matter how assiduously I hoarded them. My pleas to write with his help met with stony silence. I suggested interviewing his fellow Tiger survivors for a book. "They'd never sell their stories," he said. What about a fictionalized version, with composite characters? Absolutely not. "Each POW has his own story," he wrote in an e-mail, "and most have one question: 'Why was I allowed to survive?' I know of no simple answer or even a complicated one."

Even when I found the treasure trove beneath the filing cabinet, the challenge was formidable. Could I bear to read it? For more than two years, whenever I embarked on the project I could read only a page or two before the dull pain in my chest forced me to put it away. I set it aside for long periods. Did I really want to know? Did I really think it would be possible to tell a story that was his alone, in a way that he might tell it?

He had, in fact, several stories, sometimes conflicting: his prison experience account, written after he was repatriated; the April 1954 military interrogation by the army's war crimes division; affidavits prepared for court-martial testimony; reports published in medical journals and military pamphlets; the beginning of a memoir left on his hard drive. In the end, my cache included many more of his words than I could actually use. I had to choose.

I didn't always find the details I needed. To settle discrepancies and fill narrative gaps, I turned first to what in many ways was his first family: the Tiger survivors, who often credited Doc, their "gentle giant," with pulling them through. I reviewed personal correspondence from Ralph (Eli) Culbertson and Miss Nellie Dyer and sketches and descriptions by Carl V. Cossin. Susumu (Sus) Shinagawa's "Little Switch" informed a brief scene and dialogue in "Seoul, Korea, July 1950," and for the dialogue in "The Cornfield, North Korea, October 1950," I relied on *In Enemy Hands: A Prisoner in North Korea,* by Larry Zellers; *Valiant Dust,* by Albert Kenyon; and "The Korean POW Story," by Wadie (Jiggs) Rountree. Critiques of *Journey through Shadow* (Conley Clarke) and *The Medics' War* (Albert E. Cowdrey) by Isadore Peppe, Tim Casey, and others were helpful, as were letters and newsletters from Wilbert (Shorty) Estabrook, whose tenacious advocacy and thorough documentation of Tiger survivor history are nothing short of extraordinary.

For military background, I consulted T. R. Fehrenbach's *This Kind of War,* David Halberstam's *The Coldest Winter,* and other history books. *Korean P.O.W.: A Thousand Days of Torment,* by William H. Funchess supplied descriptive detail. Also essential were *When Hell Froze Over,* by William Shadish, M.D., and *And the Wind Blew Cold,* by Richard M. Bassett, both coauthored by Lewis H. Carlson, who also wrote *Remembered Prisoners of a Forgotten War.* The challenge of tracking my father among 7,140 prisoners, who were often moved in random batches among thirteen prison camps during more than three years, was daunting. I created time line after time line as I struggled to tell only his story, leaving out horrific ordeals suffered by those in Death Valley and other camps. It was gut-wrenching research; I worked in short spurts and worried obsessively about getting everything right.

Although Korea is dubbed the Forgotten War, media coverage at the time was abundant, in *Time* and *Life* magazines and local and national newspaper accounts, which supplied court-martial detail and dialogue for "Lawton, Oklahoma, January 1955," as did *Broken Soldiers,* by Raymond B. Lech. In later years, my father saved transcripts from occasional speeches and wrote letters to friends and relatives who thoughtfully kept and generously shared them. Bless my mother for spending her last days typing answers to my questions and for tucking away such artifacts as ocean-liner menus, train tickets, and, of course, the worn brown scrapbook. It was she who first understood that this story belonged to all of us.

This book would not exist without the help and tenacious support of my friends, family, and fellow writers. Thank you, Rick Dublin, for always believing in me and this project. Thanks to Jim Lenfestey, who persuaded me to tell both stories, and to first-draft readers Karen Olson and Cindy Christian Rogers, who kindly but firmly insisted on a complete revision. So many others toasted my small victories, guided my research efforts, and informed my decisions along the way; the list is long, and I am indebted to them all. How lucky I was to find my agent, Laurie Abkemeier, who taught me so much about good writing and whose cheerful, unflappable perseverance pulled us through haunted manuscripts, techno nightmares, and agonizing author doubt. She was always confident that she would find this book a good home, and she did.

Finally, I have to thank the man who instilled the fight in me, the need to battle through the war zone of emotions to reach a better place. Whether or not he intended to, my father left behind the tools I needed to learn not only about war and its effect on families but also about him, a complicated human being who was both noble and flawed, just like the rest of us. I had thought that when one person in a relationship dies, that relationship is destined to remain unchanged, but I was wrong. Now I understand.

Catherine Madison is a freelance writer and editor. She has been editor-in-chief of *Utne Reader* and senior editor of *Adweek* and *Creativity* magazines. Her writing has been published in the *Chicago Tribune, Minneapolis Star Tribune, Advertising Age, The History Channel Magazine, Minnesota Monthly,* and many other publications. She lives in Minneapolis and Los Angeles.